Collective Ac

Collective Action

A *Bad Subjects* Anthology

Edited by
Megan Shaw Prelinger and Joel Schalit

Pluto Press
LONDON • ANN ARBOR

First published 2004 by Pluto Press
345 Archway Road, London N6 5AA
and 839 Greene Street, Ann Arbor, MI 48106

www.plutobooks.com

British Library Cataloguing in Publication Data
A catalogue record for this book is available from the British Library

ISBN   0 7453 2180 1 hardback
ISBN   0 7453 2179 8 paperback

Library of Congress Cataloging in Publication Data
Collective action : a Bad Subjects anthology / edited by Megan Shaw
Prelinger and Joel Schalit.
       p. cm.
    Includes bibliographical references.
    ISBN 0–7453–2180–1 — ISBN 0–7453–2179–8 (pbk.)
  1. United States—Civilization—1970– 2. United States—Politics and government—
1989– 3. Politics and culture—United States. 4. Radicalism—United States. 5. United
States—Social conditions—1980– 6. Civilization, Modern—1950– 7. World politics–
–1989– 8. Politics and culture. 9. Social history—1970– I. Prelinger, Megan Shaw. II.
Schalit, Joel. III. Bad Subjects (Organization)

    E169.12.C548 2004
    973.931—dc22

                                                                      2004001897

10   9   8   7   6   5   4   3   2   1

Designed and produced for Pluto Press by
Chase Publishing Services, Fortescue, Sidmouth, EX10 9QG, England
Typeset from disk by Stanford DTP Services, Northampton, England
Printed and bound in the European Union by
Antony Rowe Ltd, Chippenham and Eastbourne, England

Contents

Acknowledgments

This volume represents a group effort of the *Bad Subjects* editorial collective and community of contributors. The collective is Cynthia Hoffman, Jonathan Sterne, Robert Soza, Joe Lockard, Rachel Swan, Mike Mosher, Geoff Sauer, Charlie Bertsch, Elisabeth Hurst, Kim Nicolini, Megan Shaw Prelinger, Joel Schalit, John Brady, Scott Schaffer, Zach Furness, Arturo J. Aldama, Frederick Luis Aldama, and J.C. Myers.

The coeditors of this book would like to extend their deep appreciation to Charlie Bertsch, who provided special assistance with the manuscript preparation, and to Aaron Shuman and Jonathan Sterne, who at different times performed essential administrative duties on behalf of the collective as this book was being prepared.

It is impossible to acknowledge every individual who has contributed to *Bad Subjects* over the past ten years. Nevertheless, we would like to thank the following people, without whom the *Bad Subjects* collective would not have reached its current manifestation: founders Annalee Newitz and Joe Sartelle; former production team members Ron Alcalay, Julia Bryan-Wilson, Carlos Camargo, Elliot Cola, Ana Marie Cox, Brock Craft, Lindsey Eck, Peter Ives, Ed Korthof, Jeremiah Luna, Paul Rosenbaum, Steven Rubio, Jeremy Russell, Jillian Sandell, Aaron Shuman, and Matt Wray.

Bad Subjects would also like to thank Ewa Pagacz, Carrie A. Rentschler, Chrysanthe Mosher, Doug Henwood, and Rick Prelinger, all of whom have made noteworthy contributions to the magazine over the years. We would also like to extend our gratitude to everyone who has contributed to *Bad Subjects* since its beginning in 1992.

Bad Subjects is an online publication that has attracted over 200,000 readers per issue. Without the web mastering, design, and layout skills of Geoff Sauer and his groundbreaking English server (*www.eserver.org*) none of this would have been possible.

Bad Subjects is also indebted to the generosity of several institutions: the University of California at Berkeley's Townsend Center for the Humanities and Graduate Assembly for ten years of financial support; Carnegie Mellon University and the University of Washington for service space and technical assistance; and Iowa State University, the current home of the English server.

Introduction

Charlie Bertsch, Joel Schalit,
Jonathan Sterne, and Megan Shaw Prelinger

There aren't many rules at *Bad Subjects: Political Education for Everyday Life*. Nobody gets paid to work on the magazine. Footnotes are a no-no. And showing off knowledge of multisyllabic words like 'polysemy' and 'envagination' is strongly discouraged. But we have never drawn a party line in the sand. If a piece seems likely to get our readers thinking about their lives politically, it will probably pass editorial muster. Given the choice between a perfectly polished essay that muffles the injunction to 'change your life,' and a provocative polemic, we have invariably opted for the latter.

Despite major changes in the membership of our editorial board and readership since the publication debuted in September 1992, the policy our cofounders Joe Sartelle and Annalee Newitz articulated in the introduction to our first issue continues to be integral to our mission: 'The purpose of a *Bad Subjects* article is to take a stand, preferably one which is defiant of conventional leftist wisdom in the service of leftist politics.' This volume represents a collective effort. The essays were selected by the entire *Bad Subjects* collective nominating their favorite essays. The named coeditors of this volume took the table of contents that had been developed by all hands and saw it through to publication.

Although the left may not be tongue-tied as it seemed to our contributors in 1992, there is still a lot of room for improvement. While we welcome the decline of both Marxist and multicultural orthodoxy around the world, leftist intellectuals continue to display a distressing herd instinct. Just because everyone is quoting Antonio Negri and Michael Hardt's breathtaking *Empire* instead of the *Critique of the Gotha Program* doesn't mean that freedom of inquiry has triumphed. At *Bad Subjects*, we remain convinced that leftists need more spaces where they are comfortable taking intellectual and political risks. They need to express themselves without the protective coating of specialized terminology. And they have to want a larger, more diverse audience instead of retreating into the comfort of familiar professional and political circles.

Obviously, we can't hope to satisfy the need for new spaces on the left in isolation. As the Louis Althusser quote from which we took our name implies, bad subjects resist the dominant ideology by refusing to work 'all by themselves.' For each of us, *Bad Subjects* is a link in a chain of affiliation, not an end in itself.

Because we are an all-volunteer organization, without advertising or distribution in the marketplace, *Bad Subjects* will never make the inroads that 'professional' publications take for granted. What we can do, however, like like-minded people in the world of independent publishing, music, and filmmaking, is lead by example. As *Bad Subjects* has gradually moved away from its student origins we have seen what real-world pressures can do to a collective organized around the understanding that no one should profit financially from its efforts. But we like to believe that the price we pay for our idealism—the inefficiency of a volunteer organization—is more than compensated for by what we demonstrate in holding on to that idealism in the face of adversity. While we recognize that nothing is truly 'free' in a world structured by global capitalism, there is still something special about labor freely given. It testifies to the conviction that people would be doing something better with their time, if they only had the time in which to do it. That's the sort of utopianism we endorse wholeheartedly.

*   *   *

As great thinkers on the left have regularly reminded us, however, the dream of a better life too readily becomes a nightmare when it is cut off from the reality of everyday life. We are the lucky ones. Our status as intellectuals in the developed world gives us the opportunity to donate time to political and cultural organizations. Most citizens of the planet never have the chance to give their labor freely to a project like *Bad Subjects*. Even as we imagine the day when everybody will able to work as they please, we confront the hard, cold facts of the contemporary workplace. In almost every respect, the situation of workers in the developed world is worse than it was 25 years ago. But for most people in Africa, Asia, and Latin America, there is no Golden Age of workers' empowerment to remember nostalgically. That doesn't mean that leftist intellectuals should wring their hands in anguish over their own privilege or, worse still, project their self-loathing onto others as Chinese leaders did during the Cultural Revolution. What we need is an awareness of history that takes account of national, regional, and religious differences without forgetting that those differences are themselves the product of human labor.

Fundamental to *Bad Subjects*' approach is the conviction that history isn't simply the province of textbooks. Marx's famous statement from the *18th Brumaire of Louis Bonaparte* that 'people make their own history,' but 'not under circumstances of their choosing' should be the foundation for all leftist politics. In a world that bombards us with the message that individuals are powerless, we need continually to remind ourselves that the power used against us is our own. But we also must be mindful of the circumstances of our disempowerment. The struggle against free market economics and state terror is as relevant as it was in Marx's day, but waging it successfully demands an attention to the details of history. We aren't living in 1850 or 1900, after all. More pertinently, we aren't living in 2000 either. As short a lifespan as *Bad Subjects* has had, we have nevertheless witnessed dramatic developments in world affairs. And we need to attend to them in their specificity if we are to take the lessons of the *18th Brumaire* to heart and not recreate the failed revolutionary past as our own desired future.

When the United States invaded Iraq in early 2003, commentators around the world remarked on the way the war recalled its predecessor, Desert Storm. The continuity editors did a bang-up job on *New World Order: The Sequel*: a Bush in the White House, Saddam Hussein playing the role of poor man's Hitler, shadowy hardliners from the Reagan era once again driving American foreign policy. And the Wal-Marts of the world urged us to party like it was 1991. But the celebration of the second Gulf war was more half-hearted than the first. Republican strategists worried that George W. Bush's approval ratings would suffer the same fate as his father's, as Democrats rediscovered the power of the economy. North Korea expressed no shock and awe over the military campaign in Iraq. And fear of SARS beat down the romance of globalization so mercilessly that news organizations started looking for file stories on consumers' response to the Black Death. In short, the euphoria of victory lasted about as long as it took to load the CNN home page on a high-speed internet connection.

Less obvious was the second Gulf war's effect on collective memory. By taking us back to the anxieties that came to a head with Desert Storm, the final days of Saddam Hussein's regime threw the last clods of dirt on the grave of the 1990s. In the San Francisco Bay Area, where *Bad Subjects* was born, the sunny days of Bill Clinton's presidency made the memory of Stormin' Norman Schwarzkopf seem as distant as the Napoleonic Wars. The stock market was climbing the stairway to heaven. Intellectuals were quitting the academy to make improbable salaries describing a future of borderless consumer satisfaction. The dominant fear for many privileged Americans, to reference a popular television commercial, was that the tow-truck drivers who had invested before them would buy up all the good islands.

It didn't take a genius to see that the bubble would eventually burst. But some very smart people, from Federal Reserve Chairman Alan Greenspan on down, gravely underestimated the force of the explosion. It is not likely that September 11, 2001 will ever dissolve into the amorphous flow of history. The images were too striking, the effect on the American psyche too devastating. Yet we are beginning to put that fateful day in perspective, to recognize that, like the storming of the Bastille, it was both a long time coming and a long time going. The war in Iraq in the spring of 2003 made it all too apparent that the relative stability of the Clinton years represented an insignificant pause in the tale of the New World Order. The confusion, betrayal, and despair that followed the collapse of the Eastern Bloc after 1989 never really went away. From Bosnia to Iraq, the forces unleashed by the disintegration of Western communism have pushed us all relentlessly toward the present crisis.

*   *   *

Responding intelligently to that crisis requires that we see it from multiple perspectives, without trying to reconcile them into one neat-and-tidy vision. A 'circumstance,' to return to Marx's formulation, is what stands around us. More often than not, it functions as an electric fence for the mind, imprisoning us in our burdens of the moment. We end up standing around. If we are to have any hope of initiating meaningful change, we have to find different ways of stepping outside of our present circumstances, without forgetting the view from within. The only way to outflank the status quo is by standing in several places at once. In practical terms, this means paying attention to the ways in which the second Gulf war was both like the first one, and was different; to the singularity of September 11, 2001 and the recognition that, as Slavoj Žižek aptly remarks, Americans had already staged the day in their fantasy lives many times over; and, finally, to the ways in which the turmoil of the past few years belongs to more broadly understood eras: post-Cold War, post-1960s, post-World War II, and, yes, post-French Revolution.

As Marx so brilliantly argues in the *18th Brumaire*, progressive political activity has to emancipate itself from the prison house of past revolutions. While we may be fighting the same war as the First International, we are fighting very different battles. Trying to make the world conform to terminology that predates the telephone is not wise. For example, the term 'globalization' may be a more effective way of describing the way imperialism has abstracted itself into a higher form of hegemony than references to explosive military power. However, as every ink-stained, newspaper-hawking Leninist at antiwar demonstrations will remind you, traditional forms of imperial expression—such as colonial occupations—are still practiced by very real nation-states such as America, Israel, and Great Britain. And they're right.

But that doesn't mean that theories of power developed outside the party door—such as the readings of globalization proposed by such disparate figures as Arundhati Roy, Naomi Klein, and Hardt and Negri—are any less prescient for the interpretive purposes of the greater left. They are part of the massive intellectual arsenal at everyone's disposal. Synthesizing the history and the varieties of progressive intellectual experience is what contributors to *Bad Subjects* have always done best. In positioning ourselves to the left of the organized left, we have encouraged our readers to see that contemporary forms of hegemony represent the sum total of hegemonies, both past *and* present.

*   *   *

Like our relationship with the organized left, our relationship with left publishing has been an agonistic one. In part, it is a result of our organization's ambiguous identity: is *Bad Subjects* a traditional magazine, like *The Nation, In These Times,* or *Harper's*? Is *Bad Subjects* an upstart counter-cultural rag, like *Punk Planet, The Baffler, Bitch,* or *Stay Free*? Or is it a website, comparable to online ventures that range from Salon.com and Slate.com to indymedia.org and ZNet? The answer is 'yes.'

Compared with the ink-and-paper left in the United States, whether we are talking about established magazines or photocopied 'zines, *Bad Subjects* occupies a strange middle space between the three poles of academia, journalism, and counterculture. Though *Bad Subjects* is not an academic journal by any stretch of the imagination, it did begin in a university setting. Because of this legacy, we have become something of a bridge between university culture and a broader cultural left of journalists, musicians, artists, and other creative intellectuals. The results have been both wonderful and painful. At its best, *Bad Subjects* has offered powerful, incisive, and theoretically informed cultural criticism in an accessible package. In short, we have accomplished the kind of 'public intellectual' crossover that many academics have longed for, and we have done it as a radical (rather than a liberal) publication. But it is not simply a romance. A glance at our pages will show that as editors and writers, we constantly struggle with how to talk about both theory and politics. Our pages have brought together philosophers, activists, and everyday people in both explosive and productive combinations. As we already noted, the fact that we don't have to sell anything—the magazine or advertising—means we are able to take chances and go in directions that other publications simply can't.

*   *   *

In a time when the established publications of the left are giving in to reduced expectations and increased pessimism, *Bad Subjects* retains a commitment to imagination, speculation, idealism, and all the other fuzzy dimensions of the left intellectual project. We are deliberately more cultural, more philosophical, more personal, and more experimental than the established ink-and-paper magazines of the left. At the same time, unlike other cultural 'zines, we are committed to the analysis of politics and culture in all their various forms, rather than focusing on a particular countercultural perspective. We occupy a position that nobody else in the US left print media can occupy because we are heterodox, hybrid, committed, and intellectually adventurous.

Our online presence has had much to do with this. As with countless other left organizations, we have found the internet to be an amazingly useful network for distribution and dissemination. We reach hundreds of thousands of readers all over the world—a feat that would be impossible for an ink-and-paper magazine run on almost no budget. Our internet presence began in so-called 'gopher space' because there was no world wide web at the time. Today, we are one of the oldest—if not the oldest—continuously running left publication online. As countless other for-profit online ventures have failed or stagnated, as the dot com sand castle of the 1990s collapsed, *Bad Subjects* has remained strong because it follows the principles of free exchange and free dissemination. As Richard Barbrook has argued in his widely circulated cyber-communist manifesto, the internet is much better suited to the free exchange of information than the exchange of commodities for money. Thus, while media conglomerates continue to struggle in their search for a stable internet profit stream, *Bad Subjects* has thrived and grown in the online environment.

So unlike many other online ventures, even some of those on the left, *Bad Subjects* is not an attempt to carve out a profitable niche for its producers. But we are also quite different from indymedia.org, commondreams, alternet, or even the many culture jammer sites out there. We retain a steadfast commitment to patient, considered, sustained, and edited cultural criticism. While we applaud the do-it-yourself attitude and accessibility of these other sites, ours is an intellectual project that allows for the immediacy of the online editorial but places it—literally—against a background of a patient and developed cultural analysis that sets its own agenda, and does not simply react to the latest in current events. We are more committed to criticism than journalism.

* * *

At its best, what *Bad Subjects* contributes to the world of progressive publications is an emphasis upon politically interpreting the world, without assuming that there is a common moral consensus that is held by our readership. This has always been of particular importance to us, as we have strived to produce a periodical that not only questions its own political assumptions, but that of its readership as well. This is one of the reasons why we take a particular interest in running interviews with philosophers and social critics whom most Americans would not necessarily believe to have anything to say to the mainstream left, such as Slavoj Žižek and Hayden White, instead of Noam Chomsky and Vandana Shiva.

By choosing such interview subjects, *Bad Subjects* is not only making an ideological point about intellectuals we believe ought to be part of the activist canon. We are also making a political point about the deficits of progressive publishing, specifically its marginalization of intellectuals dedicated to the interpretation of politics. Our reasoning is as much a product of ethical deliberation and participation in street politics as it is a product of having been trained as traditional intellectuals. If the left is going to continue to grow beyond the bounds of its own historical formations, it has to work just as hard on expanding its critical imaginary as it does assembling globally coordinated demonstrations against war.

To paraphrase Theodor Adorno, interpretation is its own kind of political practice. To separate the two, and assume that there is a necessary division of progressive political labor based on education and skill is tantamount to inscribing class relationships within the left. You can't make lettuce organic by washing it in a pristine stream. And you can't make intellectuals 'organic' by sending them off to bucolic re-education camps where they learn to suppress their tendency to think before acting. As the American writer Thomas Pynchon makes painfully clear in *Vineland*, his underrated novel about the backlash against the legacy of the 1960s, desire for purity is the bane of the left. We envision *Bad Subjects* as a counterweight against the tug of that desire.

Maybe it makes the most sense to describe *Bad Subjects* in the negative. We aren't pure. We aren't professional. We aren't for profit. And we aren't in line with a political party. The essays in this volume testify to this negative identity. It's impossible to distill a common style or message. We have nevertheless grouped the essays in six parts around some common themes. The essays in 'Politics Old and New' identify many central political currents of the present day and exemplify the eclectic and thoughtful manner in which *Bad Subjects* constructs the political. The essays in 'Remembering History' exemplify the 'Bad' approach to political historiography: criticizing popular notions of historical memory, redeeming that which is forgotten, and calling into question received wisdom about politics. The *Bad Subjects* project allows for academics and non-academics to interface and bridge the gaps between their discourse methods. By challenging academics to present complex concepts in straightforward, jargon-free language, *Bad Subjects* impels this gap to close. The essays in 'In and Out of the Academy' explore this changing boundary. In the section 'Crossing Borders,' the essays address contemporary geographies of power, class, and interpersonal and geographic landscapes. The essays in 'The Personal Is the Political' are the kind of gripping first-person narratives that provide for *Bad Subjects*' most engaging political education. And in 'Media and Response,' our authors directly address the political meanings of significant productions of popular culture.

The essays all share a broader commonality: a refusal to believe the lies of free market ideology, a reluctance to take the commonplaces of progressive discourse for granted, a rejection of the notion that there is a proper way to make love, art, or politics. Our hope, as you read them, is not that you would agree with us, but that you would be provoked to the sort of respectful disagreement that keeps both politics and hope alive.

Part I

Politics Old and New

INTRODUCTION

One of the strengths of the traditional leftist critique of ideology is its ability to demystify the idea of progress. For all the 'modernization' we have witnessed of late—online commerce and stock trading, the downloading of cultural goods, the decline of the state's role in the marketplace, and the reduction of taxes and tariffs on global trade—we continue to see a regression in the civility of political life. Genocide, ethnic cleansing, and classical imperialism re-emerged during the first ten years of the post-Cold War era, while a transnational business elite in the West rejected what remained of the welfare state as an outmoded form of income redistribution. True racial equality took a backseat to 'market multiculturalism' and the extension of economic, but not political, rights to minorities. Pundits declared that the glass ceiling had shattered, ignoring the fact that most women in the workplace never even get to see the sky. And lesbians and gays became protagonists on prime time television, but remained minor characters in the political process. Meanwhile, prison populations in the United States skyrocketed, incomes continued to decline, and people worldwide retreated to the comfort of traditional identities—religious, cultural, and nationalist—in search of imaginary redress for the injuries inflicted on them by the marketplace.

Itself a product of the Cold War's icy afterglow, *Bad Subjects* has excelled in diagnosing these patterns of regression, showing how they have instantiated themselves in transnational establishment discourses covering the implosion of the welfare state, the rapid growth of the prison-industrial complex, the postcommunist left, and the renewed vigor of the United States' imperialist agenda. The pieces selected for this first section open a window onto the diverse analyses of the New World Order that have graced our journal's pages. We take particular pride in showcasing our support for self-consciously heterodox positions. There is no ideological line to toe in *Bad Subjects*, except displaying a willingness to let one's line be tied to a network of others. For precisely this reason, however, *Bad Subjects* has provided a warm welcome to people who see no shame in returning to Marx, Gramsci, or Adorno, even as we acknowledge those classic thinkers' ideological blindspots. In an era when intellectuals win points by declaring their posterity—postwar, postmodern, post-Marxist—we take great pleasure in announcing that we refuse to jump on the bandwagon of progress.

Karl MacRae inaugurates the proceedings in this first section with a blistering critique of human rights abuses in the American penal system, taking care to contextualize these crimes by examining them in light of post-1960s social thought, and his own experiences working as a prison activist. Moving from domestic to international security, Joe Lockard proceeds to define the war-like culture that gave birth to—and was recreated by—the second Gulf war, launched by the United States and the United Kingdom in March 2003. Reading these two essays in tandem provides a compelling portrait of a comprehensive American ideology of exploitation and brutality that knows no national boundaries and is completely lacking in consciousness of its own history.

Long-time *Bad Subjects* contributors Rick Prelinger and Doug Henwood then shift our attention from the state to culture. Prelinger reflects on debates over the status of copyright in the digital age; Henwood on the appeal conservative politics held for him as a college student in the 1970s and their subsequent transformation into many young people's ideology of choice. Both authors take on ideas we too readily take for granted: the legitimacy of private property and the sacredness of conservative ideology. Together they illustrate perfectly compatible crises of capitalist hegemony, one incurred by technology, the other by personal maturity.

David Hawkes and Edmund Zimmerman descend deeper into the grime of the archaic. Reflecting on observations about religious ritualism and contemporary politics in Haiti, Hawkes' essay firmly articulates in classically contrarian fashion the horror of the mythological. Zimmerman, in turn, charts the return of the fascist repressed in Italy, with the second rise of Silvio Berlusconi and his neo-American embrace of contemporary market ideology. More concerned with the revival of classical Italian fascism, Zimmerman's portrait of contemporary Italy should give pause to those who think that the Forza Italia is simply the Tuscan version of Britain's New Labour.

'Politics Old and New' concludes with a revisitation of the legacy of state socialism in the former Soviet Bloc. Ewa Pagacz's essay looks at the re-emergence of precommunist forms of life in postcommunist Poland. What is distinct about Pagacz's vision is not so much her attentiveness to the return to power of institutions like the Catholic Church, but her facility for showing how present day Poland has fused the worst aspects of precommunist and communist Poland under the pressures of Europeanization and globalization. Poles are still poor, still ruled by superstition and still unable to buy such basic necessities as medicine: so much for the redemptive power of German auto plants.

Richard D. Wolff, on the other hand, looks at what Marxist ideology has historically achieved. He shows how it has influenced leftist politics and become a part of progressive common sense, while also reflecting on Marxism's failure to achieve social reform and eliminate the class system in the former USSR. Focusing on Soviet deviations from historical Marxist conceptions of surplus labor, Wolff concludes this section with a utopian reading of Marxism's unfulfilled historical potential.

I
Prison Activist's Notes

Karl MacRae

And what will happen in the evening in the forest with the weasel with the teeth so sharp when you're not looking in the evening.

Nick Drake, 'Hazey Jane II' (1970)

The levels referred to in this essay reflect those defined by the California Department of Corrections (CDC). If they seem confusing, you are not alone. There are levels within levels, but according to the CDC, there are only VI levels of detainment.

LEVEL IV: *Cells, fenced or walled perimeter. Electronic security, more staff and armed officers, both inside and outside the installation.*
SHU: *Security Housing Unit: The most secure area within a level IV prison, designed to provide maximum coverage.*
Warden and prison staff determine who is relegated to the SHU, not the courts. The most severe, secure, and inhumane of prison environments, living in the SHU is akin to being buried alive. Prisoners spend 22½ hours locked in a small, permanently lit, windowless cell. The prisoner cannot see any others and is under constant surveillance. No direct sun ever reaches the cell. Nothing is permitted on the walls. There is no education, no work, no recreation, no smoking.

Six guards forced Vaughn Dortch, an inmate at Pelican Bay's Security Housing Unit, into a vat of 125 degree water and scrubbed his body with a steel-bristled brush. Suffering from SHU syndrome—the deterioration of mental faculties caused from the extreme isolation of living in the SHU—Dortch had smeared his body with feces. After 15 minutes of prison hygiene, Dortch was let up. As he stood, Nurse Barbara Kuroda noted, his peeling skin '[hung] in large clumps around his legs.' She testified that one of the guards remarked, 'Looks like we're going to have a white boy before this is through ... His skin is so dirty and so rotten, it's all fallen off.'

COND. (*Condemned*)
While perhaps not as spectacular as the public drawing and quartering of Damien lovingly depicted in the opening of Foucault's *Discipline and Punish*,

Dortch's near-fatal brush with the law puts the criminal in criminal justice. When I began working at the Prison Activist Resource Center (*www.prisonactivist. org*) I knew the prison system was in crisis. What I didn't realize was that abuses such as those sustained by Dortch—and worse—are regular and acceptable, in as much as the steps needed to prevent them are rarely taken. The ease with which contemporary penology recalls medieval torture speaks volumes of our much lauded progress.

If anything we are devolving. The present trends of denying prisoners legal and educational resources, not to mention media access, bodes poorly for all concerned with civil rights. Without these, the 89 people found wrongly convicted on Death Row since 1973 might well be dead or still languishing. In these cases it was not 'the system' that saved them, but the determination of concerned citizens who fought for years, often without pay, that granted these people freedom. In an already overburdened system, denying prisoners access to resources will only increase the abuses and deaths.

LEVEL III: *Individual cells, fenced perimeter, armed coverage.*
The quotation below from Thomas A. Markus' introduction to *Order and Space in Society* describes competing beliefs in the formation of character and the individual's relationship to society during the Enlightenment: 'What both views however share is a fundamental pessimism about society, since it was either malevolent or irrelevant, and a fundamental optimism about the individual.'

That was then. I have heard prisoners defined by those who work in the prison industry as inmates, criminals, convicts, scum, and toxic waste. For those who live outside the razor wire in a landscape sorted into zones of social control, our status, power, and freedom either falls along a continuum of acquired wealth, or is determined by race. Mike Davis describes well these zones of exclusion, containment, enhancement, and abatement. To these, I would add privatization of public space (enclosure), cultural control strategies such as profiling, and low level harassment, all of which function well to regulate the flow of bodies in society. What these policies reflect is our fundamental pessimism about the individual *and* our pessimism about society.

It is almost impossible to believe that Thomas Paine could have measured a government's success by whether '[its] jails are empty of prisoners, [its] streets of beggars.' The control and incarceration of the public has reached unprecedented levels: at 1999 rates, one in 20 newborns will spend time behind bars, according to the Justice Department. The business of locking people up is moving at electron speed, with every keystroke of a bed broker or corrections consultant.

In the 1990 essay *Postscript on Control Societies*, Gilles Deleuze describes the shift away from disciplinary societies where control is maintained via sites of confinement, to control societies in which control is maintained through the use of surveillance, biometric devices, and other tracking technologies. Deleuze fails to mention the possibility that both forms of control might blossom, working in concert, in a stupefying danse macabre of remote and site-specific technologies. While some of us feel the back of our necks tingle under the gaze of ubiquitous cameras, and more have grown numb to the sensation, at least we are spared the strip search. Actually, we only think we are spared. X-ray technology, with a limited capacity to see through clothing, went into use at JFK Airport in the late 1990s. Nudity, not radiation, is the grounds on which this technology is being challenged.

RC: *Reception center—short term housing to process, classify, and evaluate incoming inmates.*

I got in my car, picked up a fellow activist, and drove to FCI Dublin, a federal penitentiary for women, to attend a pow-wow organized by the Native Americans housed there and the Four Winds Cultural Group. I could hardly find the place even with a map. I blamed my lack of directional sense on my anxiety about going inside; I knew full well that prisons are made deliberately hard to find.

We parked, met the others arriving for the event: a collection of drummers and singers, mostly Native American, and a few folks such as my colleague and I, who felt they had something to learn by attending. As some gathered their drums, I began to fill the forms required for attendance: name, organization, license plate number, social security number ... I could see the government's database grow as I wrote. In the lobby, family members waited to visit with loved ones. They lined up in front of a counter, behind which the prison official directed them one by one to step up, sign in, and walk through a metal detector. To the left of the counter was the door inside the prison. As I waited in line, the prison chaplain walked up to me and asked for my hand. He placed a rubber stamp there. I looked at my hand but saw nothing. I had been chemically impregnated; I could feel the liquid evaporating like alcohol, but had no idea what had been placed on my skin. 'What is that?' I asked, offering a meek smile. 'Oh,' he replied, 'it's really for the women.'

At the counter I surrendered my driver's license to the prison official. In groups of two we were escorted past the metal detectors and into a small ten-by-six-foot chamber. The doors were opened and closed remotely. From this room we entered the prison yard. Once inside I saw the sun glancing off what must have been miles of razor wire, like giant flesh-tearing slinkys, one on top of the other.

LEVEL II: *Open dorms with secure perimeter.*

The industry of locking people up is an ironic cancer eating away at the social body. Those most likely to fall victim to crime—people of color and the poor—

are also those most likely to be criminalized and thus fed into the maw of America's great prison machine.

The great feat of designing, building, and maintaining the prison industry reflects a remarkable convergence of disciplines: architects, lawyers, psychologists, doctors, computer scientists, biologists, chemists, MBAs, politicians, and journalists, to name a few. What Hawthorne called the 'black rose of society' has become a major growth industry.

There are growing ranks of admirable professionals and others working for social change, behind prison walls or on the outside. But as with attorneys, there are too many for the few, and too few for the many. I often dwell on the inability or unwillingness of professionals to exert their own power, however meager. I once met a doctor who told me that prison officials were denying care to people at an institution she worked in. I pointed out the illegality of this, to which she shrugged her shoulders and changed the subject.

During the pow-wow I sat next to a friend who is an attorney. He turned to me and spoke of the definitive moment when for each and every person we saw in prison garb, a juror uttered the word 'guilty', and a gavel dropped. For him, that moment defined the horror of what was now before him. For me, having been schooled in architecture, the horror was the thought of countless designers with bleary computer screen-staring eyes, manipulating electrons into lines that would spawn the housing of 2 million people. I whispered to my friend, 'For every building you see—for every cell and every bed, every isolation tank and every weld on every truss, every blade of manicured grass and every curl of razor wire—someone somewhere drew them up with accuracy and precision, knowing full well to what use their designs and labor would be put.'

I decided to research firms that designed prisons. I wanted to find out which teams of architects and engineers were responsible for places like Pelican Bay, which former California Governor George Deukmeijian called 'a model for the rest of the nation.'

Finding architects to design prisons on schedule, to 'spec.' and within proposed budgets, was far easier than I imagined. Logging on to the American Institute of Architects (AIA) website, I clicked on the 'find an architect' icon, then posed as a client seeking a designer of correctional facilities. While some architectural firms have a policy against prison work, others are brazen in what informs their professional decisions.

HDR for instance has a whopping 235 'justice projects' under their belts, including 'the design of over 150 state and county detention and correctional facilities, representing more than 100,000 beds, with a combined construction value of over $6 billion over the past 23 years.' HOK is more genteel. Their website insists, 'Our designs must go beyond pure function—they must enrich people's lives in a positive meaningful way.' How sweet: 120,000 beds full of positivity and meaning. A sidebar reassures, 'The environments are distinguished by design and functional excellence, operational efficiency and cost effectiveness,' with nary a word of the people they house or employ, under what conditions, to what effectiveness. Nor do they explain how their brand of excellence is measured.

Like concrete, the nexus of architecture and justice has hardened with time. Herbert McLaughlin, the M in KMD, a large San Francisco firm, was appointed to the Attorney General's Ad Hoc Committee on Correctional Architecture. This marked KMD's humble beginnings in criminal justice architecture. On their website they boast their 'reputation as a leader in jail, prison, and court architecture.' The smiling face of architectural integrity these firms unctuously display is little more than an investor relations ploy. Insulating the investor from what the money actually does is the name of the game.

The most chilling example I've come across assumes the most nonchalant of positions. Frank Roberts of Durrant—an architecture, construction, engineering, and financing conglomerate—promises in his caption, 'Privatized prisons built on spec? ... You bet!' He goes on to boast about his ability to predict what the correctional facility marketplace will look like into the next century.

An article by AIA architect Tom Adams entitled 'Accommodating the Unsavory Side of Society: Contemporary Jails and Prisons' contains blind spots begging to be examined. It remains unclear if architects like Adams are simply driven by profit, at the expense of all other concerns, or if they really have not informed their work with any kind of analysis, social, political, economic or otherwise. Adams attempts to describe the problems associated with prison design without any mention of which, why, and under what conditions people are locked up. Asserting there are bad people and something must be done with them would be more enlightened than Adams' article, which has the desperate feel of someone attempting to rationalize what they do.

On the one hand, Adams decries the lack of aesthetic freedom given architects who design prisons, and the difficulty of including amenities like air conditioning. Whether air conditioning is an amenity at places like Chowchilla, where women wait out 106 degree temperatures, eight to a 16 by 18 foot cell, goes unexamined. Adams blames 'public perception,' complaining that designers are told to 'ugly up' buildings to appease the anonymous public. Adams bemoans a project for which the architects had to give up their beloved, textured, colored concrete.

On the other hand, Adams notes, 'At an average cost of $50,000 per bed, this represents $13.6 billion in construction dollars with no end in sight.' Despite design constraints and budgetary concerns that stifle innovation, 'security does not come cheap.' Adams and his peers shall someday overcome these factors— and the nasty public. It's not his fault the public is so misinformed. After all, prisons and jails 'have been besmirched by images portrayed in *Brubaker*, *The Shawshank Redemption*, and *The Birdman of Alcatraz*,' Adams writes. Despite poor public perception, he still hopes his prisons can 'affect the individual's future with education, training, development of good work habits, and counseling.'

It is impossible for anyone with any experience in prison issues to believe this, given the gutting of programs for prisoners and reports of rampant abuse.

But the power of positive thinking carries Mr. Adams on to his conclusion, 'While the architecture may not make a better citizen out of those that have erred, it can facilitate the institution's ability to carry out its mission.' This is the locking key: the architect's responsibility to the institution that commissions him, not to those who people his creation. The lives of inmates or guards are hardly mentioned. The fact that architects are neck deep in a social/political project on a massive scale—one third of black male residents in both Florida and Alabama can no longer vote (a total of 3.9 million Americans can't vote because of felony convictions)—does not occur to Adams. There will be time for critical thinking after the check clears.

Granted, most of these buildings, SHUs notwithstanding, only function as environments that facilitate routine abuse; the buildings themselves are not abusive, in any strict sense of the term. Lest we forget, there are 3,500 people nationwide waiting to be put to death in a chamber designed for the task.

Control units designed ostensibly to reduce human-on-human abuse have had the opposite effect. More astounding still, the psychological abuses of those forced to live in these environments are built into the very functioning of these structures as *designed*—regardless of how those who run the facility behave. The AIA's code of ethics, which states members should uphold human rights in all their professional endeavors (section E.S.1.4 Human Rights), apparently does not apply here.

After the pow-wow I was escorted back to the chamber through which I had entered. I placed my hand under a light that shone down from a fixture on the wall. I hadn't noticed it on my way in. A spot on my hand glowed; it was green or purple. This confirmed I was not one of the women inmates. The doors opened. I walked.

LEVEL I: *Open dormitories without secure perimeter.*
I wake up and walk to the corner coffee shop. Outside is the man who sells me the homeless newspaper. We talk. When I tell him about my work with prison issues, he tells me he was once inside. Huntsville, he says. The execution capital of the country, I think. Out of the corner of my eye, I see a local, a man who was locked up for a short stint in Portland. I wait in line, and when I get to the counter, I am served coffee by a man who, while incarcerated in New Mexico, watched a man attack another man. One had grabbed the other, and in a ravenous fit, bit through his scrotum, crimson tides flooding his shorts, legs, shoes, floor.

Note: Statistics quoted are from 1999, the original publication date of this essay.

2
Iraq War Culture

Joe Lockard

CUTBACKS AND REPRESSION

The US political landscape of the Iraq war is characterized by massive cutbacks in social expenditures, together with tax structures that underwrite capital accumulation by a narrow union of social allies. Corporate, military, and government leadership have become an integrated, interlocking circle, one that promotes an ideological culture of the nation-state as the fundamental source of progress and power to consume. Yet this has been a crisis-bound nation-state in need of affirmations of its superiority. From the inauguration of the Bush administration until April 2003, the US economy lost 2.1 million jobs. The US education and health systems are in the middle of financial crises generated by astonishing military expenditures, corporate welfare, and tax giveaways to the rich.

According to a January 2003 survey by the National Council of State Legislatures, US states had cut $49.1 billion in public services, health and welfare benefits, and education in their fiscal 2003 budgets, and were due to cut another $25.7 billion. That $74.8 billion in cutbacks represents significantly less than the Bush administration's initial $80 billion budget request for the Iraq war, with many billions of future supplementary requests certain to follow. This war has quite literally been fought on the backs of schoolchildren and university students, the working poor, single mothers, hospital and home-care patients, now-condemned recipients from defunded AIDS drug payment (ADAP) programs, and entire corps of unemployed teachers, health workers, and other public employees.

Culture, conceived in the broadest sense as the social exegesis of mass phenomena, assembles, integrates, and responds to these profound and rapid social developments. Iraq war culture has been much more than its imagery of Homeland Security orange alert warnings, proliferating global protests, video shots of night-time blasts in Baghdad, or the still image of a wounded Iraqi woman caught in crossfire. This culture represents a revolving economy between violent imagery and US political hegemonism that reinforces itself through reference to the same violent imagery. As a culture, it is an accumulation of adverse phenomena at crisis point, a continuing social crossfire created by capital making markets and unmaking labor rights. It is the clearance of shared communities—from villages in the occupied West Bank to cohesive but impoverished working-class neighborhoods in Cairo that send workers to the Gulf—and labor migrations endured by peoples of color without alternatives, the unrecognized neoslaveries that support contemporary economies. This is a culture of exhibitionist violence and invisible labor.

A key linkage exists here, because the Iraq war marks the emerging division between global domains where interventionist violence is visible and labor invisible, and those where violent intervention is invisible and elite labor visible. Iraq is the site of permissible imperial violence and majority un- or underemployment, whereas military violence is nominally impermissible in the United States and its economy responds either favorably or less so to the success of overseas violence. An emergent transatlantic Anglo-American intellectual school of neocolonialism fabricates a blatant reinvention of once-discredited nineteenth-century theories of empire, providing excuses for over 20,000 war dead and the occupation of Iraq. In the United Kingdom, Daniel Kruger publishes 'The Case for Colonialism' as a cover story essay for *The Spectator*, while nearly at the same time in April 2003 in the United States, Stanley Kurtz publishes 'Democratic Imperialism: A Blueprint' in the Washington-based *Policy Review*. Both unapologetically and unashamedly cite the arguments and advocates of Victorian colonialism as their preferred models; both deny the autonomy of non-Western natives and fail to discuss imperial violence and exploitation of labor and resources; both engage in what Lawrence James describes as 'the revival of benevolent imperialism.' The native, the nominal topic of liberatory concern, would not be of concern if there were not economic advantage to interventionist violence.

Where the claims of pseudo-democrats have been established as coordinated Anglo-American policy, we have reached a new high tide mark in Western intellectual culture, which rationalizes globalist economic inequalities and the compounded advantages of Western economies that can finance information-driven war technologies. Such is the cultural hierarchy that information labor has produced. Iraq war culture is the cutting edge of American economic, military, and information culture, with its techno-aesthetic and assertion of universal dominion under an ideological banner of Freedom Incarnate. The truly liberated class today is the mercenary migrants of state violence, the global warrior class that asserts its rights of mobility and occupational freedom, with digital video uplinks from the front lines to document its work product.

Simultaneously, at a domestic level in the United States—one that can no longer be described accurately as domestic given its global integration—a set of repressive legal enactments adopted in the name of national security has been establishing new models for international imitation. Where Britain's Emergency Regulations once established the legal mechanisms for colonialism in India, Hong Kong, Kenya, Palestine, and other locales, in this still-new century the United States is framing the security legislation that is already being promulgated by other West-allied nations. If enacted, the Domestic Security Enhancement Act of 2003—also known as the USA Patriot Act II—will radically alter constitutional legal protections, already in substantial decline since the first Patriot Act. Should Attorney General John Ashcroft prevail, Fourth Amendment protections against domestic security surveillance will fade into a ghostly remnant, where surveillance would be conducted entirely at the Attorney General's discretion without judicial review.

Secret warrantless searches would expand; almost any private record would be subject to investigative demands. Secret detentions would be permitted without criminal charge and *habeas corpus* would be annulled by provisions to prevent such litigation and even forbid the release of basic information about detainees. Lawful residents could be deported without a hearing; and federal and state orders limiting police spying on community activists would be canceled. Even without waiting for legislative authorization, Ashcroft has used his existing powers to rule, in the case of a Haitian refugee, that detained aliens may be held indefinitely without trial based on national security claims. Civil rights protections in the United States have regressed some 50 to 70 years, and a significant part of the US legal community has been left aghast at this undoing of the work of generations.

While legal ideologies in the United States struggle with restrictive interpretations of national security, the means of legal discipline have multiplied near-exponentially through information technology that enforces narrowed parameters of citizenship rights. A new culture of systematic automated surveillance and Total Information Awareness has established itself, one that points to a vista of unending conflict as its self-justification. There is no particular note of social apocalypse here, only a gray statement of the rationales of perpetuation required in order to integrate an information economy with an economy that produces and exports violence, then must guard against its return. If this information culture attempts to transform the transactions that constitute social existence into a security database, it treats absence of information as an identified object of suspicion. Non-integration into the global database signifies either ungoverned or ungovernable; it represents the presence of an atavistic and potentially barbaric subject. The discipline of market control—and social cutbacks—cannot be exerted where citizens remain unintegrated into the dominant information culture. To be outside control, whether as nation-state or citizen-subject, is to invite the discipline of information technology and its potential forms of destruction.

Iraq war culture is a culture that promotes the objectivity of a consensus of power. The test of cultural validity comes in its conformity with information power. When Iraq's former minister of information, Mohamed Saeed al-Sahaf, looked into an *al-Jazeera* camera and spoke of crushing US forces, while 3rd Division tanks moved at will through Baghdad, he occupied a paradoxical—and deeply antiquated—position as a political fabulator whose rhetorical disinformation meets simultaneous disproof via live feeds from the same city. The minister was reduced to arguing that these are Associated Press rather than Arab-owned media feeds. It is as though the minister had been transplanted from the Nasserite rhetorical world of the late 1960s, part of a once-collapsed and now-revivified rhetorical bubble. Al-Sahaf's extraordinary denial of reality was in part a retreat into a fictional, could-be, and might-still-be, world, a familiar reaction to the imminence of cultural defeat. Validity and falsity are now functions of transmissibility and integration into technological networks. What matters today are US army colonels in P3 intelligence planes riding electronic shotgun with laptops and streaming video overhead their advancing columns. An incorporative disciplinary culture stretches today between the United States and Iraq, one based on the absorption of unincorporated territory into the infosphere.

NECROPHILIC CULTURE

The Iraq war occasioned more than the war itself; it was a discrete moment in a continuum of progressive regimentalization of imperial subjects. It supplied rationales of repression, demands for the subordination of counter-argument, and delimitations between permissible speech and silence that knows its place. War culture is speech in its own right, one that functions in rhetoric of demand and conquest. Yet the *geist* of attempted homogenization of opinion is unworkable home-front psy-ops, one that will fail because mass political opinion is chaotic in nature and hysterias are transitory phenomena. War culture, in all its efforts to heroicize and memorialize the dead, embraces state violence as the apogee of citizenship. Public speech responds to the demands of citizen-sacrifice.

In *Necro Citizenship*, Russ Castronovo argues that

> While US political culture revolves around intercourse with the dead—from suicidal slaves to injured white male sexual subjects, and from passive female clairvoyants to generic though lifeless citizens—the dead do not remain eternally estranged. No matter how enamored the state and its citizenry are of passive subjects, political necrophilia is also charged with an impossible desire to forget the dead.

Iraq war culture expands the discourse of state-sanctified death, but that same vision of an ennobled battlefield requires symbols, codes, and ideologies to mask its barbarism. Memorialization of the fallen-to-be proceeds before the fact and to dissent is to disgrace the memories of citizen-soldiers who have not yet died but must die. Speech that opposes unnecessary death is itself unnecessary, and political necrophilia waves its flags. Via the media, there is a collective shared experience of death that demands transformation through public rituals and ideological appropriation of citizen 'sacrifice.' 'All Americans honor your sacrifice,' George Bush told the Marines assembled before him at Camp Lejeune, honoring the collaboration pact with civil suicide promoted by classes that remain alive to make speeches.

Where opposition to necrophilic citizenship was once limited to combatant nations, the last century's history has witnessed an ever-expanding international public assertion of entitlement to oppose state violence. Jurisdictional assertions have followed entrained on that developing international consciousness, as the inauguration of the International Criminal Court evidences. Despite this development, the US invasion of Iraq, undertaken in defiance of world opinion, was underwritten by persistent State Department assertions of international legal exceptionalism for the US military and its actions. The transparent inadequacies of such US claims to national exceptionalism contribute both to immediate antagonism and continuation of global efforts to create and enforce preventative mechanisms based in international law.

In the world of opposition, Iraq war culture has been the raw emotion of street demonstrations, of myriad coffee house discussions of energy-driven US imperialism and corporate colonialism; of popular intellectual counter-hegemonism in formation and yet-to-form; of experimental thought and democratic expression. Global contempt toward the United States cites its transparent imperial interests, the hypocritical distance between its idealistic advocacies and barbaric means, and the transformation of a post-World War II model-nation into a twenty-first century *Dirty Harry* nation-state. Oppositional culture has found its antimodel, the sole remaining superpower operated as a fundamentalist Christian franchise licensee. In the days of its greatest success, US war culture has generated its greatest and most energetic opposition. Yet because 'culture' cannot be understood in itself as immanent and self-explained, its originating political and historical frameworks intertwine themselves throughout that expression. Without this simultaneity of understandings, an opposition remains inadequate to its purposes. Sloganeering critiques of US war culture mirror the simplifications and hollow cultural 'knowledges' that enable US policymakers to model a world that will appreciate its heroic necrophilia.

3

Beyond Copyright Consciousness

Rick Prelinger

A 1960s CHILD EMBRACES TECHNOLOGY

The first cheap Norelco Cassette Recorders hit the US market in 1966, when I was 13. Though it suddenly became much easier to tape songs off the radio, I lagged behind the tech curve, stuck in the land of three-inch open-reel. When I finally saved up the money for a little Sony battery-powered cassette recorder, I ditched my lovingly recorded open-reel tapes. But the format battles were just beginning. Record companies had gotten in the habit of releasing key albums as expensive seven-inch reel-to-reel tapes, highly valued by audiophiles for their excellent sound. And as the youth music market exploded, they introduced a panoply of read-only technology: little MGM 'Playtapes,' bastard cassettes with four songs; four-track cartridges destined for sad obsolescence; and eight-track tapes, those beloved 1970s relics that still litter thrift stores.

All of these machines regularly ate tapes, but not one would record them. Desiring large music libraries yet mostly unable to afford them, we kids recorded as many albums and radio shows on cassette as we could. But then I began to lose interest in rock and roll, at least until the onset of punk. Not because free music was less alluring than expensive music, but because pop music entered a long phase of boring overproduction.

I never thought about intellectual property issues when I was young; access to music was all I wanted. But today, in our business-crazed culture, 'IP' is practically the hottest topic in town. Whether it's *Eldred* v. *Ashcroft*, Napster, or music CDs we can't copy, control over content is generating highly publicized battles. We used to just go ahead and copy; now we talk about copyright, our freedom to violate it, and the latest tools that enable us to do so. (Or perhaps the entertainment industry just thinks we do, and that's why they're scared.)

ANACHRONISTIC, BUT NOT YET DEAD

Copyright may be under siege by new access technologies, but it is far from dead. The 'copyright-based industries'—publishing, entertainment, and software—contribute hundreds of billions of dollars to the US economy. IP is our second most valuable export, and more and more of us labor to create, manage, distribute, sell, and shrink-wrap what passes for 'content' these days.

Like organic beings, copyrights used to age and wither away. In fact, Congress' original intent in drafting copyright law was to grant exclusive rights for limited terms (originally 14 years, later 28) in order that content providers might enjoy the fruits of their labor while alive. This temporary monopoly was really an exchange—after copyrights expired, works were to go into the public domain, an expanding body of words, art, music, and moving images available for unrestricted use by all. Until 1978, the 28-year term could, if formalities were strictly followed, be renewed for another 28. Publication without proper copyright notice threw a work into the public domain. This is why so many older US works are out of copyright, unlike works that originate in most other countries. After 1978, the US 'harmonized' its copyright laws with those of most other countries, extending the term of copyright for new works created by individuals to the span of their lives plus 50 years, and new works created by corporations to 75 years. And in 1993, renewals for older works became automatic. The tragic death of John Lennon at age 40 was cited in congressional testimony, as paid lobbyists warned that his young son Sean might outlive the terms of his father's copyrights, and see John's works exploited without proper compensation.

In 1998, the largely undebated Sonny Bono Copyright Term Extension Act further 'harmonized' US copyright laws with our European trade partners, extending terms to life plus 70 years for individually authored works and 95 years for corporate or collective works. The Bono Act was challenged, but upheld by the Supreme Court in 2002, removing a potential roadblock to the indefinite extension of copyrights. These laws have collectively kept hundreds of thousands of US works out of the public domain, and restored copyrights to perhaps millions of foreign works. Such lengthy timespans lock works up for an inordinately long time, but then corporations often live longer than people do.

Corporate copyright holders have also pushed to limit the definition of 'fair use.' And now, under the Digital Millennium Copyright Act of 2000 (DMCA), they are pushing to prevent just about all unpaid copying, performance, distribution, and collecting of digitally based works. If today there are not thousands of people serving federal prison sentences for felony violations of copyright law, it's not because the laws aren't on the books—they're just too difficult to enforce.

NOT IN OUR NEIGHBORHOOD

Although a critique and restructuring of copyright law (and the concept of copyright in general) is immensely valuable, copyright reformism can be a diversion. Copyright reformism focuses on changing copyright law, rather than articulating a more fundamentally radical vision about how information, ideas, art, and culture might be produced and exchanged. It constrains us into thinking in limited terms, terms that might not necessarily be our own. Most importantly, it forces us into defensive positions. When copyright 'infringement' is equated with theft and terrorism, when the free exchange of content is criminalized, and when intimidating legal letters fly freely, it is easy to feel defensive, and worse, to behave reactively. When we are obliged to defend ourselves against assaults motivated by someone else's agenda, we are fighting for freedom of expression on unfriendly turf, and are unlikely to win what we deserve.

One alternative might be to think of IP as 'born free,' in opposition to the US Copyright Act of 1976. This act declares that all human works capable of being fixed in enduring form are copyrighted at the moment of their creation. That perspective would require that we place the word 'property' in quotes when talking about IP. Whether or not we choose to support that utopian idea, we should seriously consider whether the struggle over copyright is really the most meaningful struggle for cultural creators and consumers at this time. What we really ought to be talking about instead is access to works. Access is related to copyright, but is really more fundamental to our freedom to think and experience.

AUTHORSHIP REQUIRES ACCESS

'Access' to works of the intellect doesn't just mean being able to read, listen, watch, or feel them. Today, it also means being able to incorporate other people's works into one's own: to quote, rip, recontextualize, sample, appropriate, and plunder. Today's reader is also a writer; today's listener a sampler; today's spectator an editor or director. We need to appropriate material from other works and make something that is more than the sum of its parts. Unyielding copyright law limits freedom of expression for all of us. And less obviously, there are also other ways of limiting our ability to quote, cut up, and recontextualize.

Our history and culture are increasingly becoming private property rather than public resource. These collections are generally inaccessible without payment of substantial research and licensing fees. In other media, textual material, music, and works of art are now owned or controlled by a dwindling number of rights holders. It is now highly probable that most access to cultural and historical materials, especially if digitized, will follow the paradigm of 'billable events,' with few exceptions or discounts for non-profit or public users.

The function of not-for-profit entities like libraries, museums, and archives is also changing. They no longer exist simply to offer reference or read-only access to their holdings. With the proliferation of authoring tools in all media and the vast increase in all modes of cultural production, many access requests now anticipate the reproduction of materials for reuse and public distribution. This trend is running headlong into the limitations of copyright law. Although the internet is dramatically increasing the population of creators and publishers, there is less pre-existing content available for reuse.

The access problem exists for both copyrighted and non-copyrighted works. Many public domain works exist only in libraries, archives, or private collections, and their custodians charge for access. Though fees may pay for storage, preservation, cataloging, and the production of viewing copies, it ultimately defies common sense for public domain works not to be freely available to the public.

If we act to lessen or to end copyright's authoritarian control over access to culture, we must make sure that other controls don't take its place. A society that places impermeable barriers on the movement, exchange, and appropriation of culture, art, and invention places frightening limits on its ability to evolve and progress.

TOWARD INTELLECTUAL PROPERTY PRESERVES

To think about strengthening public access to cultural resources is to consider basic questions of property and its privatization. As in so many other situations, it's worth looking to history and landscape for precedents and a possible solution. In the late nineteenth and early twentieth centuries, private corporations exerted unprecedented pressures on the 'public domain'—American land and natural resources. The aggressive pursuit of extractive interests such as mining, logging, and agriculture threatened to exhaust public lands and encroach upon naturally or culturally significant sites. In response to this threat, the conservationist movement lobbied to organize a system of national forests, parks, and monuments. By preserving a limited public sphere not subject to the exercise of private property rights, the benefits of some wilderness and cultural sites were preserved for all.

Substituting culture for nature gives us the idea of an intellectual property preserve that houses words, pictures, sounds, moving images, and digital information, and protects them as public property. How might such a 'national park for intellectual property' work? First, the preserve would be a repository for intellectual property rights that had been donated by rights holders. These rights would include copyrights, or in the case of public domain materials, the right to reproduce and disseminate the materials. The activities of the preserve would be closely coordinated with existing institutions, which would often still hold physical materials.

The preserve would contain textual material, still and moving images, works of art, sounds and digital information of all kinds, plus patents. These assets would be acquired in two ways. First, the preserve might purchase certain key resources to build up a core collection of content. Second, the preserve would solicit donations of content. These donations might not necessarily include the physical materials representing the content, but would definitely include copyrights or rights to reproduce.

Why would copyright owners (or owners of public domain materials) ever cede their properties to the preserve? First, and perhaps most important, tax incentives. Amend the tax code to allow substantial deductions or tax credits for donating valuable copyrights or materials. Second, following the precedent of public land acquisitions, key donors might be compensated with private funding. Third, promote public recognition that an act of donation is an honor—a prestigious deed benefitting the national cultural heritage.

Creative Commons (*www.creativecommons.org*) is planning to build an 'intellectual property conservancy.' Among the founders of Creative Commons is Eric Eldred, the lead plaintiff in the recent Supreme Court case challenging the Sonny Bono Copyright Term Extension Act. Other organizations have pursued similar activities toward intellectual property conservancies, and my own archive has partnered with the non-profit Internet Archive to put 2,000 films online for free downloading and reuse. In just over two years, well over 1.5 million movies have been accessed by people all over the world and the images they've gathered have made their way into artworks and commercial productions alike.

There is nothing particularly radical about the practice of a preserve. It's an attempt to work within the system, a voluntary expropriation, a creation of incentives for property holders to do the right thing. Ultimately, though, its goals are to substitute public interest for private profit; to create and sustain public areas in the increasingly privatized cultural space. Preserves are experiments capable of mounting fundamental challenges to our definitions of public and private property. In so doing, they could be a greater force for change than any possible reform of copyright law.

ACCESS AND MORE

There are good reasons to take the 'property' out of IP. We might, for instance, conceive of freer content as an end in itself, as a radically different way of thinking about the distribution of knowledge and culture, and as a utopian wedge that might lead to freer ways of circulating other goods and services. We might imagine a future where content functions to increase consciousness, improve the quality of life, and integrate culture into daily life, and consider how we might get there. And, even as most high-demand IP remains under high-level corporate control, equalizing tactics such as preserves could tip the balance toward a different kind of IP landscape—a shared, profit-free body of knowledge, culture, and entertainment whose very existence might challenge long-lasting concepts of property ownership and control, and stimulate popular alternatives to winner-takes-all thinking. Culture can illuminate and demystify property relations, and changing the way that culture is distributed can lead the way to changing how property is distributed. While corporations, lawyers, and lobbyists concentrate on articulating property rights through law, let's convene cultural creators and consumers and begin to imagine the beginnings of a postproperty consensus.

4

I Was a Teenage Reactionary

Doug Henwood

I have an embarrassing confession to make: in 1972, I cast my first ever presidential votes—primary and general—against Richard Nixon, because he wasn't conservative enough. The final straw was wage and price controls, a statist defilement of the market's purity.

I wasn't always a right-winger. My eighth-grade world history teacher, who in all other respects adhered to the classic meathead-coach style, devoted a full period one day to a sympathetic lecture on Marx. When I got home, I announced to my parents that I was now a Marxist, and, supplemented by a bit of reading, thought of myself as one for the next four years.

But sometime in my senior year in high school—in 1970, when the world was largely in rebellion—I had a collision with one of William Buckley's collections and Milton Friedman's *Capitalism and Freedom*. Subscriptions to *National Review* and the *American Spectator* soon followed. By graduation I was a raving libertarian.

In those days, 'movement' conservatism was pretty tiny. It's hard to believe that now, when undergrads convene in Ayn Rand reading circles and it's considered respectable to quote Hayek. Right-wing think tanks now fund and promote positions that were considered loony and antediluvian in the early 1970s. I had no idea I was joining what in retrospect looks like a vanguard; we thought at the time that capitalism was doomed, but there was something honorable about a last stand.

The moment I got to college, I joined Yale's Party of the Right (POR). The POR was founded by Chairman Bill himself, along with a few others, which gave it lots of cachet. Buckley, like Reagan after him, was able to finesse some of the tensions in conservative thought and politics—the traditionalist v. libertarian schism. Unlike the European Catholic right, which hated the market's destabilizing, anarchic dynamism, Buckley both loved capitalism unreservedly and embraced Catholic social disciplines. After 25 years of study, I still haven't figured out how right-wingers can tout Trad Vals at the same time as they tout the market; capitalism destroys tradition and recognizes only monetary values.

In 1971, Yale's 'traditions' were under siege not from capitalism but from broad social rebellion, much of it anticapitalist. For a kid from an undistinguished suburb who (briefly) wanted to join the ruling class, this was sad; the POR served as a repository for the Old Blue heritage. And what a repository it was.

On one of my first evenings with my POR comrades, I watched as they paged through the freshman face book, *The Old Campus*, commenting on the anatomy of the women. Not their anatomy in the Heffnerian sense, but in the Nazi biologist's sense: what the shape of their skulls, particularly the brow line, told about their intelligence and character.

With any right-wing movement, the Nazi Question is never far from the surface. Publicly, most of US conservatism, given its market-libertarian bent, is anti-Nazi, because fascism is that worst of all things, statist. It's also suspiciously European; though the POR, like most US right-wing formations, was full of Anglophiles, the Continent is thought to be deeply 'unsound' (a favorite POR word, as was 'sound'). Privately, though, many right-wingers (non-Jewish right-wingers, of course) are titillated by Nazis. Nazi jokes and mock self-identification as a Nazi were part of the POR discourse. One evening a delegation of us went to the language lab to watch a German Department-sponsored screening of Riefenstahl's *Triumph of the Will*. There were about three German students there and ten right-wingers.

But more of our time was spent on discussions of Burke and Calhoun (always 'John Caldwell Calhoun') and party rituals than transgressive Nazi games. Meetings were held in Yale common rooms, with their hybrid Old World/men's club decor, with port and sherry, and the traditionalist faction in ties. No dresses to speak of; in 1971, there were only a few women at the fringes of the party; there are a few more of them now. The induction into the party, after a brief novitiate, was held in a particularly dark pseudo-Gothic room, and was offered 'for life at least.'

Monthly meetings were held at Mory's, the Old Blue hangout, and involved collectively drinking a giant silver cup of a green cocktail. The twice-yearly investiture of a new chairman—I witnessed two—involved drinking two green cups while the chairman recited the kings and queens of England from memory.

The POR was a party within the Yale Political Union, a pretty threadbare group in the early 1970s whose remnants envied their Oxford counterpart—especially the Anglophilic POR. Political Union events, debates, and guest speakers often attracted crowds, but since most people were sitting in the street to protest the war or getting high, the ranks of the hard-core politicos were pretty thin. Into this vacuum stepped the POR, which, through packing meetings and parliamentary cleverness, was able to win elections, and put the Union on record as taking right-wing positions that couldn't have gotten 10 per cent of a fair vote.

Thanks to one of these maneuvers, I was elected secretary of the Political Union in the spring of 1971 for service in the fall. That spring, the Union tried to give an award to Secretary of State William Rogers, but when Rogers came to campus to pick it up, protesters were so thick he quickly retreated to Washington. That fall, the new group of officers inherited the privilege of delivering Rogers' award, so we took the train to DC to give it to him. The right-wing contingent—there were a couple of liberals and one George Bush Republican (he was from Bush's district in Houston, and urged us all to watch this guy)—complained about having to take the 'socialist' railroad. Rogers fed us lunch in his personal dining room, showed us around a bit.

That was the high point of my flirtation with the empire. My conservative faith began to waver, I hated the work of the Political Union secretary, shirked the duty of writing press releases saying that the Political Union (in one of its stacked votes) had endorsed some horrid position or other. Watergate was breaking, and sitting in streets and/or getting high began to look a lot more attractive. Soon it was back to my eighth-grade Marxian roots.

My ex-comrades in the POR did nicely in the Reagan years. The authoritarian Catholic chairman who engineered my election as Political Union secretary picked federal judges for Reagan and then went off to be Chief Justice of American Samoa, which he promised to make the most pro-life jurisdiction in the world. Most recently, he was appointed as the first American ambassador to East Timor. Another became Dan Quayle's advisor on tort reform (the business agenda of limiting citizen power to sue corporations). Another spent part of the 1980s as a landlord's enforcer on the Lower East Side; he had gotten thrown out of Yale for gun possession. (The university had let it slide when he was busted for manufacturing speed.) And another was briefly the Republican candidate for governor of Massachusetts, but he was dropped when it emerged that he liked to hang around nude in his office.

Since I am still a member of the Party of the Right—a status even death couldn't deprive me of—I still get invitations to their annual January banquet. Every year I think I'm going to go to check them out and maybe write up the experience. But then I think of having to sit through the dinner and throw the invitation away.

5

Voodoo Politics: Tyranny and Enlightenment in Haiti and Britain

David Hawkes

During one of the frequent rebellions against his rule, the Haitian dictator François 'Papa Doc' Duvalier encouraged his supporters with the proclamation: 'They cannot get me, I am immaterial.' Duvalier was not announcing his irrelevance, but his divinity. Early in his reign he instigated a graffiti campaign, which baldly claimed that 'Duvalier is a god,' and while he held power he managed to convince most of his subjects that this was literally true. From an early age, Duvalier had studied and practiced voodoo, publishing scholarly books on the subject and ingratiating himself with the sorcerors and priests. Once elected president, he appointed a well-known voodoo 'houngan' as head of the national militia, and used the religion as an integral part of his program of terror and repression. With his black clothes, top hat and other-worldly aura, he aped the style of Baron Samedi, a particularly malevolent voodoo deity. It required only a small leap of the imagination for the populace to conceive the notion that Duvalier actually was Baron Samedi. Image became reality, as the fact that Papa Doc resembled this spirit edged into the conviction that he was actually a god in human form.

It would be very easy to portray this chicanery as the product of a primitive and underdeveloped culture. For two centuries, the West has confidently assumed that its political discourse is of a quite different nature from that which pertains in places like Haiti. Reasoned persuasion and rational debate have been the means through which the Western democracies conduct their affairs; in sharp contrast, the likes of Papa Doc have enforced tyranny by the skillful manipulation of image and perception. But as the West leaves the age of Enlightenment behind and sails into the uncharted waters of the postmodern era, it is worth challenging this glib assumption of superiority.

In recent years, political discourse in Europe and the United States has largely abandoned substantive issues, and paid an increasing degree of attention to image. In election campaigns and political commentaries, rational discussion of policy has given way to analyses of the way in which policies are presented and perceived. There seems to be a certain similarity between political discourse in pre-Enlightenment and post-Enlightenment societies. If, as seems to be the case, the West is relapsing into a superstitious, fetishistic, and magical faith in totem and image, we ought seriously to consider the political condition of other societies that currently practice what the West has traditionally viewed as superstition, fetishism, and magic.

François Duvalier was able to secure his political power by exploiting the credulity and superstition of the Haitian peasantry. He represents a phenomenon typical of pre-Enlightenment societies: the tyrant, who does not base his legitimacy on reason or democracy, but on mystical and supernatural foundations. Visiting Haiti is probably the closest one can come to visiting medieval Europe. The poverty and inequality of these societies are of comparable levels, but just as notable is the fact that most Haitians do not think in a post-Enlightenment manner. They do and say things that strike a Westerner as irrational. This is hardly surprising: most Haitians are illiterate subsistence farmers who speak only Kreyol, a language that was not written down until the 1950s. Education is largely unavailable; malnutrition and even starvation are constant threats; male life expectancy is 42 years. In such circumstances it is not hard to understand why the values of enlightened reason have failed to strike deep roots.

Founded in 1804 as a result of the only successful slave rebellion in history, the Republic of Haiti was ostracized and ignored by the rest of the world for over a century. One result of this ostracism was to violently impede Haiti's journey toward what the West likes to call 'progress.' The freed slaves associated labor with bondage and land with freedom: they subdivided the plantations into tiny individual plots and lived off the fertility of their country's flora and fauna. Soon the soil was eroded, the jungles destroyed, the fish eaten, and Haiti began to starve. A kind of society emerged that was just in the process of finally being eradicated in Europe: feudal, with a huge class of desperately poor share-cropping peasants, and a tiny elite of gangsters and soldiers.

The benefits of Enlightenment have been much denigrated by recent Western philosophy. The schools of thought often grouped under the loose label of 'postmodernism' suggest that Enlightenment rests on assumptions which were patriarchal, repressive, and hierarchical. Postmodernists celebrate what they see as the crises of reason and referentiality, and the triumph of signification and difference. Figuration and imagery are portrayed as ludic and liberatory; rationalism and logic are arraigned as oppressive. And it is certainly true that philosophical, economic, aesthetic, and social developments in Western societies have combined to bestow a pronounced importance on matters of perception, presentation, and signification.

In the United Kingdom's general election of 1997, the most controversial political issue was whether Tony Blair, the leader of the Labour Party, had 'devil eyes.' The Conservative Party advertising campaign featured a close-up of Blair's eyes, hideously distorted and reddened in archetypically Satanic fashion. Labour responded with furious denunciations, and countered with a media blitz that stressed the warm, sympathetic qualities which, it was claimed, were clearly visible to any impartial observer in Mr. Blair's eyes. A visitor who entered the country in the middle of this discussion could not but be struck by the a-rational quality of the debate. It was not so much that the parties were being irrational as that the question was not one which could be resolved by reference to the standards of rationality. It was a superstitious debate. It was a debate that took place on the same plane as the belief that François Duvalier might be Baron Samedi. It was a debate from the other side of Enlightenment.

It would seem that the West, having passed through an age in which reason and democracy were the ideals, if not always the reality, of political practice, now seems to be moving toward a system in which the random, irrational fluctuations of the market are the only forces that will be allowed to influence the political direction of nations. Luck, chance, rumor, and perception dictate the vagaries of stocks, bonds, and currencies, and the shifting relations between these are given a supernatural, unquestioned, tyrannical power over the lives of individuals. Social and personal responsibility has been abdicated, and bestowed upon a capricious, almighty pseudo-deity to whose whims all must bow. The techniques employed by the market to further its ends—advertising, the manipulation and perversion of human hopes and fears, opinion polling and market research—have migrated from the economic sphere and colonized the political. The new irrationalism is the product of capitalism and relative abundance. The old irrationalism is the legacy of slavery and dire poverty.

I arrived in Port-au-Prince on a fine April morning in 1996 with a suitcase full of tuna fish. My fellow passengers were loaded down with similar goods. I'd been warned by the friend I was meeting there that food, especially protein, was hard to come by in much of Haiti; this turned out to be true. There is no working telephone system in Haiti, and the electricity cuts off regularly, even in the capital. There is no public transportation other than 'tap taps': converted pick-up trucks, usually open to the elements and with standing-room only. The distance from Port-au-Prince to Jacmel is about 30 miles; such is the condition of the road that the journey takes six hours. There is no police force; the streets are sporadically patrolled by UN troops and cops who are supposedly training their Haitian replacements. Visibly and severely overpopulated, the entire country is pervaded by an atmosphere of turmoil and chaos.

Most Haitians firmly believe in and practice voodoo, despite determined visible campaigns against it by American missionaries. One man I met in Les Cayes had tried to get a job as a cook for the UN garrison. They turned him down. He went for advice to the local houngan, who instructed him to smear his face with a foul-smelling green ointment and try again. They turned him down again. He couldn't understand why. In Gelee, a man offered my companion and me beds in a single room with no running water. His asking price was 600 US dollars a night. We explained that this was excessive, and offered him ten. He thought about it for a while, then offered us the room for five.

In a hotel in Cap Haitian, there were 50 or 60 Chinese guests. None spoke a word of English; none ever left the hotel. It was impossible to find out what they were doing there. Eventually, an American fisherman told us that unscrupulous Chinese ship owners often charge exorbitant fees to smuggle their compatriots into the United States. Rather than face the patrols and police of American waters, however, the captains drop their passengers on a beach in Haiti and tell them they're in Miami. I wondered whether the hotel guests had realized the truth of their situation yet. 'What happens to them?' I asked. The American shrugged: 'I guess they just turn into Haitians.'

In context, his meaning was clear enough. The attitude of the average Haitian, he implied, is fatalistic. It involves the sense that the course of events is not within human control. The idea that the systematic application of reason and logic can influence and alter the objective world seems to be absent. Instead there is the belief in magic, the determining power of the supernatural. In recent Haitian history, this belief has been closely associated with political tyranny, and has served as the means through which tyranny has justified and maintained itself.

It is deeply ironic that what the West calls 'superstition' has achieved such prevalence in Haiti. The nation was founded on the rational republican principle that government should be based on a reasoned constitution, rather than on arbitrary, capricious rule, or 'tyranny.' This tradition of republicanism originated in Rome, was revived in Renaissance Italy, and achieved its first importance in a modern nation-state with the English Revolutions of 1642 and 1688. The constitutional theories elaborated by Milton, Harrington, and Sidney in seventeenth-century England inspired the politics of the French Enlightenment, and were invoked by the revolutionaries of 1789. It was the French Revolution that gave rise to the Haitian revolt of Toussaint L'Ouverture and the 'black Jacobins.'

In Haiti, republicanism immediately gave way to Caesarism, largely because there was no significantly skilled or educated middle class. In England too, the victory of republicanism was incomplete, due to the fact that the seventeenth-century revolutions took place before the bourgeoisie was powerful enough to win victory outright. However, by 1688 the principle was established that the state ought to be guided by reasoned debate and rational persuasion, as opposed to the irrational rule of an arbitrary tyrant. The association between irrationality and tyranny had become a vital element of European political theory.

It may be worth remembering that association in the postmodern era, when spin and sound bite, image and perception, have come to dominate political discourse. I grew up in the United Kingdom, and when I left in 1987 it still seemed that the various political parties could be differentiated on the basis of their substantive arguments on rational issues. This is no longer the case. Shortly after visiting Haiti, I went back to Britain for a month. The 'devil eyes' controversy was in full swing. Watching Tony Blair perform for television, a resident of 1990s United States could not avoid a shock of recognition. Blair was 'doing' Clinton: the studied avoidance of settled positions, the talk of following the dictates of 'principle not policy,' the advertising slogans about a 'stakeholder society,' the marketing man's gambit of referring to his party as 'New' Labour, the attempt to minimize the difference between the parties, the superstitious faith in opinion poll and focus group.

In short, the economic realm has invaded and conquered the political. Expertise in advertising and marketing is the most valued skill in a political advisor. The philosophy of the marketplace dominates political debate. Rational discussion has been replaced as a means of persuasion by the manipulation of images; referentiality is rejected in favor of empty signification. In this context, it seems rather arrogant for a Westerner to criticize Haitians for fatalism or gullibility.

Philosophers such as Guy Debord and Theodor Adorno have connected this hegemony of the image to the rise of fascism in prewar Europe: Hitler was the supreme manipulator of representation and perception. Formal fascism may be dead in the West, but the irrationalism and idolatry which characterize that mode of politics are stronger than ever. To allow the market to dictate the course of politics is to give up human agency to an irrational force. It is a fundamentally superstitious position. In seventeenth-century England, Francis Bacon wrote of the 'idols of the marketplace,' thus establishing a connection between religious fetishism and commodification, which informs many subsequent analyses of market ideology, most notably that of Karl Marx. If Haiti exemplifies the potential political influence of religious 'superstition,' then the contemporary West illustrates the enormous power of commodity fetishism. They have much in common, including an irrationality that historically has been associated with the theory and practice of political tyranny. Postmodern thinkers should bear this connection in mind before attacking the principles of Enlightenment as patriarchal and repressive.

6

When Neofascists Storm into Government (a Context for Genoa)

Edmund Zimmerman

THE BATTLE OF GENOA

Proponents of 'liberalized' global rules that promote free trade as an inalienable right have embraced some troubling methods to defend their gains against increasingly vocal popular opposition. Dissent, long simmering in the southern hemisphere, is finally spilling north. At the July 2001 G8 summit in Genoa, Italy, the industrialized world revealed a chilling tendency to rely on tactics once commonplace in Europe's not so distant totalitarian past. Public chaos and violence trigger fear and insecurity among the populace; this lesson is being rekindled among the ashes of a political movement long discredited but never extinguished.

International media accounts portrayed Genoa as an armed camp patrolled by a dizzying array of aggressive uniformed forces: military, paramilitary, and police. Huge crowds of non-violent protesters were repeatedly attacked, often without provocation, but sometimes in response to chaos reportedly orchestrated by extreme right-wing thugs who had infiltrated the 'black bloc' of self-styled anarchists. When the smoke cleared in Genoa, one young protester was dead and dozens were imprisoned amid charges of torture and abuse—charges since verified in the Italian courts.

The ideological underpinnings of this brutal show were provided by Italy's Prime Minister, Silvio Berlusconi, and his hand-picked Council of Ministers. The council is led by the Alleanza Nazionale Party; unrepentant, historically accurate fascists.

LO ZIO AMERICANO

During the waves of emigration from Europe to the United States generations ago, the expression 'Lo Zio Americano' ('the American uncle') referred to the stereotypical émigré, a newly successful relative who sent money back to his village, presumably along with snapshots of his Cadillac cruising the 14-karat causeways of the new world. But rank and file American travelers can attest to the changing attitudes of Western Europeans toward the United States in recent decades. While the United States is considered a good place to make money, few Europeans harbor hidden dreams of Ellis Island anymore. Italians are as enthralled as the rest of Europe by the unique popular trappings of what has come to be known as American culture: blue jean cowboys and chewing gum GI Joes blasting through their cinema screens, but 'globalization' is a decidedly less glamorous affair. As promoted by the G8 and by the World Trade Organization (WTO), globalization is the forced opening of healthy local markets and systems of resource distribution to pure Yankee capitalism. It manifests as profit crazed feed lots in England exporting their diseased livestock, and as genetically manipulated pollen sailing on the scirocco to the mistral. It appears as the golden arches sleazing up the Piazza di Spagna, and as Disney littering the Loire Valley with its revisionist history. Time and again the US-led WTO has proven that its complex formula of money, threats, and maxi-media frontal assault is the gold standard in the promotion of all that glitters. Obviously a few Italians have profited mightily from this American fueled onslaught. None have done so more than Silvio Berlusconi.

Berlusconi has flourished as a peddler of old American TV shows, dubbed into Italian: 'Gli Angeli di Charlie,' 'Le Strade di San Francisco,' and 'Baywatch' are broadcast non-stop on his three national stations sandwiched between bombastic advertisements and sensationalist 'newsbreaks,' which often flog his own interests. His billionaire status alone is enough to earn him kind, albeit condescending, treatment in the American press. In a fluffy profile in the *New York Times Magazine* on April 15, 2001, he is said to possess 'the kind of engaging good humor shared by the best Italians.' This is presumably different from the type of humor his corny sit-coms share with the rest of the population. How the seemingly innocuous Zio Americano of Italian media came to be the overseer of the brutal police riots outside the G8 conference is primarily a story of concession and ruthless coalition building. But it is also a story of globalization as the last resort of billionaires.

The richest man in Italy embraces an astonishing array of Mussolinian attributes, personal as well as public, and takes some ideas far beyond what even Mussolini was willing or able to do. Berlusconi has created through media and public relations trickery his own 'Cult of the Personality,' a phrase coined to describe Mussolini. A shamelessly self-promoting clown in public, he is alternately engaging and critical to suit his purposes, often with the same people. Leading up to the recent war with Iraq, Berlusconi appeared at press conferences with visiting heads of state from Rumsfeld to Chirac to Putin supporting whatever position his visitor was in Italy to promote. His first desire seems to have been to stand by Bush and Rumsfeld—'for a seat at the victory table,' as Mussolini once said after an early incursion into France in World War II—but Berlusconi was certainly hindered by overwhelming opposition to the war among the Italian populace. Rome hosted what was possibly the largest antiwar demonstration in history in February 2003.

Berlusconi has been indicted dozens of times, for corruption, bribes, mafia connections, buying a multimillion dollar villa from a young orphan girl for a fraction of its value. This summer, in the days leading up to the verdict in a huge bribery case many years in the making involving the sale of the SME food conglomerate, Berlusconi's allies in parliament rammed through an immunity from prosecution law, effectively protecting him from his imminent conviction. (For a detailed account of the case see *The Economist* online, 'An Open Letter to Berlusconi,' August 2003). Since the passing of that law he has been attempting to oust the judiciary involved in his prosecution, criticizing them collectively, individually, personally, every day in the press. In an interview published this week in the conservative English newspaper, *The Spectator*, Berlusconi called the public magistrates 'mentally disturbed and anthropologically different' from normal people.

In the same interview Berlusconi also defended Mussolini saying, 'He never killed anyone,' and, in reference to the mass expulsion of Jews at the end of the war, claimed that Mussolini had 'just sent them on vacation,' alluding to the now plush resort islands of Ponza and Maddalena where many Jews were imprisoned while awaiting trips to death camps. The European establishment, conservative as well as neoliberal, is highly critical of Berlusconi and disgusted by his public antics. At his first convening of the European Parliament with Italy in the rotating spot of president, he rebuked a German member of parliament for being a 'Kapo,' a concentration camp guard.

'A JUDICIAL COUP'

In the twentieth century Italy was at ground zero in the struggles between the authoritarian and populist trends that racked Europe in the wake of the Industrial Revolution. Italy was the ideological spawning ground for fascism in the first half of the century as well as the home of the largest, most popular communist party in Western Europe in the second half. Mussolini first wrote for a 'socialist' journal and his ultimately iron-fisted totalitarianism was based on a rhetoric of elevation of the masses to their rightful place in society, in the world, in history. Hitler idolized Mussolini and both rode to power on the backs of post-World War I industrialists and monarchies terrified by the revolutionary fervor sweeping Europe. After fascism was crushed in World War II, communist agitation, real and perceived, caused the center-right coalition that ran Italy from 1948 to 1994 to make notable concessions to social welfare. The large, popular, and intellectually fluid Italian Communist Party (PCI) educated generations of Italians and to some extent inoculated them against the ad agency driven simplification of modern Western politics. Until Berlusconi.

Berlusconi, who describes his politics as 'Thatcherite/Reaganite,' ran a glitzy American style campaign full of jingles and sound bites during which he spoke of little more than 'tax cuts and free markets.' Owning the media proved invaluable: his TV and radio outlets refused to run ads for his opponents, his newspapers were unflinching in their editorial support, and his publishing house, 'Mondadori' (Italy's largest), sent a glossy 130-page book to every potential Italian voter. This book, 'An Italian Story,' has 114 photos of Berlusconi on the cover alone and another 132 inside.

There is no popular or ideological base for Berlusconi's party, Forza Italia, apart from the dependents, the chroniclers, and the wannabees of his vast business empires. He became the richest man in Italy during the era of 'Tangentopoli' (bribe city), an ongoing scandal that was devastating to Italian politics. Tangentopoli caused the total collapse and disbandment of the ruling Christian Democrats, prison sentences for ministers and businessmen alike, and the death in exile of Berlusconi's most valuable political ally, Prime Minister and Socialist Party leader Bettino Craxi. Berlusconi dismisses Tangentopoli as a leftist inspired 'judicial coup.' Regrettably this is not the worst historical rewrite his government is now involved in; he seems to think that historians have perhaps been too hasty in condemning fascism itself.

OF FASCISTS AND XENOPHOBES

Berlusconi lacks any political vision beyond the protection of his businesses from regulation and his own ass from a jail cell. He handed over the business of governing Italy to two extreme right-wing parties with minimal popular support but lots of tenacity. A center-left coalition had been governing Italy since the fall of Berlusconi's first corruption-plagued government of 1994. In order to gain electoral victory over them, he renewed ties to a bizarre gang of xenophobic, homophobic northern Italians known as the 'Lega Nord' (Northern League), as well as a group he single handedly rescued from the brink of history's dustbin, the neofascist 'Movimento Sociale' (MSI). The members of the Lega Nord, headed by Umberto Bossi, the new Minister for Institutional Reform, fear and despise not only immigrants from Africa and Eastern Europe but southern Italians as well. They have called repeatedly for secession of various provinces from the Italian republic while arming themselves for an expected purge, even as neighboring Yugoslavia was dissolving into the most brutal killing fields Europe has seen in 50 years. Luckily for Bossi's bigots, Mr. Berlusconi offered cabinet posts as well as credibility for their dangerous demands in exchange for a few crucial votes.

The anabiosis of Italian fascism came when Berlusconi revived flagging Italian interest in the MSI. The MSI was born from the ashes of Mussolini's cadres in 1946 and routinely drew about 5 or 6 per cent of the national vote until judicial inquests around Tangentopoli shed light on many of their shadowy organizations and nefarious activities. In 1990 they reached their electoral nadir at only 3.9 per cent of the vote nationwide. Berlusconi's media boys, experts at 'buying short,' singled out MSI leader Gianfranco Fini and created an Italian version of compassionate conservatism for him to embody. This vision succeeded in spite of the fact that in 1992 Fini had proclaimed Mussolini 'the greatest statesman in Italian history.' Fini had also run a thuggish campaign for mayor of Rome with moshpits of Nazi skinheads at every rally. But with their new name, Alleanza Nazionale, and newly polished jackboots, their vote totals have soared and Vice President Fini is Berlusconi's right-hand man.

To appreciate the immediate danger represented by the re-emergence of unfettered fascism, consider the numerous police and paramilitary forces arrayed against the demonstrators in Genoa and the function of state- (Berlusconi-) controlled media in presenting and coloring the tragic results. Any neofascist pronouncements about the instigators of violence in Genoa must be weighed against the historical record of right-wing violence perpetrated by fascist gangs in the 1970s and 1980s. Minister of Communications Maurizio Gasparri, along with Forests and Agriculture Minister Giovanni Alemanno and Vice President Fini, all boast in their official government biographies of membership during the turbulent 1970s of the 'Fronte Della Gioventu.' This gang of young fascists was widely known for their brutality and racism. The police who raided and terrorized the center for non-violent protests in Genoa were singing a favorite Fronte song, 'La Facetta Nera' ('Little Black Face'), which commemorates Mussolini's brutal domination of Ethiopia in the 1930s with a message of racism and rape.

NOTES ON THE ARCHITECTS OF NEOFASCISM

At the end of World War II, British and American Secret Service officials began planning their follow-up war with the Soviet Union by cultivating friendships with many of the most notorious Nazi and fascist war criminals. Presumably they wished to take advantage of their savagery as well as their expertise concerning their long-time Russian foes. Allied intelligence services set up secret escape routes known as the 'Ratlines' through the Vatican in Rome by which many of these newfound friends of freedom were allowed to escape to the Americas. The escapees included Klaus Barbie, Adolph Eichmann, Joseph Mengele, Martin Bormann; and Mussolini's emissary to the Goerring SS, Licio Gelli. The operation for which some of these war criminals were being prepared was code-named 'Gladio.' Referred to in English as 'stay behinds,' fascists and Nazis throughout Europe were organized into cells with buried arms caches to be used to thwart an imminent Soviet invasion.

From his post as head of a secret neofascist Masonic lodge known as P2, Gelli, known as the 'puppet master,' incorporated treachery and terrorism into his newly respectable position. P2 grew to include many prominent right-wing DC ministers and members of parliament including one time President of the Republic Francesco Cossiga and the ubiquitous Prime Minister Giuglio Andreotti. Much of Gelli's handiwork was implemented under the watchful eyes of the US and NATO security apparatus headed by Henry Kissinger and General Alexander Haig.

As the PCI's brand of electoral communism became ever more popular in the 1960s and 1970s, Italy's right wing became convinced that this was the communist invasion for which they had been preparing and they became increasingly bold. They attempted two outright military coups, and reinvented a traditional fascist tactic of orchestrating chaos and fear in order to increase public demand for authoritarian control. After the dramatic communist victory of 35 per cent of the vote in 1976 (a landslide by Italy's electoral standards), a series of monstrous bomb attacks rocked the country including a 1980 attack on the train station in Bologna that left 85 dead. Four avowed fascists were later convicted of planting the bomb with Gladio materials and even the 'puppet-master' Licio Gelli was sentenced to prison for creating an elaborate scheme to protect the bombers. After seven months, higher courts overturned the convictions prompting the original trial judge, Liberato Mancuso, to lament (as reported in the *Guardian*, August 3, 1990):

> It is now understood among those engaged in the matter of democratic rights that we are isolated, and the objects of a campaign of aggression. In Italy there has functioned for some years now ... a control of our national sovereignty by the P2 ... which was literally the master of the secret services, the army, and our most delicate organs of state.

NEVER AGAIN

Minister of the Interior Claudio Scajola was architect of the 20,000-strong police defense of the fortified summit of economic leaders in Genoa. He was unapologetic about the death of one demonstrator and the beatings, false imprisonments, torture, and unprovoked attacks on countless others. He boasted that, 'A state must never lose the monopoly on the use of force.' (Not surprisingly, in his government biography he was a 'militant antileftist in the

60s.') The pattern here is unavoidable. Italy, Europe, and the world ignore it at their peril. Some would have us believe that fascism didn't get a fair reading by history. One of Fini's boys, Franco Storace, is now president of the region (similar to state governor in the United States) of Lazio, which includes Rome. He is leading an initiative to rewrite schoolbooks, which he says unjustly glorify the partisans who struggled against fascism during World War II.

Fascism had its chance. It had an entire era with its own calendar still commemorated on the sides of numerous buildings throughout Italy. It cut its murderous path across the planet, enslaving great swaths of Europe, Africa, and Asia. It initiated a holocaust against a religious group of non-combatants, women, and children that systematically killed 6 million. It was not thrown out of power by some sort of electoral reform. It had to be crushed by an uprising the likes of which the world had never seen. Millions died at its bloody hands and millions more died to destroy it.

Neofascists do not renounce racism, nor do they renounce brutal, authoritarian tactics—not in Italy, not in Germany, not in Japan, not in the United States. They claim that racism doesn't get a fair hearing in the court of world opinion, and that the state deserves its monopoly on force for the sake of strict order. Silvio Berlusconi understands this as well as Blair or Schroeder or George W. Bush (OK maybe not Bush), but has assets apparently immense enough to shelter him from deals with the devil himself.

7
Blacks and Reds in Polish Technicolor

Ewa Pagacz

One of the jokes in communist-era Poland was that the grass in heavily polluted Silesia was painted green whenever the First Secretary came to visit.

In postcommunist Poland, the difference is that the grass gets painted green whenever the Pope comes to visit. The blacks have triumphed over the reds, and it's the same difference.

Postcommunism in Poland has led to a renaissance in the political power of the Catholic Church. Theology has replaced secular ideology. Poland is only today discovering the broad outlines of the Church's vision for its future, a frightening retreat from social rationalism and progress. The Church, which takes primary responsibility for the national defeat of communism, is building its own authoritarian structure in the midst of a new Western-style economy based on cheap labor.

The civic pacifism of Polish Catholicism protects the growing maldistribution of wealth. Forty per cent of Poles live in poverty and 13 per cent in extreme destitution. The rate of malnourishment among children is rising rapidly while schools shut down their cheap canteens because they lack necessary funds. More and more orphanages are opened to shelter infants abandoned by mothers who cannot support their children, frequently their tenth child or greater. In villages, people do not have enough to buy even basic groceries: they rely on what they can grow in their small plots. Pensions are too low to let the old have a decent meal every day, and under privatized health care they cannot afford to buy medicines.

In the midst of this poverty, the Church is building an Empire of the Spirit. Since the early 1980s, when Poles could again openly attend church without fear of repercussions, new churches have literally mushroomed throughout the country. They are huge and gloomy edifices, usually made of red brick, with parish houses of almost the same size. The parish house has replaced the party branch office as a center of social power. No social event, no opening of a new public institution, can take place without a priest arriving to give his blessing, which is as important as any establishing legal documents.

This singularization of power is the realization of Church policy following the installation of the first real postcommunist government in 1989. In the previous year, a leaked internal document written by Cardinal Glemp, the country's senior prelate, attacked the idea of neutral civic institutions and called for the Catholicization of the state. Glemp specifically rejected the concept of tolerance inasmuch as this limited the diffusion of true Christian values; he termed atheism 'abnormal'; and he called for a ban on the right of non-believers to organize their own institutions. The core of Glemp's worldview and his insistence on the future centrality of the Church in national policymaking brought his vision close to that of Iranian theocrats. So far, he has failed only in his proposal to have the constitutional separation of church and state eliminated. Glemp and other major Catholic voices, like theologian Joszef Tishner, are calling for redemption of Poland's 'national soul' from the secularizing effects of Marxism and for the substitution of a monopolistic faith.

HOLY CLASSROOMS

As a teacher, whenever I look at another new church and its towering walls of brick, I can only think of how many schools or libraries might be built with the same material and human effort spent on another priest's workplace. There are hundreds of uncounted new churches under construction, but not even one new university. An old–new system of social control is being built to replace the party's control, and it is a culture of domination that relies equally on imposing its dictates through the educational system.

State and religion have become synonymous in the classroom, as state and party once were. In 1984 the clergy began a campaign to require school authorities to hang a crucifix on the front wall in every classroom, insisting that it should be affixed over the national emblem. They suggested that classes begin with a prayer, the same prayer as they proposed should serve as the opening paragraphs of the new constitution.

Beginning in 1991, Catholicism became a regular subject taught in state primary and secondary schools. The Church prevailed on the government to introduce this change by administrative means, avoiding a parliamentary vote and public debate. Although attendance was supposed to be optional, in practice it is difficult for students to get released. The latest initiative is to introduce Catholicism classes at the preschool level ('Hey, mom! We did Jesus show-and-tell and I got these neat stigmata!').

Priests and nuns now serve as regular—but privileged—school faculty. They catechize bored children who take notes for memorization, because the religion exams are thorough. Failure in homiletics means being held back a grade. Religion classes provide the New Morality with its center. They are devoted specifically to the 'proper' upbringing of youth and creating 'good Christians' resistant to the wickedness of the world.

And what is wickedness if not sex? The Church successfully pressured the Ministry of Education in 1988 to withdraw all textbooks containing any information on sex. Priests list sins on the blackboard for students, among which are the use of contraceptives, premarital sex, or sex within marriage for reasons other than procreation. Students who demand some explanation or who express a different viewpoint are usually told to leave the classroom. Still, the clergy must know what it is talking about: newspaper articles frequently appear about priests fathering and nuns bearing children, and clergymen seducing young boys.

MORALITY FOR THE MASSES

I have never needed my alarm clock to wake me on Sunday mornings. When I lived in Poland the low, mournful sound of nearby church bells woke me at 6 a.m. Masses are available until noon, so whenever you look out the window on Sunday mornings there are crowds of people either going to or returning from church. In small provincial towns like mine, a large majority of the population attends mass; in villages, hardly anyone fails to attend.

The reason is not only religious zeal. In this heart of Europe, there remain many places where sermons are one of the major forms of social entertainment. They are sermons that offer up visions of God's anger together with promises of eternal suffering for hundreds of sins committed daily. Sin's definition is all-inclusive. A sin is what is done and what remains undone; what is read and what is not read; what is thought as well as acted. One wonders why no priest has translated the works of Jonathan Edwards or Michael Wigglesworth for sermon material; mere anti-Protestant prejudice, for the content is little different.

For all its status as a site of patriarchy, a church in provincial towns and villages is almost the only social exchange available. Pubs are another, but since patriarchy is even stronger there, women—and especially women without male company—are a rare and unwelcome sight. Forget about coffee houses, bookstores, sports centers, theaters, concert halls, et cetera: they don't exist. In smaller communities, any attempt to break out of the custom of attending masses, let alone public assertion that you are an atheist or not Christian, is to become an outcast. The atmosphere is 'miasmatically puritanic,' similar to that which Theodore Dreiser attributed to his nineteenth-century hometown of Terre Haute in his autobiography *Dawn*, a place where, 'An atheist is a criminal.' An invisible line fences off any religious (and hence social) non-conformist. This is a smaller world, removed from the larger cities, one that the party once governed but could never change.

In the tiny mountain villages of southern Poland, Sunday mini-pilgrimages are a common sight. When I took my son on weekend hiking trips in the mountains, whatever village we passed through we encountered groups of people descending from the hills, walking narrow country roads toward the village church. All of them wore their Sunday best and walked for an hour or two to worship, even longer during winter. There were lines of villagers walking on both sides of the road and since we were headed in the opposite direction from church, we received angry looks. Secular aliens heading for damnation, their looks said.

ABORTING EVIL SHOPPING MALLS

There is little coherent, identifiable, or effective opposition to political demands from the Church, largely because the generation of politicians elevated by Solidarity owes its success to support from the Church. The intellectual attacks of an aging, radical anticlericalist like Lescek Kolakowski have given way to isolated journalistic animosity, such as that from Jerzy Urban and the newspaper *Nie* (No). The real difficulty the Polish Church faces does not come from left-wing dissenters or anticlericalists. There has been expanding access to urban infrastructure and economic changes that promote secular materialism with a rapidity far, far greater than under communism. Given such an emphatic growth in materialism, how will the new morality plays of spiritual virtue be performed? How will the Church remain the paramount force in this consumerist Poland?

Open capital investment markets since the 1980s have attracted western European—mainly German and Austrian—firms that have built supermarket chains and shopping malls. They have been multiplying in large towns and cities as fast, possibly even faster, than the churches, and are often built next door. Malls are open on Sunday mornings and are pulling in more and more customer traffic, especially because Sunday is the only day off for workers who remain on a six-day workweek. In consequence, attendance at Sunday masses has dropped and the malls have become an official Church enemy. Not only does mall consumerism divert the attention of the faithful. It also diverts their contributions to the Church.

The major political struggle in Poland today concerns the introduction of a ban on Sunday sales on the grounds that 'true Christians' must not work on the Sabbath. A bloc of Catholic deputies in the Seym has prepared this national Blue Law for enactment. The current obstacle does not concern the specter of a state-enforced religious norm, but rather the consideration that a Sunday sales ban will become a major obstacle in Poland's effort to join the European Union. In the meantime, impatient and infuriated priests have launched their own private religious war against Satan's malls, not only sermonizing against them as sources of evil but also instigating window-smashing campaigns.

Together with targeting Sunday shoppers, the Church has continued its campaign against women and their reproductive health. Even before its faithful servant Lech Walesa swept into office, a Church-sponsored initiative succeeded in outlawing abortions that had been available under the communist government. The law affects only poor women, since wealthier women can have the procedure performed in the Czech Republic or Germany, or by bribing a physician (an everyday practice—the current market price is about $500, or two and a half months' average salary). The results are tragic and common: corpses of newborns wrapped in plastic bags and dumped in trash bins, abandonment of infants in clinics, death and near-death of women from septicemia and non-medical abortions. Because labor protections have almost disappeared in the new market economy, women who do bear children frequently lose their jobs because of work absence and their families sink into greater poverty. The Church presses its campaign forward: one of the latest legislative initiatives would criminalize parties to an abortion—a woman and the medical personnel—as responsible infanticidists and murderers. Another proposed law would ban prenatal examinations entirely.

The Church's self-proclamation as the Great Defender of Human Life resolves into mere words shouted from the pulpit. Words cost nothing. At the dawn of the new millennium, a regressive theo-politics has seized the country, one that tells Poles to accept their miseries and pain, and that specifies God's will as the reason for poverty and income inequalities. Sexuality and the elaboration of a divine morality have become religious cudgels for social control. Religious intolerance of gender orientations other than heterosexuality is inseparable from this control regime: outside a couple of urban areas, gay and lesbian life remains entirely underground. When a deputy minister of health was dismissed after announcing that distribution of condoms would not be sanctioned even as protection against AIDS, since only 'deviants' contracted the disease, Cardinal Glemp protested vigorously and compared the dismissal to Stalinist tactics.

The power to make desire legitimate or illegitimate is one of the Church's greatest skills. Desire is the point where the material and the emotional meet to emerge as the conditions of life. Desire is the point where the Church searches for its instruments of control. The historical results of rampant religious triumphalism were apparent some 50 years ago to Witold Gombrowicz, who recorded in his *Diaries* his dismay as a rationalist: 'We were horrified to see that we were surrounded by an abyss made of millions of ignorant minds, which steal away our truths in order to pervert, diminish, and transform them into instruments of their passions.' The drive toward theocracy relies on social rationalism both as an ally and as an enemy. To achieve material desire, theocracy relies on rationalistic production and social conditions; to achieve its immaterial desires, theocracy seeks to demonize secular ideologies.

8

Marxism, Class Analysis, and the USSR: a Y2K Perspective

Richard D. Wolff

The new century and the historic shifts of recent years invite—indeed, they demand—that we weigh the strength, achievements, and prospects of Marxism against its weaknesses, failures, and problems. The *goal* remains to struggle against capitalism and for communism. But communism will henceforth mean something very different from what it meant in the last century. The *strategy* is to ally this Marxist goal with the compatible goals of other social movements such as those for democracy and equality. In so doing we will construct an effective new left movement. Such an alliance will aim to take power from those who have it now and enact an agreed set of social changes including the class transformations that Marxists seek.

Among the achievements of Marxism since 1850 are:

- The construction of explicitly Marxist organizations (trade unions, political parties, journals, newspapers, mass organizations) and Marxist components of other organizations;
- The struggle to replace capitalism with socialism in opposition and in power;
- The production of a genuinely global literature of social analysis derived from countless practical struggles for socialism and communism; and
- An influence on several generations of workers and intellectuals to think in class terms.

The weaknesses and failures of Marxism can be summarized simply: it could not yet displace capitalism. This essay focuses on one major reason for these failures: the overlooking of surplus labor value. Unlike the other major reasons, this one has not received the attention it deserves.

Marx developed a new conception of class that took surplus labor value into account because he believed the understanding of class held by his fellow radicals was incomplete. More importantly, Marx believed that this incompleteness directly undermined social movement beyond capitalism toward socialism or communism. I believe the new understanding of class initiated by Marx still eludes opponents of capitalism today, including those who are otherwise Marxist. Like Marx then, it is urgent for us now to address the failure of radicals to absorb and apply Marx's new class analysis. The urgency is driven by the same reason now as in Marx's era: all radical projects are hobbled from passing beyond capitalism to communism.

Marx respected and used existing concepts of class. Yet he was compelled to develop an understanding that differed from those historically employed by other radicals to criticize capitalism, to work out strategies for displacing it, and to define the socialism or communism they sought to construct. His contribution was largely lost in the tumultuous crises of Western capitalism that almost overwhelmed it from the 1870s to the 1950s: from the Paris Commune to the post-World War I socialist upheavals in Russia, and from the Chinese and the Cuban to the Vietnamese revolutions. Marxists everywhere during this era suddenly faced real opportunities to take power from capitalists. Swept up by such heady openings and by mass agitations for social change, they relied upon entrenched concepts of class for their strategies, slogans, and programs. They did not worry about the implications of Marx's new class concept with regard to their goals or strategies. Capitalist societies seemed obviously split into two great groupings: a vast majority without property and power confronted a small minority who owned and ruled. Marx's writings could be, and were, read as endorsing old dualistic concepts of class.

Long before Marx, at least as far back as early Greek thought, radicals interested in changing societies had often classified populations into groups. These groups, or classes, were organized according either to how much property they owned or how much power they wielded over others, or both. For such early radicals, social ills flowed from a small minority who owned most of the property, wielded most of the power, and used both to maintain their status quo no matter what the cost in social waste, injustice, and suffering. Historically, radicals have often identified change in class structure as the solution to these costs. The social distribution of property and power has been considered to underlie that class structure. Eventually, socialism and communism came to stand for that social change. Property was to be redistributed equally, or collectively owned, and power was to be equally distributed. Socialists and communists thus widened democracy to include property as well as power: it became 'social democracy' or 'democratic socialism.'

Marx partly embraced this radical tradition. His critiques of capitalism, feudalism, and slavery rooted many of their injustices, wastes, and inequalities in the unequal distribution of property and power. He too sought a movement of the propertyless and the powerless for social democracy. But Marx also addressed the question of why the large majorities without property or power had tried but failed, both before and since the arrival of capitalism, to achieve socialist or communist goals. His major works, *Capital* and *Theories of Surplus Value*, answer that question. In them, he theorized that the struggles of radicals had been severely weakened because they had not understood an important feature of the societies that they had tried to change. Where radicals won political power, efforts to construct and sustain social democracy eventually failed because they did not attend to this feature.

Marx labeled this feature 'class.' The term had been widely used before, but Marx meant something new. Instead of a property and/or power definition of class, he offered a *surplus labor* definition. In every society, he argued, a portion of its members—the laborers—work; using brains and muscles they transform nature into useful objects. They not only produce such objects in quantities sufficient for their own consumption (fruits of their 'necessary' labor in Marx's language); they always also produce *additional* (Marx called them 'surplus') quantities of output. The latter are fruits of the laborers' 'surplus labor.' If sold in markets, surplus output yields 'surplus value.' Marx referred to the organization of surplus labor as society's 'class structure.' He then asked the following questions of all societies: which people produce the surplus? Who receives it? How is it organized? And to whom is it distributed? He also asked what the social effects are of this organization of surplus labor. In Marx's new conception, class refers not to a set of people grouped by their access to property or power, but rather to the set of processes by which surplus labor is performed, appropriated, and distributed.

The ways in which societies organize their production, appropriation, and distribution of surplus labor differ from the ways they distribute wealth and power. Surplus labor, wealth, and power are interdependent, but they are not identical. Before Marx, radicals had focused on wealth and power, hardly ever on surplus labor. Having overlooked surplus labor and the influences of its organization, their projects for social transformation ignored it. This proved to be a fatal error. Likewise, when constructing new societies, radicals focused on changing wealth and power distributions. When the organization of surplus labor was left intact, the changes in wealth and power distributions that had initially been achieved were undermined.

Marx stressed how capitalist societies organize the who and how of producing, appropriating, and distributing surplus labor. Capitalism entails *exploitation*: social organizations where those who produce the surplus do not also appropriate and distribute it. Others appropriate the surplus and then distribute it—to themselves and to others—to perpetuate their position as exclusive appropriators. Proletarians produce the surplus. Capitalists appropriate and then distribute it, first to themselves as profits, then to others as taxes to state officials, budgets to managers, fees to advertisers and lawyers, and so on. The latter provide the social conditions that enable capitalist exploitation.

The most ambitious and long-lasting effort to date to replace capitalism with communism, the USSR, illustrates the costs to radicals of not recognizing the role of surplus labor in social life. In the decades before 1917, Russian industry was mostly private capitalist. Private citizens, Russian and foreign, owned and operated corporations that hired other people, laborers, to produce commodities. The boards of directors of these private corporations then sold those commodities. They used a portion of the proceeds to pay wages, another portion to replenish used-up raw materials and tools, and they appropriated the final portion (the surplus). The boards then allocated part of this surplus to themselves as profits and the rest of the surplus to others who enabled their enterprises to continue and grow. This pre-1917 private capitalist class structure coexisted with an extremely unequal distribution of property and power. A small number of individuals owned most of the corporations and a Czar dominated politically.

World War I collapsed the Russian economy. Given the prior history of mass exploitation and privation, workers and peasants lost confidence in both capitalists and the Czar. Radicals suddenly found mass support to take political power. The Bolsheviks did so together with other socialists, and all were influenced by Marxism. Because they all understood class in the classic sense of property and power, they focused on transforming the distributions of wealth and power in the new USSR. Land taken from its few former owners was distributed roughly equally among millions of peasant families. The USSR abolished stock markets and deprived private owners of their industrial wealth. Henceforth, industries would be the nation's collective property administered by the workers' state (and the vanguard Communist Party). Revolutionary leaders believed they were replacing capitalism with socialism because of these certainly monumental changes in the social distribution of property and power.

But the basic organization of surplus labor did not change when Russian industry became Soviet. Before 1917, workers had performed surplus labor in Russian factories and offices for private capitalist boards of directors who distributed the surpluses to maintain that exploitative system. After the revolution, those same workers performed surplus labor whose fruits were again taken away by others and distributed. Instead of private capitalist boards of directors, it was state officials who appropriated and distributed the workers' surplus. In Marx's sense of surplus labor, Soviet industries' class structures had not changed. A *private* capitalism had been supplanted by a *state* capitalism.

Lenin partly recognized this, arguing that state capitalism was needed until conditions allowed a transition to a genuine socialism and then communism. But he did not express this in terms of a surplus labor theory of class. He too had not found that part of Marx's work sufficiently important to use it in a practical way. Likewise, the revolutionary workers who seized the Russian factories thought they had vanquished capitalism by giving the Bolsheviks state power and giving the factories to the new state. Everyone operated with a class analysis of capitalism and communism based on property and power. No one worried much about the organization of surplus labor. In the name of socialism, workers welcomed Soviet state officials who replaced the private boards of directors. Stalin later formalized and enforced a definition of socialism as exactly what existed in the USSR.

Marx had argued that the exploitative class structure of capitalism alienated workers and fostered economic waste, cultural inequities, and social injustices. Exploitation continued in Soviet state capitalist industry (and increasingly in agriculture too) through to the collapse of 1989. Soviet leaders never addressed the class structure of their industry in the surplus labor sense. They insisted that no classes existed in the USSR because the state owned the industry. No Soviet strategy could or did emerge to cope with how a continuing exploitative class structure was undermining the 1917 changes in wealth and power. The 1989 collapse included the USSR as a nation, the state as exclusive owner of industrial enterprises, the Communist Party's monopoly of power, and the dominance of state planning over markets as the means to distribute resources and outputs. What did not collapse was communism in Marx's class sense: it had never existed in Soviet industry. Soviet state capitalism is what collapsed.

Marxism's last century provides two major lessons for its future. First, the capitalist class structure can take both private and state forms. Capitalist class structures have coexisted with private as well as state property, with markets as well as state planning. Establishing collective property and planning need not abolish capitalist exploitation or its social effects. Indeed, Soviet history suggests even more. Wherever capitalist class structures have come to prevail socially, they have oscillated between private and state capitalist forms. When private capitalisms have engendered serious economic downturns that provoked mass suffering and criticism, demands have arisen for the state to intervene: to regulate, control, and sometimes even nationalize private capitalists. Circumstances of time and place overdetermine how far and how long each swing to state capitalism occurs. Likewise, when state forms of capitalism engender similar social crises there are frequently calls made for an oscillation toward something like private capitalism. The USSR oscillated in one direction in 1917 and in the other in 1989. During the twentieth century, many capitalist economies oscillated, first toward state capitalism in the crises of the 1930s and then back toward private capitalisms in the neoliberal last decades.

The second lesson of Marxism's last century concerns the Marxist goal of communism as it will be articulated once it is no longer confused with state capitalism. If henceforth understood in terms of the surplus labor value, communism will mean that the workers who perform surplus labor must also themselves be the collective appropriators and distributors of its fruits, the surplus. That is how Marx defined the absence of exploitation. To establish communism then means fundamentally to alter the organization of surplus labor inside each enterprise, thereby transforming work and life. That goal offers a distinctive improvement and differentiation in relation to the agendas of allied social movements for economic equality, collectivized property, and democratized power. To affirm that goal will distance Marxists critically—and precisely as Marxists—from the different 'communism' of the USSR and its imitators. Marxism might then recapture the utopian impulse and longing for community that attracts and inspires all who believe that human society can do better than capitalism.

Part II

Remembering History

INTRODUCTION

Bad Subjects returns to history in this second section. To critique ideologies of progress properly, we must pay equal attention to the other side of that theoretical coin: memory. Bringing the fractured shadows cast by post-Cold War reconstruction into the light, the contributors to this section of the book make a compelling claim for memory as an essential left-wing concern. But they also reject neoconservative arguments about the necessity of historical consciousness, which hold that without tradition there is nothing, because we cannot know ourselves without it.

John Brady starts things off by reflecting on a New Year's Eve celebration of the new millennium on the Alexanderplatz in front of Berlin's city hall. Surveying the party that unfolded in front of him, contrasting it with the history of the buildings and the layout of the neighborhood, Brady uses the experience as a window onto the radical political complexities of German history after Berlin's reunification. Megan Shaw Prelinger considers the tenth anniversary of the siege of the Branch Davidian compound from the perspective of the American security state that has emerged since 9/11, seeing the federal government's violent seizure of the Waco compound as a preview of the internal imperialism that has made meaningful dissent a death warrant for radicals on both sides of the political and religious spectrum. Prelinger argues that progressive politics needs to remember Waco in order to recognize that the terrorist attacks on the World Trade Center and the Pentagon did not end the New World Order declared by the first President Bush, but rather confirmed the paranoia that set it in motion a decade earlier.

The physicality of history that inheres in Brady and Prelinger's accounts of Berlin and Waco reappears in Tomás F. Sandoval and Jason M. Ferreira's essay on the significance of the Free Speech Movement (FSM) begun in 1964 at the University of California in Berkeley. Sandoval and Ferreira unpack the troubling institutionalization of the FSM in the form of the Free Speech Movement Café, dedicated by Chancellor Robert Berdahl at UC Berkeley in 2000. Reflecting on parallel crackdowns on contemporary student organizing, Sandoval and Ferreira see this café as a reification of the legacy of the Free Speech Movement. Elisabeth

Hurst takes a different approach to speaking about history. In her ruminations on working in Vancouver, Canada, during the economic summit APEC '97, Hurst surveys the security apparatus in place to protect the non-democratic leadership of Pacific Rim nations such as China and Indonesia. She uses this contrast between the freedom of Canada and the repressiveness of its trading partners in order to show how economic integration obscures authoritarianism, past and present.

J.C. Myers concludes the section with an essay revisiting the political 'choice' offered to social theorists during the Cold War: who are you going to use as your methodological foundation, Marx or Weber? Myers comes down in favor of Marx, but with a nuanced reading of the importance that Weber's work still holds for progressive academics. However, Myers is less concerned with scholars' choice of methodology than he is with the way that political climates influence this sort of decision. Indeed, Myers concludes the question isn't so much who is better, but what made us have to choose between them?

9

New Year's Eve in Berlin: Firecrackers, Fascist Light Shows, and Witnessing History in the Hauptstadt

John Brady

I

I rang in the millennium standing in the square in front of Berlin's city hall with my sister and friends of mine from the capital. City Hall, or the Red Rathaus ('Das Rote Rathaus') as Berliners call it, a designation that refers to the building's nineteenth-century red brick exterior and not necessarily to its denizens' political inclinations, sits near Alexanderplatz in the middle of downtown Berlin. The rathaus has a clock tower and thus was a good place to count down to the new year.

In the spirit of the dawning corporate millennium, Berlin's city fathers contracted out the organization of the city's official New Year's Eve festivities to a private firm, New Year's Eve in Berlin Ltd. With capital raised through the sale of advertising sponsorships, the party company organized a four-kilometer millennial party strip featuring 15 stages, numerous video screens upon which people could check to make sure they were having as much fun as everyone else, two Ferris Wheels, 500 beer and bratwurst tents, and 1,000 toilets. The strip stretched from Alexanderplatz and City Hall, down the famous tree-lined boulevard Unter den Linden, through the symbol of the city, the Brandenburg Gate, and finally ended at the Victory Column, the monument commemorating the German army's victory in the Franco-Prussia war of 1871. This monument is probably best known to the American intelligentsia as one of the many perches occupied by Wim Wender's angels in his film *Wings of Desire*.

It was at the Victory Column that Mike Oldfield entertained the crowds with his vocal stylings before the searchlight spectacle 'Art in Heaven,' designed by local artist Gert Hof, projected a cathedral of light into the millennial night sky. As Germany's part of the globe rotated into the next thousand years, Berlin was shrouded in a thick fog and thus the *Lichtkathedral* was not even visible from nearby Alexanderplatz. This was, in the end, probably better. As a number of querulous Berliners noted with discomfort, 'Art in Heaven' was strikingly reminiscent of another event in which Berlin and Germany appeared before the global public sphere, the light spectacle organized by Nazi architect Albert Speer at Berlin's Olympic Stadium during the 1936 Olympics.

Despite the obvious allure of, on the one hand, witnessing the continuing difficulty Germans have trying to really learn from their past and, on the other, listening to Mike Oldfield warble in the new year, we passed on the main celebration at the Victory Column. Nonetheless it is interesting to speculate about what exactly Berlin's movers and shakers were thinking in putting on such a spectacle. Ever since the political *sturm und drang* that accompanied Germany's transition from two partial nation-states to one unified nation-state has waned, Berlin's elites have dreamed of returning Berlin to the pantheon of great European cities. In their civic fantasies, Berlin will regain its status as a political and cultural leader in Europe's firmament, attracting talent, money, and publicity like it did during the days of the Weimar Republic. Berlin's new-found neo-Weimar vitality will come, of course, without all the messy revolutionary violence and economic chaos of the interwar years.

II

Instead of taking in Oldfield and company, we staked out a place in front of City Hall, standing in the nearby Poseidon Fountain in order to better take in the scene. Part of our decision to stay at Alexanderplatz was motivated by a very banal reason. After the big New Year's Eve meal we prepared before hitting the streets, none of us wanted to fight our way through four kilometers worth of people in order to get to the middle of the Tiergarten, Berlin's central municipal park, and the Victory Column's location. But our decision was also motivated by loftier goals. We wanted to witness the millennium at Alexanderplatz because it is one of the most historically significant spaces in the entire city.

In a city that has no shortage of important plazas, squares, and buildings, Alexanderplatz is one of the richest in historical meaning. Standing in the middle of the square that once served as the city's ox market, it is possible to construct a web of associations that link Alexanderplatz with key moments and periods in Germany's past. It is at Alexanderplatz that one can see the traces of the events and struggles that have shaped and continue to shape German everyday life.

During the Weimar Republic, Alexanderplatz came to symbolize modern, big city life in Germany. Indeed, Alfred Döblin used the square as one of the main settings for his novel *Berlin Alexanderplatz*, a classic of modern German fiction. It was on and around Alexanderplatz that Döblin's hero Franz Biberkopf—ex-con, hustler, chump, fatty, windbag, amputee—was buffeted and finally conquered by the social, economic, and political winds that kicked up such a storm during Germany's chaotic interwar period.

The postwar division of Berlin and Germany placed Alexanderplatz in East Berlin, capital of the German Democratic Republic (GDR). The square became one of the most important public spaces in a regime whose leaders tried to tame the forces of exploitation, human misery, and greed that had gotten the best of Biberkopf. Alexanderplatz was the social heart of the GDR. Here weary tourists from the provinces mixed with regular East Berliners, socializing, relaxing, and passing the time. Of course, Alexanderplatz wasn't just a harmless oasis amid the bustle of greater East Berlin. It was also bound to a repressive regime of control and surveillance. The East Berlin authorities, fearing disorder and perhaps the birth of the next incarnation of the Sex Pistols, banned East German punks from using the square. And lest any of the 'normal' occupants of the square act on any subversive ideas of their own, Alexanderplatz was under constant surveillance by the state security apparatus, the Stasi.

With the fall of the Berlin Wall, the reign of the Stasi came to an end, only to be replaced by a different sort of control, that of Western-style consumer capitalism. Like many of the other public spaces in the city—Potsdamerplatz, Friedrichsstrasse Station, Breitscheidplatz—'Alex' is now a bustling commercial center with glitzy stores, overpriced restaurants and cafes, and tourist attractions. In this respect it is thoroughly Western. But it is also significantly more than just the hunting ground upon which consumers pursue the latest commodity fetish. It is also a reminder of Germany's divided past and its sutured present. And in this important respect it is unique.

Solidified into the square's built environment is the legacy of 40 years of communist government and politics. Standing on the square one can see the low-slung concrete prefab buildings built by the regime during the 1960s to house the Hungarian and Polish cultural centers. Off in another direction the concrete high-rises built to house East Berliners shoot out of the earth. Standing at the south-east corner of the square one can look down Karl-Marx Alle, which turns into Frankfurter Alle, itself an historically significant street in the brief history of East Berlin. It was here that the East German regime undertook one of its first great building projects in 1952 and 1953, turning the Alle into a wide boulevard in grand communist style. Huge Stalinist housing blocs hulk on either side of the boulevard, demanding that you be impressed and cowed by the collective power of the triumphant working class. Ironically, it was in working on this project that the triumphant working class rebelled on June 17, 1953, prompting the Soviet commanders of the city to declare a state of emergency. But the greatest reminder of the past is the television tower. Rising 365 meters into the sky, it is the result of the communist government's largely successful attempt to dominate Berlin's skyline and show that they could build tall things, too. The built environment of Alexanderplatz is the shoals upon which the West German inclination to run roughshod over the memory of the German Democratic Republic continues to founder.

We chose Alexanderplatz in order to witness the passing of the millennium in such an historically rich atmosphere. We chose the Poseidon Fountain because it was a good place from which to launch fireworks. And launch them we did. As fast as we could light them, we would throw out our firecrackers beyond the fountain's edge, waiting expectantly for the pay-off: the loud bang and flash accompanied by the bits of paper debris that would shoot off from ground zero in pleasantly elliptical arcs. With each explosion we would laugh and then quickly light some more.

We celebrated on the streets, got lit, danced to the early hours in a sweaty, smoky club, stumbled home, fell into bed, slept late, ate a big breakfast, and nursed our hangovers the next day. It was the kind of experience I had wanted to have. In planning to celebrate the millennium I had wanted to do something a little more exotic than sit around the rainy Bay Area. So I told my friends I was coming, cajoled my sister into letting me flop at her apartment, and off I went, ending up in Berlin on New Year's Eve.

III

While the desire to go someplace different for the millennium might not be too hard to understand, my plan to spend New Year's Eve in Berlin does raise the question: why that particular city? One reason had to do with personal history. While I was doing fieldwork for my dissertation, I spent a substantial amount of time in the city and grew very fond of it. In the time that winter break afforded me, I wanted to go back and spend some time there, visit friends, and reinvigorate my ties to a city I like to think of as a second home. The second reason for going also had to do with history, but in a broader sense, namely in the sense of the history of Berlin as a city and as the new capital of Germany. When I left Berlin in 1997 after my fieldwork was complete, the city was, as the cliché had it, still under construction. The many projects ranged from refurbishing East Berlin's housing stock, which had fallen into disrepair, to the construction of the consumer pleasure palace at Potsdamerplatz, to the restoration of the Reichstag, and the construction of the buildings to house the federal government after it pounded the dust of Bonn, the old capital, off its shoes and moved to Berlin. When I left many of these projects were still not finished and I wanted to see how they had progressed in the three years since I had been to the city. I wanted to witness the passage of time, the making of history, and see the difference between the present and the Berlin I had known in 1997.

A similar desire to witness history was at work in the popular fascination with the passing of the millennium. As an historically constructed unit of time, the millennium is a rare event, one that comparatively few people are able to experience. Moreover, the millennium is an event that a person will only be able to experience once. A very few individuals who are able to forgo fat, alcohol, tobacco, and sausage live long enough to witness the beginning and end of an entire century. Although if the science of antiaging, which biotechnology firms are rushing to exploit, indeed pans out, more and more of us may get the chance to experience an entire century's worth of history. But unless they figure out the secrets of time travel or discover the fountain of youth sometime very soon, none of us will have the opportunity to experience the dawn of the next millennium. Thus in a popular culture in which individuals often establish their identity in terms of their participation in special events—a particular sports game, a star sighting, a political convention—the millennium, as such a singular event, offered people a very valuable opportunity to bolster their individual uniqueness.

Yet there is something problematic about approaching the millennium as an historical event to be witnessed. In the first place, the millennium was a highly artificial happening, propped up and given legitimacy by cities hungry for tourists, corporate sponsors hungry for name recognition, and revelers thirsty for champagne. As sticklers have pointed out, the real millennium was actually at the end of the year 2000. But beyond this surface and calendric artificiality, there was something more fundamentally false about the millennium as an historical event. History is not a natural process that just happens. It isn't something that just passes us by and that we watch and witness. Instead, history is something that we collectively make, and make with more or less conscious intention. What is more, not all of us have the same resources and the same interests in participating in the historical processes that shape our lives. History isn't some populist spectacle. It consists of real struggles between groups to shape the institutions, norms, and rules that govern their everyday lives.

As my stay in Berlin progressed, my perspective on witnessing history shifted. I no longer looked to events like the millennium or to completed construction projects to get a sense for the historical development of the city. Instead, I looked to how Berliners were relating to one another. I also stopped thinking that there was one history which all of the inhabitants of Berlin were participating in equally. Instead, I began to see the conflicts and fissures that exist in the city and divide its inhabitants into different groups, classes, and cultures. I began to see that there isn't just one history in Berlin, but many histories, not all of which follow the same logic or advance at the same speed. And I saw that the history of Berlin isn't just something that flows along like the river Spree flows through the city. No, history in Berlin is marked by political conflict and struggle.

Berlin's groups struggle to determine the economic fate of the city. The German majority struggles with the city's many minority groups to fashion some kind of common life together. And the political elites and the populace struggle to establish Berlin's place in the rapidly changing European and global contexts. These conflicts aren't always easy to see. They involve shifting alliances and dirty tricks, and are fought out on a far from level playing field. They can't be packaged as a popular festival, but they, unlike the millennium, will determine the future of Berlin.

10

The Tenth Anniversary of the Siege at Waco and April 2003

Megan Shaw Prelinger

Ten years ago this spring, 80 civilians died in Waco, Texas, following a prolonged assault on their home by the army's elite Delta Force. It was the greatest loss of civilian life in conflicts with federal forces in American history.

The Delta Force staged its assault with Bradley armored fighting vehicles (AFVs), armored personnel carriers best known for their use by American forces in the last two Gulf wars. The civilian dead included many immigrants, people of color, elderly, and children. They were members of the Branch Davidian church, and when they died they had been trapped in their home by federal forces for 51 days.

The tenth anniversary of that tragedy occurs amid a national crisis of civil rights and a war against terrorism that could become the next world war. It cannot escape its context within the current wartime wave of inward directed aggression. While war continues to rage in the Middle East, the long reach of the Patriot Act is continuing a long-standing pattern of wartime federal aggression against immigrants. The FBI is holding round-the-clock informal 'conversations' with Arab-Americans. The Department of Homeland Security (DHS) has absorbed the functions of the former Immigration and Naturalization Service (INS). Immigrants from 26 predominantly Muslim countries are required to register with the government.

The specific targeting of Muslims frames the current anti-immigrant initiatives in bold terms of a religious opponent. The army is not yet knocking at the door of suspected Muslim fundamentalists with flash-bang grenades and open gunfire. But ten years ago this is exactly how the chosen Other was treated.

THE SIEGE

The siege of the Branch Davidians began with a botched raid on the group's home by the Bureau of Alcohol, Tobacco, and Firearms (BATF). The BATF had come to serve a warrant for illegal weapons. Its warrant ignored the fact that the group's gun holdings were within normal limits for residents of Texas. It ignored the fact that the group was on good terms with its local law enforcement, and had invited weapons inspections at any time. Using militarized police tactics, the raid was staged as a 'dynamic, no-knock entry,' which means entering with flash-bang grenades and open gunfire. The BATF killed six Branch Davidians that day, lost four agents in return fire, then called in the FBI for reinforcement. The FBI called in the army.

At the conclusion of the eventful 51-day siege, the army used heavy duty Bradley AFVs to punch holes in the walls of the church complex and insert CS gas. When exposed to flame, CS gas produces hydrogen chloride, the gas used in execution chambers. Three months prior to the siege at Waco, in January 1993, the United States had agreed at the Chemical Weapons Convention in Paris not to use CS gas during wartime. Unfortunately peacetime use against civilians was not ruled out. When the gas met the kerosene lanterns the group was using for light, firestorms and gas clouds erupted.

HOW IT WAS FIRST REMEMBERED

In 1993 the United States was awash with panic about gun-wielding cultists. Fear of Islamic militants was just entering the mainstream as a result of the first attack on the World Trade Center, but Islamophobia had not yet eclipsed fear of the enemy within. When Sheik Omar Abdel-Rahman, whose teachings inspired the 1993 attack on the World Trade Center, was featured on the cover of *Time*, he shared the cover with David Koresh, leader of the Branch Davidian community. The Davidian community was perceived as an equal threat to the wellbeing of the United States, on a par with World Trade Center attackers, even though the group had never attacked anyone.

The mass suicide of 900 cultists at Jonestown, Guyana, 15 years earlier was still within reach of public memory. In the 1980s there was heavy reporting of militant white supremacist separatist churches such as The Covenant, The Sword, and the Arm of the Lord. Fears that loved ones could be kidnapped by crazed cultists, or killed by white supremacists, were real to many people. Mainstream, coastal-dwelling Americans looked with an anxious eye to the heartland for hordes of a dangerous Other.

The BATF was humiliated in the initial raid and the news media defended them. The Branch Davidian community was dismissed as a cult in local, national, and international news, both print and broadcast. The siege and prolonged assault of its members was publicly framed from coast to coast with several broad prejudicial discourses. Runaway gun culture, dangerous millennialists from the heartland, and the specter of another Jonestown confirmed the threat supposedly posed by the Branch Davidians. These discourses were so totalizing that they diverted all attention away from the staggering civil rights violations of the siege.

Early advocacy for the Branch Davidians was limited to civil libertarians whose lobbying centered on gun rights. These lobbyists faced a cultural divide separating them from ruling antigun opinionmakers and government officials. Opinionmakers and officials were answerable to the suburban conventions of their electorate. They had no need to take up the cause of people who had come to symbolize a significant perceived threat to their constituents. The tragedy at Waco was ghettoized for years.

Yet while the mainstream was sleeping, filmmakers, independent journalists, sociologists, media critics, scholars of religion, and historians began slowly to reframe public memory of the event. Many of their books, films, and other interpretive works have proliferated since the mid-1990s. The 1995 book *Why Waco? Cults and the Battle for Religious Freedom in America* sympathetically contextualized the group's history and beliefs. The 1997 film *Waco: The Rules of Engagement* exposed the brutality of the bias inherent to most of the reporting about the siege. Most recently, the film *Urban Warrior* (2002) mentioned the tragedy at Waco in its most appropriate context for a secular audience: the rise of domestic militarization.

THE MILITARIZED PUBLIC SPHERE

As explicated in Christian Parenti's *Lockdown America: Police and Prisons in the Age of Crisis*, the initial raid on the Branch Davidians is consistent with the style of militarized policing to which immigrants and the poor became regularly subjected in the 1990s. Starting in 1995, technology transfer amendments enabled the Department of Defense to begin offloading disused military equipment to civilian police forces. Between 1995 and 1997 the department distributed more than 3,800 M-16 assault rifles, 73 M-79 grenade launchers and 112 armored personnel carriers.

The presence of these armaments in the hands of civilian officers has disabled any last thought that the fabled Posse Comitatus Act might save the populace from the deadly force designed to vanquish foreign armies. In 1807, Congress declared the army to be the enforcer of national law. But in 1878, following a bloody period of post-Civil War reconstruction in the south, the army was removed from everyday peacekeeping duties by the Posse Comitatus Act, which gained a mythic weight over subsequent decades. The act became endowed with the widespread and utopian misconception that it designated the US's standing army exclusively for wars against foreign armies.

But the act only removed the army from ordinary law enforcement. It did not prohibit the army, or other federal forces, from other inward-directed acts of aggression. The army remained on legal standby for intervention in domestic disturbances, and it developed an involved domestic intelligence gathering and intimidation force.

During World War I, the army formed the MI-4 intelligence service to spy on civilians. Recent European immigrants were under suspicion of harboring traitorous loyalties to their former home countries. Together with labor activists whose projects were perceived as threatening to the lines of mechanical production upon which the war effort relied, they were heavily spied on and reported on. During World War II Japanese-Americans and to a lesser extent German-Americans were targeted. The army's forced incarceration of thousands of Japanese-Americans between 1942 and 1945 is unequaled in the US's history of immigrant oppression.

In 1965, the US Army Intelligence Command was formed to focus inward aggression on civil rights activists. And in 1968 the army created the Civil Disturbance Collection Plan to spy on civilians suspected of being associated with the civil rights and antiwar movements.

The Posse Comitatus Act was amended in 1986 to allow the army to fight the domestic 'war on drugs.' It was through this loophole that the Delta Force ended up surrounding the Branch Davidians at Waco with high power Bradley tanks left over from the first Gulf war. Earlier tenants of the Branch Davidians' property had once used one of its buildings as a meth lab. The presence of Delta Force in American streets is not unique to Waco. In 1999 this high-powered unit was again used against civilians, this time against anarchist protesters at the WTO meeting in Seattle.

APRIL 2003

The tenth anniversary of the siege of the Branch Davidians occurs in the context of a brutal war and a sinister series of compromises on civil liberties. Since the attacks on New York and Washington of September 2001, the government's jihad against Islamic fundamentalists has assumed epic proportions. For example, during the week of this essay's writing, George W. Bush framed his conquest of Baghdad as 'God's will.' The home front of this war has predictably focused in on Americans of Middle East descent; 26 'at-risk' countries have been identified as possible sources of immigrants who might promulgate terror.

The FBI is questioning Iraqi-Americans door-to-door; other 'at-risk' immigrants are merely required to register. The Department of Homeland Security has absorbed the functions of the Immigration and Naturalization Servise; collapsing the historic distinction between the granting of civilian travel visas and defense screening. For everyone else, there are the department's new spying powers. This department's chief weapon of terror is the power to strip individuals of their citizenship based solely on suspicion of association with so-called 'terrorist' groups. The department is equipped with an officer of Civil Rights and Civil Liberties, but this officer is not empowered to investigate abuses by department officials.

Right now, the religious war at home is being waged with civility. After all, many Muslim immigrants to the United States are well educated and hold white-collar jobs in research and engineering. The war on immigrants that is waged by spying and tracking tends to follow a class line that distinguishes it from the war waged on immigrants with Department of Defense hand-me-downs. The tanks and guns are largely reserved for working-class immigrants from Mexico and Central America, and for the American underclass.

CONCLUSION

In 1970, the American Civil Liberties Union sued the army, arguing that the Civil Disturbance Collection Plan amounted to illegal spying on civilians. Amazingly, in 1971 they won their case. The Civil Disturbance Collection Plan was rescinded, and the data that had been collected was destroyed.

Encouraging as this bit of history may be, it cannot be presumed that history will happen again in this same way. The DHS's spying program has been born even with the full knowledge of this recent history. Although no groups of immigrants or religious Others are currently facing federal forces down the sight line of a Bradley AFV, history does tend to repeat itself. The United States repeatedly constructs new immigrant groups as dangerous and builds public fear about them. It routinely subjects them to harsh hazing rituals. It is the survivors of these hazing rituals that are assimilated into the melting pot.

It is also noteworthy that the tendency of the US government to militarize its relationships with immigrants and marginal groups is intact throughout history irrespective of which party is in control, or whether the ruling party has a reputation for being 'liberal' or 'conservative.' The siege of the Branch Davidians occurred during the Clinton administration, as did the technology transfer of equipment from the Department of Defense to civilian police forces. To see our way out of this repeating bitter loop will require a deeper break from tradition than our customary rotations of power are prepared to manifest.

REFERENCES

Parenti, Christian, *Lockdown America: Police and Prisons in the Age of Crisis*, New York: Verso, 2000.

Tabor, James, and Eugene Gallagher, *Why Waco? Cults and the Battle for Religious Freedom in America*, Berkeley: University of California Press, 1995.

Urban Warrior, documentary film, directed by Matt Ehling, 2002.

Waco: The Rules of Engagement, directed by William Gazecki, written by Michael McNulty and Dan Gifford, 1997.

11

The FSM Café: History, Memory, and the Political Legacy of Coffee

Tomás F. Sandoval, Jr. and Jason M. Ferreira

In the fall of 1964, students at the University of California's flagship campus rose in protest and began what is now famously known as the Free Speech Movement (FSM). The Berkeley students who spearheaded this movement were protesting against the university administration's attempt to limit their political advocacy on the campus. In time, the students succeeded in amending the speech policies of the Berkeley campus while contributing to the more general radicalization of campus politics at their home campus and also nationwide. In that respect, the FSM is remembered as a glowing success of student empowerment.

However, the FSM represented more than a push toward free speech. It was part of a broader movement that increasingly recognized the ubiquitous limits of liberalism: rampant and violent societal racism, a lack of government response to inequality, and the emerging contradictions of the United States' involvement in Vietnam. The FSM represented a radical step in the critique of the complex of social forces that were characterized at the time as 'the system.'

Mario Savio was the most prominent leader of the FSM, and he articulated this developing ideology in a speech titled 'An End to History.' In 1964 Savio had recently returned from Mississippi where he participated in the Freedom Summer political programs of the Student Non-violent Coordinating Committee (SNCC). In 'An End to History' he demonstrated a skill for acute social commentary, linking the racially oppressive federal government to the politically repressive university in their shared reliance on a 'depersonalized, unresponsive bureaucracy.' He asserted that these bureaucracies believed that history had ended, that 'no events can occur now that the Second World War is over which can change American society substantially.' He attacked the university's unwillingness to change, and its inability to recognize that both it and society still needed to change.

At the time, the Berkeley campus and the University of California (UC) system as a whole were in fact undergoing substantial changes. Campuses expanded as the flood of baby boomers began pursuing higher education, while the California state government revised its relationship to its educational components. The resulting policy, contained within the state's Master Plan of Higher Education, created a multitiered system sometimes called the 'multiversity.' Heralded by UC President Clark Kerr, a former industrial relations professor, the plan defined distinct roles for the Community Colleges, the State College system, and the University of California system as it sought to increase the synergy enjoyed between higher education and private industry. To students like Savio, the plan reflected the 'conception that the university is part and parcel of this particular stage in the history of American society; it stands to serve the need of American industry; it is a factory that turns out a certain product needed by industry or government.' In this conception, speech (or students) that ran contradictory to the status quo disrupted that relationship and threatened the very production of the UC machine.

In the more than three decades since the beginning of the FSM, its political and historical legacies have been invoked numerous times in support of different causes. From the Third World Strike of the late 1960s to current movements surrounding the repeal of affirmative action policies, the implicit belief common to these many movements is that students have not only the right but also the responsibility to play a role in the bettering of their society. The university usually plays an opposing role, representing the societal status quo and opposing that betterment.

The FSM altered the relationship between utopian student movements and the university because it recognized the ways in which the university system played a part in the maintenance and reproduction of the proverbial 'system.' Whether calling the university to task for its production of research that serves the military-industrial complex or for its policies that reproduce and maintain a racially segregated society, the students of the FSM also represent a movement against the static, corporate university system. On this front, perhaps, a meaningful success eluded the FSM.

Moving forward to the dawn of a new century and millennium, a revealing turn of events demonstrates the point. On February 3, 2000 the very same institution that a young Savio compared to an 'odious machine' marked the history of the FSM by dedicating the 'Free Speech Movement Café.' The dedication ceremony was attended by several members of the university's administration, staff, a large contingent of FSM alumni, and a small group of students. At the dedication Chancellor Robert M. Berdahl, a historian, delivered his remarks placing the FSM critique within the American paradigm. He said that 'contrary to popular belief, the students desperately—and with great fervor—aspired to embrace American values. They believed that the nation's finest hour had not yet arrived. And the prism of their views was marked by a distinctly American constitutional idealism.' Berdahl continued as he argued 'for the need to understand the movement, to not place it in a sealed box of misunderstanding and miss out on the values and the lessons it could still teach three decades later.'

But what are those lessons? Entering the café, one is instantly surrounded with the images of students protesting on the walls. An electric message strip runs the repeated phrase 'Welcome to the Free Speech Movement Café' over and again as if a newswire in Times Square. Just beneath that, an excerpt from Savio's famous speech imploring students to 'throw your body upon the gears and cogs of the machine' is printed on the wall, superimposed over the faces of the protesting masses. On the opposite wall, a collection of art that is supposed to represent some aspects of the era hangs behind glass. And in the realm of the present, in the seats and on the tables that fill the space, the modern masses of students sit and sip their coffee, chat on their cell phones, sneak in a quick study break, and visit with friends.

Of course, this café has little to do with the actual history of the movement. The FSM directed little effort, either directly or indirectly, at the growing need for more coffee. The café attempts to remember the past by institutionalizing it on the Berkeley campus, by creating a physical space that can serve as an acknowledgement of 'the impact and the values of the movement and its participants.' The result of a generous donation from a Berkeley alumnus, the café is only one expenditure of a funding source that will enable the library to maintain its archives of the FSM and make them available to a wider audience. Both are noble goals that help to serve the preservation of history. The café, however, is less in step with the legacy of the FSM.

While Berdahl's remarks placing the FSM within the context of American idealism are true, the movement (as demonstrated in its sustained critique of the equally 'American' values of jingoism, racism, corporatism, and the like) also tried to problematize much of that idealism. By calling the university system to task for its role in the furthering of societal evils, the FSM tried to change that very system. But the historical trajectory of the university proved far more powerful than the student voice, as the 1996 slogan 'UC Means Business' attests. The concept of the multiversity is alive and strong today, and is rarely questioned. Today, the UC seeks to enhance the relationship its research has to the private sector, even so far as encouraging academic departments to forge new partnerships with corporate America on a direct grant-funding basis. As for the critique that the university is engendering the forces of societal inequality, the recent repeal of affirmative action and the strike for Ethnic Studies reveal that change is still needed. For that matter, the continued fight against the university's labor abuses with its Graduate Student Instructors and its habitual support of the use of sweatshop labor stand as symbols worthy of Savio's scathing critiques.

History is a living, breathing organism that is shaped by the present as much as by our memory of the past. It is not a fixed set of events that exist only in the past. There will be no perfect recreation of the past in the present, but as a society—or a university—we must still make attempts. The Free Speech Movement Café can mean many things, too. To the Chancellor and the gathered alumni it meant the preservation of the past. To others, the commercialized form and substance of that particular preservation stands as a glaring contradiction to the meanings of the past. Perhaps the real issue lies a bit deeper than competing interpretations of a café. To whom does the movement belong?

While FSM alumni naturally have some stake in the memory of their efforts, this movement is also 'owned' by the masses of students who continue the fight for a better university. To many of them, what makes the institutionalization of the FSM in this café so disturbing is that it took place during the same year that the Chancellor ordered the arrest of students carrying banners in the name of social justice and equality, and as the university faced continued pressure to divest from sweatshop labor, maintained relations with the expanding prison-industrial complex, and failed to rectify the decline of students of color enrolled at the university. Perhaps just as the lack of the visible oppression of blacks with hoses and dogs doesn't mean that there isn't racism in Mississippi, so too the establishment of a Free Speech Movement Café doesn't mean that students' voices are considered in the shaping of the university system.

The disagreement is more than interpretive. History is not an esoteric exercise but part of the living debates of the present. The type of historical commemoration embodied by the FSM Café is dangerous to the healthy life of the past when the past can be used to sell a cup of coffee and to make customers think that the goals of the movement were institutionalized in the system. The 1960s have been historically packaged and made safe and sanitary. At times, the fixity of the past in the café borders on a scary revisionism. For example, one of the glass-encased art pieces is a poster from the Third World Strikes of 1969. A direct outgrowth of the culture of radicalism that the FSM engendered, the Third World Liberation Front (TWLF) also fought for a utopian goal of a better university. Advocating for a new Third World College along with curriculum reforms, the goals of the movement never materialized. In a caption underneath the artwork, a brief statement misrepresents the TWLF as a movement for affirmative action. Instead of seeing affirmative action and the Ethnic Studies Department as a compromise, if not an outright cooptation of the movement's goals, the reader is left to believe that the TWLF achieved its goals. In that way, the establishment of the café stands as a vibrant example of Savio's critique that the university has reached the end of history.

To stay true to the legacy of the FSM we have to do more than drink coffee. We—the students, the professors, the staff, the community of people who stand for a just society and university—need to take back history. As Savio said, 'the university is the place where people begin seriously to question the conditions of their existence and raise the issue of whether they can be committed to the society they have been born into.' That process of questioning as much as the movement itself are both connected to a body of principles, a set of values to which the university will never adhere unless it is pressured. They are the values of justice, equality, and tolerance. They stand in opposition to the modern university of corporate standardization and mass production. And it has nothing to do with a latté. If the FSM is to be remembered then let it be remembered for this. And if it is to be immortalized, then let it be in the hearts of the men and women who 'have shown that they will die rather than be standardized, replaceable, and irrelevant.'

12

Are Diplomatic Ties with Tyrants More Important Than Civil Rights? Life During APEC '97

Elisabeth Hurst

The 1997 Asia Pacific Economic Cooperation (APEC '97) summit was a major international economic conference in Vancouver, Canada during November 1997. Eighteen world leaders attended that conference and hardly anyone in North America knew about it.

During that conference, American President Bill Clinton, Canada's long-running Prime Minister Jean Chrétien, Indonesia's President Suharto, and China's Communist Party leader, President Jiang Zemin, endorsed a deal that supplemented the International Monetary Fund to prevent financial meltdown in the Far East, and discussed trade, business infrastructure, and other matters that impacted your future.

I couldn't avoid APEC '97. I worked in the third building of the Waterfront Complex, next to the conference headquarters and the Waterfront Hotel where President Clinton, Secretary of State Madeleine Albright, and the US delegation stayed. The conference PR people called it a 'secure zone.' It felt more like a war zone. APEC security analysts identified every potential threat, then set up precautions to prevent them. Too bad if those precautions suborned the civil rights of ordinary citizens whose tax dollars paid the bill for the conference.

We voluntarily give up those rights in small, unnoticed ways almost every day in government buildings, office towers, and airports. Every time we meet a flight or fly on an airplane, we are subjected to camera surveillance, metal detectors, x-rays, and searches. Our bags can be confiscated if we put them down in the terminal and walk away from them for a minute too long. No search warrant needed—we are deemed to consent to those invasions of privacy when we enter the airport. You can refuse, but if you exercise that right, you're denied entry and forfeit your plane ticket.

It's hard to condemn airport security designed to stop people from taking weapons or bombs onto planes. But security is a delicate balancing act between ensuring safety and curtailing public freedoms and rights. Too much emphasis on one side or the other, and everything tumbles down, usually hurting the public in the process.

My introduction to APEC '97 came a month before in a series of melodramatic memoranda circulated by the APEC management committee: don't use too many couriers, because they dress strangely and may not get through the Royal Canadian Mounted Police (RCMP) checkpoints; don't carry long narrow objects near the windows because it makes US Secret Service agents nervous and they shoot first and ask questions later; don't drive into the area unless you've got photo identification and a monthly parking decal to prove that you're allowed in the public car park beneath the building; allow extra time however you travel because street closures will change bus routes and cause traffic congestion throughout downtown. Oh, and by the way, don't be late for work.

Two weeks before the conference, I realized that it would be worse than I expected. A man with a grenade in his hand luggage was captured at Vancouver International Airport in a spot check. The next day the newspapers announced that the cost of security for APEC had more than doubled.

On November 19, concrete barricades, chain link fences, and gates surrounded the three buildings in the Waterfront Complex. In one way, I was lucky. My bus route had not changed. I only had to walk four or five extra blocks around sealed-off streets. Others had to walk 15 or 20 blocks.

As I walked to work, eyes followed me everywhere: the eyes of the police and RCMP officers standing in clumps on every street corner; the eyes of the RCMP officers manning the concrete barricades at the outer checkpoints; the eyes of the RCMP officers manning the gates at the inner checkpoints; the eyes of the RCMP officers in the lobby; the eyes of the police, RCMP, Canadian Security Intelligence Service (CSIS), and US Secret Service agents congregating in the food court—holding meetings, eating McDonalds, drinking Starbucks coffee, listening to instructions through their ear wires and muttering into walkie-talkies. Eyes that made sure that I didn't go anywhere, that I didn't belong and that I wasn't interested in the security personnel.

By the time I'd bought a mocha and made it up the elevator, my hands were shaking. A lesbian, feminist, anarchist, and occasional activist, who just wanted to be invisible.

The ignorance and willful blindness of my coworkers added to my stress. Didn't they realize that the concrete barricades on Cordova Street were there to prevent car and truck bombs like those used by terrorists in Lebanon, in London, and in Oklahoma? That there were bomb-sniffing dogs wandering around because someone expected there to be bombs? That the plethora of handguns holstered on uniform belts and beneath suit jackets were there because the officers expected to need and use them? That the security was there to protect the APEC delegates and we were just potential innocent bystanders?

I ended up feeling responsible for them, even the woman who, with all seriousness, told me at the end of that first day that she had never felt so safe in her entire life. I endured the teasing from those who thought I was being 'funny' and unnecessarily paranoid. I pushed them to move away from the windows facing Canada Place when I looked down and saw fire trucks idling on the street and military personnel scrambling around. Afterwards, when the TV and newspapers announced that the military had dealt with two bomb threats that day, they realized that I hadn't been joking. And yet they still felt safe.

On November 21, the security tightened even further, and every pore in my body was aware of the guns. As I got my morning mocha, I received a smile I will remember for the rest of my life. It was casual day at the office, so I wore my usual uniform of jeans, shirt, Doc Marten boots, and black leather motorcycle jacket. At the end of the coffee line was a US Secret Service agent with a wire, in his ear, cell phone in hand, and gun distorting his suit jacket. As I stopped behind him, he turned and smiled at me. It was the scariest smile I've ever seen. His mouth moved but his eyes remained cold, alert, assessing. I wanted to crawl off and hide. But I didn't. I had no doubt that if I did anything except wait in line and get my espresso, I would set off his alarms and he would take me some place private to find out why I changed my mind.

While I worried, stressed, and fretted about the safety of everyone in the office, the grumbling started. 'How inconvenient,' was a common complaint, 'making us walk 16 blocks to the office instead of two.' 'That's unfair,' was another, 'how dare they search my car and demand proof that I have the right to use the parking lot beneath our building.' Even the protestors caught their ire, when a march down Granville Street delayed their commute home. 'Couldn't they have chosen a less-busy street?' They complained about inconvenience, about delays, but not about how their civil rights were infringed every day. When I broached the subject, they were incredulous and disbelieving. This was for their protection and safety. How could it hurt them? How could it erode their civil rights?

How could they not see what was happening? We couldn't all pick up placards and take to the streets in protest, but we could defend those who did.

Indonesian immigrants and their supporters ignored threats of retaliation from President Suharto and his Foreign Minister Ali Alatas against family members in Indonesia, and took to the streets. And, before you dismiss these threats, consider that some observers estimate that Suharto and his allies have slaughtered 400,000 communists, suspected communist sympathizers, and East Timorese peasants.

Many Chinese joined the protests, taking a stand against Jiang Zemin. In an interview with the publisher and two reporters from *The Globe and Mail* shortly after APEC '97, the Chinese President claimed that he was a democrat, and that he was 'quite open-minded.' Interesting protestations from a man who governs a country that encourages forced abortion and the murder of female infants; who approves the use of organs for transplants without prior consent from executed prisoners; who believes that the bloody military crackdown in Tiananmen Square, in which hundreds and possibly thousands died, was necessary. In his words, 'Had the then-Chinese government failed to adopt resolute measures, then we could not possibly have enjoyed today's stability.'

APEC '97 protestors also included the People's Summit, the No! to APEC Coalition, First Nations people, students, and Canadians from every walk of life who objected to the presence of dictators in Vancouver and to the removal of civil rights to protect those tyrants.

All protests were unacceptable to the security organizers for APEC '97. Minds conditioned to look for conspiracies, assassins, and terrorists saw ample opportunity in even the most peaceful demonstration. Barricades, fences, and a small army of police kept the protestors far away from the APEC leaders who met in the Museum of Anthropology. They arrested a demonstrator for posting signs with subversive messages like 'Democracy' and 'Free Speech' outside the security perimeter.

On November 25, when demonstrators got too close to the security fence, when some, in their frustration, tore at the wire fence, the police entered the fray. Forcing their way into the crowd with bicycles, the police used pepper spray indiscriminately on protestors, bystanders, and reporters.

When it was over, 40 people were arrested during the protests and the attempts to block roads used by the motorcades. Most were demonstrators, but two were members of the Indonesian security team protecting Suharto. Why were they in the middle of that protest? The press releases and news articles said only that they were arrested for breach of the peace during a demonstration. Why were those brutes allowed to get so close to Canadian civilians?

An unidentified someone told Canadian law enforcement officials that to serve and protect Canadians was not their most important duty. The security of the summit delegates was paramount. Sections of Vancouver became miniature police states without freedom of speech and assembly; where potential conspiracies, born in the minds of security analysts, took precedence over the obligations of police officers to obtain warrants before they searched private property, before they confiscated driver's licenses and possessions from people going to work.

APEC '97 did not change everyone who survived it, but many otherwise apolitical Vancouver residents have spoken up against the subornation of their civil rights. Neither the late, unacceptable explanations of the police media liaisons, nor the complaints filed on behalf of the students by constitutional experts can expunge our memories.

My questions all start with why? Why did the Canadian government want to chair APEC and sponsor APEC '97? Why did Canadian taxpayers pay many millions of dollars for luxury accommodations and protection for thugs who are only interested in human rights for themselves and their lackeys? Why did the security of these tyrants take precedence over the civil rights enshrined in the Canadian Charter of Rights and Freedoms? Why compromise civil rights for a forum that is unlikely to include human rights on its agenda?

The answer to every question is money. Experts agree that, in an ever-shrinking world, Canada must expand its trade horizons. APEC estimates the 1996 combined gross national product of its 18 member countries at over $22 trillion, or approximately 52 per cent of total world output and 40 per cent of global trade. To Canada, with its globally integrated economy, APEC represents a trading bloc that cannot be ignored by a government which is not willing to see this country, with its struggling dollar, become poorer.

I'm far from an expert on global economy, but after reading Prime Minister Chrétien's official news release, the results of APEC '97 seem more ephemeral than concrete. Except for the financial bailout for troubled Eastern countries, almost everything is geared toward encouraging future work.

It's not enough. No amount of money or promises of future benefits can possibly make it worth my while to give up my civil rights.

In a *Vancouver Sun* article titled 'Stephen Hume: Denounce the Tyrants,' Mr. Hume talks about the willingness of Canadian politicians and financiers to deal with leaders like Suharto and Zemin, to ignore human rights, environmental standards, and workers' rights in return for discussions of freer trade and financial considerations. In his words, 'Out in the blunt-spoken hinterlands we call this whoring, but this week in the sophisticated city it will be called a necessity of protocol.'

I mostly agree with Mr. Hume. However, to me, Canada is worse than a whore. At least when I walked the streets and sold my body, I was paid in cold hard cash, not vague promises couched in flowery language.

13

Marx v. Weber: Uno Mas!

J.C. Myers

Most of us who grew up in the United States during the Cold War years were indoctrinated with the dogmatic and inflexible party line that Marx was wrong. By the time we reached college, the crude Pavlovian conditioning had done its work well. 'Marx ... ' our teachers would begin, 'was wrong!' our collective subconscious would chant in unison. One dangerous radical teaching a philosophy course I was enrolled in as a college student went so far as to begin a lecture by telling us, 'Marx ... isn't so bad.' The Cold War may have ended, but the conditioning settled in, deep and resonant. Is there another political thinker who can elicit such a quick and visceral response? But what, exactly, was Marx wrong about? Was it his savage, unsparing critique of Bruno Bauer that we were instructed to reject? Or perhaps his musings on the organic composition of capital? No, the answer is much simpler, of course, and we all know it, don't we? Marx was wrong because he failed correctly to predict the future. Marx predicted a future of capitalist decline and proletarian revolution, neither of which happened, thus sealing the fate of his 'social theories.'

There has been, I think, too little reflection on the Cold War years so far; on what we knew and why we thought we knew it. For instance, let's get one thing straight: Marx's prediction of a future of social revolution wasn't far off. Not long after the ink had dried on the pages of the *Communist Manifesto*, revolutions broke out across Europe. In the aftermath of their defeat, things went quiet for 70 years or so before revolutionary struggles rose to power in Russia and were turned back in Germany and Hungary. After that, Asia, Africa, the Caribbean, and Latin America. Let's be clear: it is one thing to point out that in most places revolutionary struggles that have thought of themselves as socialist or communist or Marxist have been turned back. It is quite another thing—and an abominable historical inaccuracy—to claim that they never happened.

Surely, a more outrageous prediction was the belief (cheerfully circulated by left-liberals and social democrats circa 1990) that once the Cold War had come to a close with the West firmly victorious, reasonable, clear-headed social-democratic criticisms of the market could come to the fore without the red warning label being slapped across them. With the Soviet Union gone, it was often said, real reforms could take place in the West without knee-jerk reactionaries fighting tooth and nail against anything that might put us on the slippery slope to socialism. Nothing, it turned out, would be further from the actual course of events. 'Reform' in the United States and Western Europe quickly came to refer to the process of dismantling what few social welfare protections those societies once enjoyed. Social-democratic parties became liberal centrists, liberal centrists became unapologetic free-marketeers, and just about everyone else to the left of Bill Clinton or Tony Blair went out for cigarettes and never came back.

Neither did it turn out to be the case that rational, reasonable considerations of Marx as a political thinker would become the norm once the red flag had been hauled down from over the Kremlin. Take, for instance, an article focused entirely on the work of Alexis de Tocqueville, which opens by slamming Marx for having failed to 'accurately describe, analyze, and explain the late-modern and early-post-modern world.'[1] Criticizing Marx for his failed fortune-telling is a tired routine. Wheeling in Tocqueville to do the job, however, is a bold new innovation. Traditionally, that task had been reserved for Max Weber. If Marx was wrong about what lay ahead for Western capitalist societies, Weber was right. For those of us schooled during the Cold War era, this was sure and certain knowledge. As sure and certain as the knowledge (obtained from where, no one can quite remember) that supermarket lines in Kiev were longer than those in Cleveland.

During the 1950s and 1960s, Weber's superiority over Marx became the bedrock of American social science. And while the champion's belt has gone uncontested for years, if those two old German duelists were with us today, surely they'd be ready for a rematch. So, in the interests of reflection and contemplation at the beginning of the twenty-first century, why not bring 'em back into the ring?

ROUND ONE—SOCIAL ORDER

One of the central questions on which Marx and Weber were traditionally brought head-to-head concerned the sources of political order. Just why is it that the masses of people at the bottom of steeply unequal societies go along with the program, day in and day out, rather than rising up in rebellion? Marx's answer was not that the ruling class exerted such power through its steely grasp on the state that all expressions of proletarian political aspirations would be quickly snuffed out. Although, after the liquidation of the Paris Commune, he had no illusions about the ferocity with which capitalist states were capable of defending themselves, either. Nor was his answer that workers were too hopelessly deluded by 'false consciousness' to act in their own interest. Marx's real candidate for the source of social order in modern, capitalist societies was far more mundane than either force or fraud—it was what he called in *Capital* the dull compulsion of economic forces: rent and groceries. Compounding this was the fact that in both production and politics workers become alienated from any meaningful control over the material conditions of everyday life. Rather than a sense of patriotic fervor, what Marx suggests capitalist society breeds under normal conditions is a sense of isolation and powerlessness. Life seems entirely accidental—booming economy one day, mass layoffs the next—and what can one individual do but try to make ends meet and take care of number one?

This doesn't seem to be a wildly implausible description of life in the 'early-post-modern world,' but the Weberians have maintained for years that their man had a better answer, with far greater explanatory power when applied to the trajectory of modern politics. The source of mass obedience was the belief in a system of legitimate authority. In early societies, legitimacy was based on tradition. We do things this way because we've always done things this way. When a society went into crisis and its system of legitimacy was disturbed, a charismatic leader would arise and step into the breach. But in the long run, the system of legitimacy bound to dominate modern societies was rational administration. We follow the rules and obey authority because we believe that the powers that be are rational and legally constituted. For all the stones that have been hurled at Marxists over the question of 'false consciousness,' there is quite a bit riding on collective belief here. But the rationalization and bureaucratization of the state was unquestionably a central political trend in the developed countries for most of the century.

Two plausible descriptions of social order in capitalist society. Some good punches thrown by both fighters. Let's call round one a draw.

ROUND TWO—THE DIRECTION OF HISTORY

What was Marx's prediction for the future of capitalism? Why, the impoverishment of the proletariat—says so in black and white in the *Communist Manifesto*. The proletariat would sink deeper and deeper into poverty while the bourgeoisie ruthlessly enriched itself until the day of the revolution, when the expropriators would be expropriated. Weber, on the other hand, predicted a future of progressive rationalization. Capitalist societies would manage their contradictions and overcome their crises with the tools of rational administration. They would reform, if necessary. They would supply the masses with sufficient amounts of material wellbeing so as to stave off revolution. In the Marx–Weber debate, this was always the Weberian knock-out punch. Capitalism wouldn't impoverish the working class. It would rationalize. It would reform. It would survive. After the arrival of the Western European welfare states, the New Deal, the War on

Poverty, and the Great Society, it was hard not to be convinced and most scholars were. Weber's analysis had stood the test of time.

Until our own day and age, that is, in which Marx's counter-punch finally seems to have landed. For what Marx predicted about the future of capitalism, first and foremost, was the spread and dominance of the market. Finding its way into every pore of social life, the market would leave no human relationship unaffected. Capitalism would transform personal worth into market value and convert revered professionals into wage workers. It would expand to reach every corner of the globe in the search for profits, slipping out of the nation-state's grasp and forcing every country to adopt its way of life. Could there be a more accurate way of describing the conditions of post-Cold War globalization? In place of the cornerstone of the US welfare system, Aid to Families with Dependent Children, we have now the Personal Responsibility Act. In need? Hit hard times? Tough luck, go find a job. Public schools falling apart? Here's a voucher, go talk to the private sector. National health insurance? We've got something even better, it's called 'managed care,' run by private companies for a profit, of course. Laid-off? Downsized? Jobs moved to a cheaper labor market overseas? Well, what did you expect? Competition leads to the generalization of technological innovations and rates of profit decline. Somebody has to make up for the losses and it certainly isn't going to be the stockholders. A whole world filled with workers, firms, and governments tearing at each other's heels to remain 'competitive'? You can find descriptions of contemporary capitalism like this in the business section of any major newspaper—or you can find them in Marx.

In the 1950s and 1960s, Weber's great advantage as a social theorist was his fascination with bureaucratization—unquestionably the name of the game back then. But whereas Weber saw market capitalism as inseparably linked to a broad, totalizing, rationalization of society, what Marx recognized about the market was its irrationality. His inspiration here was drawn from none other than Adam Smith himself, who taught that commercial society was organized by the collision of independent economic exchanges: unplanned, unconscious, and unhindered by the iron grip of rationality. Marx, however, foresaw a slightly less benign result to this process than did Smith. Market capitalism, Marx suggested in the *Manifesto*, is like the sorcerer no longer able to control the dark powers summoned up by his spell. What is lost in capitalist society (rather than gained, as Weber held) is precisely the ability to use the tools of reason in matters where our collective material wellbeing is concerned. Just as the worker's conscious control over the act of production is lost when he or she becomes nothing more than an abstract laborer—a burger-flipper, a cubicle drone—society's conscious control over investment, employment, and the environment is lost when we give over those decisions to the market. As the political tools once used to rein-in market forces have been steadily dismantled and disorganized, capitalism once again comes to resemble a ship on the high seas whose captain has gone mad.

ROUND THREE—NATIONALISM, INTERNATIONALISM, AND REVOLUTION

To be sure, Marx's most outlandish prediction was that of a growing internationalist consciousness among the working classes of the world, and their eventual rise to power in a global revolutionary struggle. 'The workers,' the *Manifesto* famously declares, 'have no country.' It was internationalism, Marx argued, that would separate communist political practice from that of other nineteenth-century socialists. For his part, Weber recognized the existence of proletarian internationalism, but saw it as a force in decline. Nationalism looked to him far more likely to spur the passions of modern societies and in a world still firmly divided by national borders and cultural boundaries, can we doubt the accuracy of his insight?

There are a few things to say about Marx's understanding of nationalism and internationalism before awarding this round to the dueling-scarred sociologist from Erfurt. Marx's internationalism was rooted in a critique of any partial identity's ability to deliver a meaningful form of emancipation. We may all be citizens of a proud and free nation, but the day you find yourself unemployed, that and a dollar will buy you a copy of the want ads. For Marx, in order for human beings to live a genuinely human sort of life, physical necessity would have to be brought under control and relegated to its proper place. We would have to spend less time slaving for rent and groceries and more time thinking, acting, and creating freely. The nation-state *qua* nation-state can't deliver this, nor can any type of identity-based social solidarity—including, we might add, an internationalist proletarian identity. But international working-class solidarity was never meant to be a form of emancipation in itself. Freedom, for Marx, would only be the result of a massive reorganization of production, not a quick change of social identity. What stands in the way? Capital. And capital, Marx maintained, was far too powerful to be overcome by a working class in one country, acting alone. Even a European social revolution, Marx wrote, would founder on the rocks of British capital. A lone, isolated socialist country, he predicted, could never stay afloat economically in the world of global capitalism.

Marx's 'prediction' of the rise of proletarian internationalism, then, was never really a prediction at all, but a deadly accurate assessment of what it would take to overcome the power of capitalism. It was the survival of the Soviet Union for 74 years, not its collapse, that flew in the face of Marx's analysis. As for Weber's prediction that proletarian internationalism would wither away, this too turned out to be correct, but only 90 years or so after it was supposed to have happened. The organization of the International Brigades in the Spanish Civil War—to take just one historical example—and the sacrifices made by more than 35,000 volunteers from 53 countries are inexplicable apart from the recognition that proletarian internationalism was rising to its high-water mark through the first half of the twentieth century, not falling into decline as Weber thought.

One of Marx's lesser-known predictions, underscored by Eric Hobsbawm in his introduction to a 1998 edition of the *Communist Manifesto*, was the failure of revolutionary struggle and the 'common ruin of the contending classes.'[2] Social revolutions have come and gone. Proletarian internationalism lived and died. It fought and lost, and for the moment at least, has disappeared from our world. We have by no means reached anything resembling common ruin. But we are certainly closer to common ruin than to any more sustainable, more humane way of existence. We are also far closer to it than to the 'iron cage of rationality' predicted by Weber. The post-Cold War world is not one of planning and control organizing every aspect of existence and snuffing out the human spirit. It is one in which the market has thrown planning and control to the wind. It is one in which every guarantee of security, from the welfare state to lifetime employment, has been sacrificed to 'competitiveness.' It is one in which personal freedom has been ground down to our choice of dwelling and adornment. Marx said that. And Marx was right.

The winner, and new champion ...

NOTES

1. Daniel J. Elazar, 'Tocqueville and the Cultural Basis of American Democracy', *PS: Political Science and Politics*, v. 32, n. 2, June 1999.
2. Karl Marx and Frederick Engels, *The Communist Manifesto*, New York: Verso, 1998, p. 16.

Part III

In and Out of the Academy

INTRODUCTION

This section of the book intervenes in debates about the place of the academy in a world dominated by the marketplace. *Bad Subjects* itself began life in an institution of higher learning and has been sustained not only by the work of professors and students, but also by the less visible labor of those workers who keep university computer systems and funding programs running smoothly despite massive pressures of time and money. We recognize the value of academic life. At the same time, our journal first found its purpose in the attempt to bridge the 'discourse gap' between scholars able to communicate only with each other and ordinary people resentful about being excluded from the intellectual concerns of the academic conference. We continue to struggle with the tensions between our own academic and non-academic editors and contributors, but with the firm conviction that we need to keep the conversation going.

We couldn't imagine a better piece to begin this section than Lisa Archer's reflections on being a sex worker in order to pay for graduate school. An autobiographical piece, Archer's story may be extreme, but it epitomizes the lengths to which graduate students will go to fund their studies. Bitter, ironic, and at times sadly amusing, Archer comes across as the Platonic form of the exploited apprentice-scholar. Continuing the theme of masochism, though in a completely different light, Matt Wray recounts his trip to the Left Conservatism conference, recounting the coming-to-blows of 'soft' poststructuralist progressives and 'hard' Marxists. Sympathetic to both alleged sides, Wray provides a fascinating account of the factional debates that riddled left-wing scholarship in the humanities during the 1990s, usually at the expense of engagement with the conservative power elite.

Mark Van Proyen's impressively far-ranging essay tackles the paradoxes that attend teaching art students how to propagate the avant-garde. Painfully aware how little tolerance contemporary American society has for pursuits that don't translate to the bottom line, he makes a plea for the value of a superficially impractical practice. Art, he argues, may begin as therapy for the damaged life, but it still has the potential to be a new source of life for a damaged society. Scott Schaffer follows Van Proyen with another sympathetic portrait of left-wing academics struggling to reconcile their belief in the possibility of a better society with the pressures of this one. He details the difficulty they encounter trying to keep a progressive political point of view in the classroom, without giving the professionally and politically damaging impression that they are indoctrinating their students.

Wayde Grinstead returns to the themes of Archer's piece, providing another take on exploited academic labor. While Archer entertains clients, Grinstead pours them their drinks. By no means easy to swallow, Grinstead's essay reminds us of the more traditional forms of fundraising that have to take place before teachers like Schaffer can commence their struggles in the classroom. Finally, Katie Simon's essay provides an important moment of relief, moving away from the depressing realities of exploitation and factionalization in the academy to advocate manageable changes in the classroom. Offering a pointed critique of the way college students are taught to write, Simon singles out the lack of sensuality in academic prose and what its absence suggests about its practitioners. She argues that the dehumanizing effects of learning to write oneself out of one's writing can be countered with an approach to composition that makes room for feeling without forsaking analysis.

14

San Francisco: Dangerous for Whores

Lisa Archer

At the end of 1999, I wrote the essay 'I'd Rather Be a Whore Than an Academic.' The world has changed since then. I am no longer a happy hooker—or any kind of hooker at all. I haven't converted to Dworkinism, undergone exorcism, or otherwise renounced my sinful life. Rather—like all US citizens—I've lost my constitutional rights.

As I revise the essay for inclusion in this volume, the Bush administration is sending federal agents and funds to the Bay Area to target 'trafficking' in women and children. According to the *San Francisco Chronicle*:

> The Bay Area is a key port of entry for foreign women and children kidnapped or lured here under false pretenses to work in prostitution or pornography ... President Bush issued a directive to crack down on the sex trade during a three-day international summit hosted by the State Department and the War Against Trafficking Alliance ... to fight human trafficking, which ... could involve as many as 4 million people worldwide, half of whom may be children. (Carolyn Lochhead, Feb. 26, 2003, A3)

Like many threats to civil liberties, Bush's directive presents itself as a heroic effort to protect children from prostitution and pornography. I fear that when federal agents don't find thousands of child prostitutes, they will justify their funding by arresting consenting adults.

I also have faith that San Francisco sex radicalism will survive recent assaults on civil liberties. As for sex work: if the 'oldest profession' hadn't outlived greater obstacles, it wouldn't be the oldest.

I'D RATHER BE A WHORE THAN AN ACADEMIC
Anonymous, Ph.D

The editor who solicited this piece suggested I write about a 'community of whores' and the advantages and obstacles to this kind of community. Because prostitution is illegal in the state of California, the chief obstacle to a community of currently working whores is the risk of arrest. Any organization and any

---

visibility heighten this risk. This is why I cannot write about a community of whores. It's up to each individual whore to decide whether she wants to make herself visible and how. But people who share common oppressors tend to find each other—even if they gather behind closed doors. This piece is dedicated to those who do find each other.

Imagine you're a whore in a society where whoring is the most exalted profession, and academia the most degraded. At a meeting of fellow whores, you confess your darkest secret: you've applied for academic teaching jobs. Your prostitute colleagues exchange shocked glances. Here's what they might say:

'I don't understand why you're doing this. I've heard a lot of women get into this kind of work because they have some kind of drug addiction.'

'Why else would you want to do something that intimate with strangers?'

'You're smart. You've got a good education. There are lots of things you could do for a living without having to sell yourself in that way.'

'Think about what you *have*: a high-paying job. You can choose your own hours and hourly rates. Why would you leave all this for a job where you can't make your own schedule and have to work long hours for considerably less pay?'

'You're in a helping profession—at the highest end of the service sector, and your skills will always be in demand. Can you say that of academic work? There's little use for most of it. You won't be able to choose where you live. You'll have to search all over the country to find people who will pay for what you do, and everything you write, teach, say, and think will be entirely dependent on what those few people are willing to pay for. You'll be so desperate for work that the people who finally hire you will exploit you to no end. They'll give you part-time positions with no job security. You'll have to move from one lectureship to another year after year. How can you give up a respectable job for something so degrading? How will you feel as a feminist—being objectified in that way?'

Unlike the character in this fiction, I'm not a whore coming out as an academic. I'm an academic coming out as a whore.

In fact, I'm not coming out at all. I'm still writing from the closet—not giving you my name. This is because the way I make my living is illegal. Under the California Penal Code, it's illegal to provide sexual services in exchange for money or 'other considerations.' What are these 'other considerations'? Do they include dinner? Drinks? A wedding ring? It could be claimed that marriage sanctions an exchange of sex for financial support.

But I don't call myself a whore because I'm someone's financially supported wife or girlfriend. I sell sexual services, and if I make myself too visible, I may get busted. That's why I'm writing anonymously.

My anonymity serves another purpose as well. Since you don't know my name, I may be your neighbor or your best friend. Even if you don't know me, you've met others like me. Prostitutes who pass for respectable are far more common than street hookers. We make up an invisible class of unmarked whores.

Since most of us prefer to remain invisible, the prostitutes who show up on most people's radar are the stereotypical streetwalkers—forced into whoredom by poverty or drug addiction. Their pimps rent them out, beat them up, and take their dough.

Feminists who denounce prostitution as an 'objectification of women' often invoke this stereotype: male johns and pimps exploit the helpless female victim—reducing her to a commodity bought and sold on the market.

Although traditional Marxists rarely advocate for the rights of sex workers, this critique of prostitution sounds like a limited and perhaps displaced version of a broader Marxist analysis. In Marxist terms, the prostitute isn't the only one made into a commodity. Instead of men (pimps and johns) objectifying women (prostitutes), capitalism transforms all workers (rather than just women) and their labor (sexual or otherwise) into commodities for sale on the market. Marxism doesn't blame the worker for 'objectifying herself.' You've probably heard Marxists say that someone 'sold out,' but a factory worker doesn't sell himself or his body. The capitalist system makes us into commodities and sells us on the market.

Sex work opponents sometimes blame the prostitute for being a commodity. They accuse her of 'selling her body,' as if she willfully transforms her whole being into a commodity with no socioeconomic pressure. The prostitute, they say, embraces her commodity status: she makes herself a pretty object to be judged on the basis of her looks. Most of us do this sometimes, but it's considered evil when a woman does it to sell sex.

In most cases, this argument is blatantly sexist. Men, even male whores, are rarely blamed for 'selling themselves.' Only women who sell sexual services are said to 'sell their bodies.' The phrase is imprecise, since the client doesn't buy the prostitute's body. She still has her body after the economic transaction.

When the whore is not an evil self-objectifier, she's a helpless victim, robbed of agency and power. Her pimp lives off the profits from her labor. This kind of exploitation is typical of the capitalist–worker dynamic. Like the stereotypical pimp, the capitalist's objective is to derive the most profit from the worker's labor, and pay the worker as little as possible.

This brief analysis puts arguments against prostitution within a broader context of capitalist exploitation. Why do these opponents of sex work displace this critique onto prostitution? Perhaps prostitution is so silenced and taboo— so little known—that it serves as a blank screen onto which our culture projects the abuses of the capitalist workplace. This projection distracts us from the fact that we're all implicated in many forms of exploitation on a daily basis. We may think that the most extreme forms of objectification only affect the most visible examples: the hookers we see on the streets fighting with their pimps. It's true that these people are exploited, but exploitation happens behind closed doors in the 'straight' workplace as well.

Does this mean we're all 'prostitutes,' since we are bought and sold as commodities? Is academia, for instance, a species of whoring?

Not quite. Academia is only whoring if 'whoring' is simply another name for the exploitation that affects us all. The scarcity of academic jobs makes this objectification more blatant, because job-hunters have to concentrate on making themselves marketable. Like many grad students, I loved scholarly work. I still do. In many ways, I felt privileged in this society to be able to spend so much time reading and writing. But in grad school, I also learned I would have to cut off much of what I loved to carve myself into a marketable commodity. The institution I attended also exploited my labor by saddling me with a full-time job at a part-time salary with no benefits.

Despite the apparent socioeconomic differences, academia can resemble the stereotype of street prostitution. The power that universities wield over faculty and staff is like that of a pimp renting whores out to different johns and confiscating their profits. There's no question that my experience as a whore is far less degrading than this. I get to choose where I want to live, I'm far better paid per hour, and I often get a lot more respect. I'm still a commodity bought and sold on the market like everyone else in this capitalist world. But my value as a commodity has increased, since there's more demand for my services. Ironically, I feel less like a commodity and more like a person.

For this reason, I'm reluctant to equate academia with prostitution. Calling academics 'whores' is a denigration of whoring. It buys into the stereotype that the prostitute is the most objectified person in our society, more object and less person than anyone else. It also suggests that academics suffer from the whore stigma, whereas academic privilege is almost the reverse of the whore's trade-off. The high-end prostitute sacrifices status for profit; the professor gives up profit for prestige.

As an academic, you spend years in grad school for a slim chance at a relatively low-paying drudge job in the wilds of Wisconsin. This drudge job is, however, shrouded in Ivory Tower mystique. This is a gain in cultural capital. You wear threadbare clothing and fret that you will never get tenure. But people see you as 'cultured,' and they think your absent-mindedness means you're thinking lofty thoughts.

In prostitution—at least in high-end prostitution—you sacrifice social acceptance for a very high value and respect among a privileged clientele, and, if you're fortunate, a community of like-minded people. You may be a super-prostitute, jet-setting around the world and earning a thousand dollars an hour, even in transit. You may have a doctorate in the science of jurisprudence and be secret advisor to the Prime Minister of France. But if you tell the folks back home what you do for a living, they'll still think you're a street hooker. If you act absent-minded, they'll probably think you're stupid or on drugs.

We can't all be whores, but when we watch 'whores' in the movies, we can learn about the abuses we endure and perpetuate. Capitalism transforms all workers and their labor (sexual or otherwise) into commodities for sale on the market. Whores are no more objectified than anyone else. Our culture projects the abuses of capitalism onto prostitution, and this allows it to deny exploitation in the 'straight' workplace.

15

Left Conservatism: a Conference Report

Matt Wray

Left Conservatism: A Workshop
Saturday, January 31, 1998
Panelists: Paul Bové, Wendy Brown, Judith Butler, Joseph Buttigieg
Moderator and Convener: Chris Connery

STEPPING INTO THE RING

'"Left Conservatism" or Left Factionalism? Who invented this strange and wondrous new term, "Left Conservatism"? And why have they done so?' So the flyer began. Black ink on glowing neon red paper, it had been thrust into my path by a bespectacled graduate student just as I crossed into the lecture hall where the Left Conservatism conference was getting underway. 'Counterprogram?' he offered, although his hushed voice carried none of the usual rising intonations that signal a question. It was more of a flat statement of fact, a non-committal if slightly conspiratorial declaration. Suddenly, I felt like I was being offered drugs by some suspicious looking dude in the park. I hesitated, but only for a split second. This shit looked too good to pass up! The counterprogram, the two-page, single-spaced document I now held in my hand, asked the important questions: where had this term come from and why was it circulating now?

Email and snail mail flyers advertising the conference had shared the alarmist tone:

A specter is haunting U.S. intellectual life: the specter of Left Conservatism. Within academia and without, in events such as the Sokal affair, in the antitheory polemics in *The Nation* and the *Socialist Review* ... there is evidence of a phenomenon that might properly be labeled Left Conservatism: that is, an attack by 'real' leftists on those portrayed as theory-mongering, hyper-professional, obscurantist pseudo-leftists.

This really did seem a bit over the top—hyperbolic to the point of parody. Maybe it was just good advertising copy, designed to spark interest in an otherwise tired old debate. Of course the point of the conference and of both the program and the counterprogram was that the debate was far from tired and worn out—it has, it seems, only just begun. Or better, it has just rekindled itself. For, in the end, there seems to be agreement on both sides that this is turning out to be just the latest episode in the periodic internecine war with itself that the left has always had.

In his opening remarks, Chris Connery credited Paul Bové with inventing the term 'Left Conservatism' a few years ago. Bové had apparently dropped the phrase in reference to liberal philosopher Richard Rorty, cultural studies assassin Alan Sokal, and the poetry editor of *The Nation*. Left Conservatism, according to Connery, is supposedly marked by a belief (always unspoken) in unmediated access to reality (aka empiricism); a pragmatic belief in the transparency of language, and a desire for some kind of foundational truth(s) upon which to build political identities, broad-based social movements, and to reinvigorate public, democratic discourse. Opposed to Left Conservatism, Connery argues, is the antifoundationalism of poststructuralist intellectuals, who reject all claims to philosophical essences and who are primarily concerned to interrogate the linguistic and epistemological preconditions under which certain political ideas and political identities come to be regarded as 'true,' 'necessary,' or even as 'useful.' In some ways, this seems like a fair characterization of the debate, since it is equally unfair to both sides. The Left Conservative types are not as antitheoretical as Connery would have us believe, nor are the paragons of poststructuralism unconcerned or ignorant of immediate political contexts and issues. In what follows I offer a brief summary of the remarks offered by some of the panelists.

PAUL BOVÉ: ENTER THE CONVERSATION OR CHANGE THE SUBJECT?

Bové's talk focused on North American philosophers Richard Rorty and Charles Taylor. Both present interesting case studies for the present debate because they are known to be both antifoundationalist and prominent figures on the liberal left. And both at times have criticized poststructuralists for their obscure theories and difficult if not impenetrable prose. That is, both Rorty and Taylor would seem to be simultaneously poststructuralist and Left Conservative.

Bové tackles Rorty and Taylor by arguing that they are not as thoroughly antifoundationalist as they claim to be. Embedded in their philosophical pragmatism, Bové claims, is a narrative of movement toward the types of philosophical language that can create and sustain communities of scientific knowers. This forward movement, Bové argues, can only really be understood as a kind of evolutionary development of language, as a kind of progress toward a state where secular knowledges freely compete for truth status in the arena of rationality. Of course, this notion of progress is, in Bové's eyes, a foundationalist myth, an outmoded modernist metanarrative. This attachment to progress undercuts Rorty and Taylor's claims to be antifoundationalist. Their foundation is tied to the disciplinary concerns of an Anglophone philosophical tradition, one that poststructuralists like Foucault implicitly and explicitly critiqued. In Bové's punning phrase, Foucault was not so interested in entering that particular philosophical conversation. Instead, he wanted to change the *subject* (both the subject of the conversation and the notion of subjectivity).

With his talk, Bové opened up the fight on the philosophical front, dragging Rorty and Taylor into the ring and subjecting their texts to poststructuralist rigor in the same fashion that they have subjected Foucault to their rigorous analytic pragmatism. Of course, one could argue that Bové's fantasy of a text purged of all foundationalisms is as unattainable as the pragmatist's dream of a philosophical statement purified of all non-analytical categories. Where then does that leave us?

JUDITH BUTLER: REMARX ON ENGELS AND SEX

Judith Butler began her comments by pointing out that antifoundationalism can neither secure nor destroy politics (or any given political position). This is, in fact, precisely the point of antifoundationalist critique: that nothing, including antifoundationalism, can serve as a firm and stable foundation for building politics or political identity. She went on to say that the point of deconstruction (one of the main methodologies of antifoundationalists) is not to eliminate categories of thought or being, but to interrogate them. When we do so, she argued, we are inquiring about categories we absolutely cannot do without, since the very language of our inquiry depends upon the categories we are attempting to interrogate.

Butler went on to identify what she feels are the two complaints most often leveled against postmodernism:

1. Marxism has been reduced to cultural politics. This is, in a nutshell, the 'Cultural Studies sucks' argument. In this line of complaint, culture has replaced economics (understood here as the struggle over resources and the processes of production) and politics (understood here as the struggle over the control of state power) as the proper realm of struggle. This has led, the plaintiffs say, to excesses of discourse analysis that completely miss the materiality of *real* politics.
2. New social movements have been too concerned with the cultural domain. This has resulted in increased factionalism, seen chiefly in the rise of identity politics and identitarian movements and in the gradual disappearance of the common goals, ideals, and language that once gave (some) unity to the

left. This complaint is usually accompanied by a call to return to a mode of economic and materialist analysis, or as Butler dismissively termed it, 'an anachronistic materialism as the basis for a reinvigorated Left orthodoxy.'

Butler takes up these complaints as they appear in the work of feminist philosopher Nancy Fraser (who, Butler was at pains to say, is not a Left Conservative!). While Fraser has written that identity politics and political correctness are little more than derogatory slurs for feminism, antiracism, and antiheterosexism, she has also located the struggle of gays and lesbians strictly in the realm of a struggle over cultural recognition. That is, Fraser identifies gay and lesbian politics not as a struggle for material equality, but as a struggle for full inclusion in a pluralist democracy.

Butler countered Fraser by citing Engels' classic text on the origins of the family, the state and private property, which places the heterosexual family at the heart of the system that reproduces (both in the biological and social senses of the word) capitalist labor and capitalist property rights. Butler claims that, contrary to Fraser, Engels' insight places the politics of sexuality directly at the heart of any left agenda for social change and social and material equity.

One wonders, however: does merely citing the authority of Engels lay the question to rest?

WENDY BROWN: CONSERVATIVE DESIRES

Wendy Brown offered what was perhaps the most conciliatory approach to addressing the poststructuralist/Left Conservative split. She positioned herself as someone who was deeply ambivalent about the terms of the debate and as someone who understood not only the intellectual stakes involved, but also the affective and libidinal stakes as well. She spoke of her own conservatism, explaining that her pedagogy had been described more than once as conservative and traditional. She also spoke of her belief in politics as a semi-autonomous realm, one that cannot simply be reduced to the personal, a belief that has apparently garnered her the label of conservative in some circles. In these meandering opening remarks, Brown almost seemed to be saying, 'Don't take offence at being called a conservative, all of us on the left have our conservative impulses. At least have the intellectual honesty to admit these moments when you are confronted with them.'

Brown then went on to offer a definition of Left Conservatism as essentially a reaction to and a refusal of theory. The theoretical insights of poststructuralists include, among others: the decentering of capitalism (or any single force as determinant of social life); the Foucauldian notion of power as everywhere, rather than the old formula of who? Whom? (i.e., who wields it? Whom does it affect?); the abandonment of revolutionary politics; and the emphasis on language, its priority over deeds, words, and social forces.

Left Conservative rhetoric tends to portray poststructuralist rhetoric as 'too hard, too dense, and thus insufficiently political.' These complaints, Brown remarked, often take the form of nostalgic desire for something imagined to be lost: for a unified social movement instead of the fractious nature of identity politics and new social movements; for historical materialism instead of discourse analysis; for a clearer account of accountability and human agency instead of the complexities and indecipherabilities of the postmodern subject; and a desire to have real working-class heroes instead of the deeply ambiguous and flawed heroes we have now. Brown ended her talk by insisting that it is a mistake to conflate academic and political work. What we do in the academy, she claims, is think. To constrain thought to what has immediate political application is to constrain our imaginations.

LEFT OUT OR LEFT OVER?

In my judgment, what was not said at the conference is far more telling than what was. There was no real concern expressed for the effects this may be having on the younger generation of left intellectuals and academics. Many of us were there at the conference, many of us have been following these debates with interest and with a strong sense of investment in the future of the debates. The counterprogram penned by graduate students was an expression of concern and maybe even something like a cry for help. Many of us in the younger generation have enormous respect for the intellectual and political work of combatants on both sides of the current debate. Perhaps as a child of divorce, I personalize this debate too much and project too many of my own complexes on this, but really, how is this situation any different from the child who wants the parents to stop fighting and to take some responsibility for parenting: for raising the next generation, sharing intellectual skills and political organizing tactics in a spirit of love and affection? There is a pedagogical and political responsibility here not only to pass on the wisdom and learning of the elders, but to help create the kind of community where that wisdom and learning can take root and flourish.

In my view, the following things are needed if this debate is to move forward:

1. Crash courses in the intellectual and political history of the left that has preceded this moment of struggle, and an analysis of the discourses that make up those traditions. What was distressing about the conference was that for all the poststructuralist talk about self-reflexivity, the participants

did little by way of contextualizing their own intellectual claims or positioning themselves in relation to specific intellectual traditions. Bové came closest to making a contribution in this area when he said, in closing, that 'poststructuralism is a technical term' that has a complex intellectual history deriving from the philosophy of Husserl and other continental philosophers. How does this intellectual history shape contemporary debates about politics, identity, and culture? To answer this query we need to review the events of May 1968, or the 1970s debates of the British new left over Althusser and structural Marxism, or the more recent debates over deconstruction within the North American left in the late 1970s and 1980s.

2. A robust analysis of the ways these intellectual fault lines within the left are contributing to the ascendancy of the right and the continued rise of market forces in university life. Attention to the commodification of education in the university is a perfect example of the kind of institutional analysis that was largely missing from the conference. This unexamined institutional context is, in large part, going to determine the outcome of these debates over the new millennium. While the left sidelines itself with more factionalism in the form of *ad hominem* debates, the right succeeds in further marketizing and privatizing education.

I think the real casualties of this particular battle in the academic left will be the younger generation of scholar/activists (myself included) who will be left to reconstruct a notion of left politics long after the warriors of poststructuralism and Left Conservatism retire to their respective Valhallas of tenured deadwood. We need intellectual history and conjunctural analysis, not personal vendettas. We're all tired of the 'Jerry Springer meets MLA' atmosphere that these acrimonious debates have created. We need help from both sides. I'm talking about a division of labor that has as its goal the production of a new form of interdisciplinary knowledge, one that is neither rigorously poststructuralist, nor structuralist, neither modern nor postmodern, but simply oppositional. That is, by the way, what we here at *Bad Subjects* try to do. We often fail, but at least we can still talk to one another.

16

Caretaking the Echo Pond:
the Practice of Art in the Fin-de-Siècle Academy

Mark Van Proyen

For some individuals, the efforts put forth to earn one's socioeconomic keep are conceived as a kind of 'toiling in the vineyard.' The expenditure of effort is guided by an expectation of a fruitful harvest and a concluding Dionysian celebration. Others conduct their labor to the syncopated tune of Lee Dorsey's 'workin' in a coalmine, goin' down, down, down,' knowing that when 'Saturday night rolls around, [they're] too tired for havin' fun.'

The real journey of the American worker from a 1960s consumer paradise to our current techno-dystopia is charted along the waypoints represented by these popular epithets. Our downward path begs the depressing question of just who will be left to sing the Internationale when the new globalism concludes its postideological economic consolidation. It will certainly not be members of the techno-managerial elite crooning from their gated communities as they operate society's servo-mechanisms by remote-internet-control. And it will most certainly not be the growing population of the socially excarcerated, hypnotized by endless spectacles of mock redemption broadcast by corporate jumbotron.

That leaves only a small minority of the psychically disaffected, and they are quietly falling through society's cracks. Each is the victim of a game of economic musical chairs that is slowly eroding the very fabric of civil society. Fortunately, in my little neck of the coalmine, all I have to do is find out who can sing in visual form and endeavor to help them sing better. Job title: Art Teacher. Job description: teach students how to make art. It's not as easy as it sounds, because the task includes the subtextual mission of teaching students how to conceive of themselves as a specific kind of subject ('the artist') in a world that suddenly seems to have left art behind.

Fortunately, that world remains sufficiently guilt-ridden to invest sizable institutional energy in the pretense that it still values art. Therefore the idea of being-an-artist-so-as-to-garner-patronizing-administrative-attention remains momentarily intact. But even this gambit seems to be quickly growing stale, with no persuasive alternative yet to appear on the horizon. The end of the Cold War brought with it the end of the reigning myth of the avant-garde artist as a person dedicated to innovation and a mythical freedom of expression. It left behind an art world of administration-for-the-sake-of-administration standing momentarily naked without any fig leaf of higher purpose. This change in circumstances subtly impacts how we define the proper place that art education might hold in the larger scholarly community of the university. That position has always been complicated by the fact that being-an-artist (like being-an-intellectual) is in itself a practice and could never claim the true status of an academic discipline.

The distinction is worth pondering: a 'discipline' represents a stable and communicable body of taxonomized knowledge and organized methods of inquiry. It assumes that intelligence (i.e., the recognition of patterns operating in lived experience) can benefit in clarity and purpose from the programmatic manipulation of standardized, time-honored abstractions. Conversely, a 'practice' operates by giving priority to the patterns gleaned from lived experience, even if they might contradict disciplinary assumptions. Even though a practice must have a vocabulary of methods and a history of purposes (which can and should be taught), these things are both limited and subject to revisionist debate. In practical terms, this means that art education boils down to facilitating the process of students 'standing around until they catch on,' privileging a curriculum that has been designed to minimize the standing around so as to maximize the catching on.

But what exactly is it that students are supposed to be catching on to in the post-avant-garde artistic climate? Pragmatism provides the only answer, defining art as vernacular expression redeemed by the codes of high style. The vernacular expression part of this equation cannot and should not be taught. It stems from the symbolic thematics that are imbricated in the student's sense of individual, generational, and cultural self-definition: it represents an individual mode of marking time and space that is taught by lived experience. As for the codes of high style represented by technique and a historically derived visual grammar (themselves subtly coded with presumptions of class, gender, and ethnicity), they are now subject to so many historical fluctuations that they may be too elastic to teach in the context of a detailed curricular program.

Does the art student's arrival at the aforementioned state of praxis mean anything more than a partaking of an institutional opportunity? Is more attained than the inflation of said student's grade point average while he or she takes a playful and reflective break from the dehumanizing business of school? A break from passively sponging up endless lectures addressing endless subjects from endless perspectives? It says much about the present moment that these questions are now at the fore. For not too long ago it was assumed that such a break made a positive contribution to the larger educational mission of shaping individually integrated and socially engaged human beings.

Now the presence of the art studio in the university seems doubly vulnerable to hostile scrutiny from both right-wing budget slashers and left-wing death-of-the-author types. To this, add the need for ever-more elusive approval from accreditation agencies. The requirements of these agencies have grown incrementally more exacting over the years, no doubt in response to the political gutting of the National Endowments for the Arts and Humanities, and the fear that a similar inquisition might be directed at the Department of Education.

Here, a longer historical view can be instructive. As society transformed itself from tribal organization to civilizational empire, the preparation of artistic practice can be perceived as having evolved from an insular shamanic inheritance to chain-gang piece work done under theocratic supervision, as was the case in Pharonic Egypt. As the piece work became more technically challenging, guild systems evolved to develop and convey necessary skills on an earn-while-you-learn program where technique was passed on like inherited property, with apprentices and journeymen laboring hard to queue up for elusive master status in pre-union shop environments dominated by senior practitioners who were not disposed to encourage competition.

As the humanistic ideals of the Renaissance gave way to the iconoclastic/iconophilic political battles of the counter-reformation, the first art academies were founded, substituting an efficient pay-while-you-learn model of artistic education for the older conditions of skill gained from apprenticeship. This change signaled a larger change in what society expected from the artist, for at that point 'high art' had clearly distinguished itself from applied craft. The cult of the artist as an ideal and exemplary human being had at that point taken full political flower in a society that grew both literate and anxious under the information glut made available by the printing press. The ideological stakes were high, and the myth of the heroic artist was pressed into service for a dramatic pre-emptive strike against a succession of iconoclasms, even though the institutions that sought that service were undeniably corrupt and in decline.

As the papal patron withered, the need for bourgeois images grew and schools teaching the strategies and techniques of imagemaking became commonplace in most large urban areas. At that point, the modernist reformation came into play because the academies had become self-serving and internally politicized. They had lost contact with the emerging condition of experience emanating from a collective reaction-formation to urban society's new emphasis on regimentation and photographic surveillance. A new kind of artist hero came to the fore, an aristocrat-of-the-spirit who could recover a mythical human essence in a world that was geared to programmatic dehumanization. By definition, the academies could not produce such an artist, for academic etiquette was viewed as being at odds with the discovery of such an essence. The emerging artist hero reaped a supreme narcissistic reward of illusory immortality.

My use of the term 'narcissistic reward' is central to my assessment of the state of art and art education, and it is also central to how I conduct my own practice of both. There is a durable mythology suggesting that modernism was born fully and autonomously formed from history's brow. However, the modernist, avant-garde artist has always sought to accept history rather than society as a judge, thus bespeaking the antisocial imperatives of the pathological narcissist who is decked out in the tattered cloak of a hypocritical idealism. This artist lives like an eternal child so that the rest of us can face the adult death of unavoidable social servitude as a kind of noble sacrifice; a bleak inversion of the Christ myth.

It is nice work if you can get it, and many try. Hence the formation of avant-garde art schools. These schools are devoted to the preparation of avant-garde artists, all of whom are in the business of selling the unlikely potential for such an advent. This is where the plot thickens. Rarely does anybody meditate on the oxymoronical status of the term 'avant-garde institution' (or for that matter, 'institutional avant-garde'), and when they do they almost always become postmodern cynics who side with the institutional side of the term. This alliance supports the idea of continued employment. Continued institutional employment, I might add, in service to an institutional patron seeking its particular type of self-confirming image. The image confirms the administration itself, and is usually expressed in visual terms as something called (with decreasing precision) conceptual art.

The conceptual art of deploying ideas as visual material into institutional space is the presentational equivalent of the managerial talents that make up administration. The difference is that in the new scenario, the administrators operate in a condition of gainful employment, while the administrator manqués (i.e., artists) gain only notches on their resumes that might lead to the occasional fellowship or teaching position. This new chapter in art and its patronage follows shortly after the historical point when the university art department added the most recent and controversial chapter to the history of art education. The coincidence is not accidental, for university art education always privileged art history and theory in a way that art school education never did, and this distinction represented the inevitable lingua franca of political survival in a university life socially geared for the education of administrators.

This is the backdrop for the shift between a modernist and postmodernist art education. The shift can be described as a change in focus away from the students' crystallization of materials and experience into a unified and essential whole. Students now instead learn a way to signify experience via the art of code. These are the established polar coordinates for art and art education: on one hand, the narcissistic imperative of gaining an elusive totality (using art to heal the narcissistic wound gained from the daily humiliations of being but another cog in the collective nightmare). On the other hand, a cynical imperative of operating effectively amid the new academy of omnipresent administration via the presentational algebra of code manipulation: postmodernism by another name.

I have repeatedly emphasized the importance of the narcissistic basis of creativity. That's because I believe this basis begins as therapy for the damaged life, then transforms into a critique of a damaging society, and then resolves as a view of a better world. At least, I believe it can do so when it is not sidetracked by the siren song of administration envy. This dialectical tension between narcissism and administration serves the socioeconomic world of transnational capitalism very well by providing the image industry within that world with an enclosed petri-dish for research and development: a forget-how-to-think-tank for the translation of impulse control problems into fashion's latest set of stylistic pseudo-metaphors.

17

In-between Days: Intellectual Work and Intelligent Life at the Crossroads

Scott Schaffer

When I decided to become a professor, my vision was singular: to be rigorous, challenging, and the kind of professor to whom former students sent 'thank you for improving my life' cards ten years down the road. I've worked hard to do this. But increasingly, that vision of my professional self is being beaten down by forces larger than me: concerns for student–faculty ratios, changes in institutional and student attitudes toward educational 'content,' and the need to be 'productive' (i.e., engage in lots of research) while at the same time teaching an increasingly heavy load. More and more, my sense is that higher education is being turned into a commodity, and people dedicated to the intellectual endeavors are increasingly 'in-between' larger and alienating social forces.

I'm not alone in this. 'Education,' 'thought,' and 'intellectual activity' have become lofty ideals relevant only to the musty castle turrets that made those heavy academic robes necessary. According to conventional wisdom, what's needed now is a corporate sensibility to the entire endeavor. In other words, I should think of my lone skill set—to challenge others' ideas, to figure out how it is other people understand the world, and to help them see the world in an entirely different way for better or worse—as lending itself more to The Gap than bridging the gap between individuals and the world they create.

THE LUNATICS AND THE ASYLUM: THE COMMODIFICATION OF EDUCATION

The academy has in recent years turned into a battle zone between two different forces in our society: the ideational force of education as a liberatory praxis, and the actual force of corporate necessity.

Put bluntly, the university as an institution is being turned into a corporate training mill, motivated by parallels to the profit motive and to post-Fordist private sector-style industrial restructuring. From the president on down, the message sent to everyone within the ivory tower is this: make your course 'content' immediately applicable to 'the real world,' and immediately and thoughtlessly consumable, or be downsized. Being an educator in Freire's critical sense is an economic loss activity, whereas giving the students 'what they want,' their degree with a minimum amount of labor, ensures the expansion of the department, the hiring of new faculty, and the amassing of new resources. The lunatics have taken over the asylum.

This transition from education to popularity contest, inverting what used to be the power relations in the university—giving students the ability to toss out faculty they see as 'too tough'—can't be blamed on any one group. In my twelve years as a student and five as a faculty member, numerous structural factors impacted higher education and have made this manifestation of corporatism seem inevitable. The economic recession of the late 1980s and early 1990s increased tuition at public universities dramatically, drastically reduced state funding, put hundreds of thousands of people out of work, and forced more and more people to beg for decreasing pools of financial aid.

In the late 1990s, 'fiscal austerity' became the watchword for governments, corporations, universities, and students alike. Universities, facing increasing enrollments due to the lack of post-high school job possibilities, have to hire new faculty, though with the same small quibbled-over pool of money that was available during the recession. To save money, most universities hired part-timers and kept them 'in check' by making their rehiring process dependent on the number of students they kept in their classes.

Students too have bought into the austerity mindset. Knowing that they can't afford a university education, many of them take 'overload' course schedules and work nearly full time to support their education. This leaves them in the unfortunate position of having too much academic work to do and not enough time in which to do any of it well. To boot, their exposure to the corporate world reinforces the idea that a university education is good only to make a bigger salary. In addition to taking more courses than they can bear, they come in with the attitude that is anathema to a university education: get me out of here; they don't want to challenge themselves or others. Can you blame them? They feel the need to approach the university like clients, paying for a service, and they see nothing wrong with doing whatever is necessary to get their degrees, even finding the time required to do an internet search for essays. Whether one follows Merton's analysis of 'blocked goals' or a Marxist line about alienated labor, it comes down to the same thing: students are as in-between in the academy as everyone else.

So what has caused this shift in the approach to higher education? There are more players here than simply fiduciary malaise. The culprits are cultural and ultimately structural: the anti-intellectualism of North American society, and the sad and ultimately detrimental rise in relationships between the university and corporations.

THE McDONALD'S-IZATION OF MENTAL WORK: EDUCATION AS BRAND NAME

America has always been an anti-intellectual country; even de Tocqueville saw that. It's a rare thing to see an academic on television. American society simply doesn't think that intellectuals have anything to offer the public. They want their children to grow up, attend a good university with lots of Nobel Prize winners, and graduate; they want their kids to have good jobs. But the American public doesn't want to see what we see, hear what we have to say, or engage in the same kind of mental work we do, since it's not really 'work.'

At the same time, there has been a gradual disengagement of intellectuals from social life over the last 30 years. The demise of the student revolts in the late 1960s left many people in the academy disillusioned with the idea that any radical doctrine could be an efficacious model for political change and the notion that intellectuals could have any place of importance in American society. The 2000 edition of *The Socialist Register*, entitled 'Necessary and Unnecessary Utopias,' shows this much, calling, begging, and pleading for us to get the next generation, whose minds are in our hands, to think of something outside the cubicle. We occasionally get the flicker of 'light bulbs' when we say something in a classroom; but if the consensus is that intellectuals are useless, what effect does this have on our students and the rest of the world?

Add to this less-than-encouraging situation the increasing corporatization of the university. Beyond the treatment of classroom materials and pedagogical approaches as things to be quickly produced, easily disseminated, and easily consumed, the university is becoming more and more corporate-run. Large corporations have taken it upon themselves to endow chairs or establish research institutes in order to support research and teaching that will, ultimately, benefit them.

This is no accident. The recession made it necessary for universities to find funding outside the normal channels, and corporations were all too willing to help out. The exchange appeared even: the university could expand its research prestige and cultural capital by establishing a corporate research facility, and corporations win by getting immediate access to cutting-edge research and helping to train future employees, even before they fill out a job application. The motives of these two social organizations don't readily mix, and when thoughtful culture and capital collide, capital wins. Corporate culture infects the university culture, resulting in the rethinking of education as consumable 'content,' new positions based on sales/enrollment figures, itinerant labor, and the mass delivery of product, and the screwing of faculty and students in the process.

But the complaint we get from the very same industry types that wanted control over the institution, if not the curriculum, is that we're not educating our students. They're not 'self-starters'; they can't 'think outside the box'; they lack the kinds of critical skills necessary to help corporate America maintain its dominance, innovation, and planned obsolescence strategies. The post-Fordist approach to production hasn't translated well into the academy. We're turning out drones—the very same cogs in the machine that leftists say capitalism needs to reproduce and expand itself. Ironically, capital is not happy. Our kids can't think outside the cubicle, and we all suffer for it.

JOBS V. DUTIES: REWORKING INTELLECTUAL WORK

Higher education is at a crossroads. The question for us becomes: must we sell out our ideals, our standards, and our vision of the intelligent and thoughtful life simply because our students and administrators want us to?

The answer is a resounding no. But the reasons differ from those offered up by presidential candidates, theorists of the 'postindustrial society,' or anyone else. As the postindustrialist mantra goes, we should now have more time to concern ourselves with affairs of the mind, spirit, and soul. Education rather than class warfare should become a pressing concern for us since industrialization gives us so much more 'free time' (even though this isn't the case at all). For those who make a living talking about education, education is the good to be attained—but that's not how it works at all.

University education is not now serving as a good in and of itself. Keeping in mind the purpose of the university—to create new knowledge and to educate future members of society—reminds us of our real importance in the world. Education is a means to a better world. To think critically and work to induce that same kind of thought in those who follow us in history enables us to improve the human condition and enables our students to rethink their place and agency in the greater scheme of things. *This* is the resource that teachers ideally give to students for questioning the legitimacy of the status quo.

When education is seen as a commodity, though, we fall into the capitalist production process best outlined by Marx. We create a product, distribute it through a socially agreed-on process, and see it consumed in the production of other products. And our patterns of consumption these days demand instant feedback. We want our Paxil because we want the quick fix to our alienation; we want our MTV to catch this week's trends in fashion. Education doesn't fit this bill at all. It is a long, slow, painful process, requiring us radically to reshape our entire being. Its benefits don't appear until years down the road, when our students are no longer in contact with us and not in the academic world at all.

Teachers are alienated, stuck between liberation and outright exploitation, between working with the future of the world and being just another cognitive cog in the educational-industrial complex, in part because we've been forced to see intellectual work as a job. We're compelled to sell our intellectual labor to someone else in exchange for a wage. But we need to see educational labor as a duty, to see ourselves as more than factory workers of the mind, as people oriented to the possibility of positive social change. The university and national climate tries to force us into seeing teaching as just a job. But teaching, if it critically engages students and their inertial, corporatized set of ideas and compels them to account for their beliefs and actions, becomes our contribution to that kind of change.

If the one thing the thousands of students we work with in our career take away from our courses is an expectation of accountability, a call to take stock of themselves, then we've done what we must do in order to be successful at our work. We've trained them for the future, and we've satisfied the ethical demand to improve the world. The situation of higher education today has provided us with two options, both lacking any kind of security. Institutionally, economically, and culturally, we are in the 'in-between days,' so we do our best to walk the lines. But as Merleau-Ponty once said, 'there is really no "in between" in any political situation.' Even by not choosing sides, we take a political position. If we are to see any kind of change in the world, we *must* take a side. Teachers *should* work against the corporatization of the university, of our students' minds, and of society at large.

18
Make It a Double:
My Dual Lives as Barkeep and Grad Student

Wayde Grinstead

A rare winter sunlight sifts through the nicotine stained windows of an old city bar. On his usual perch at the end of the bar, Wes rolls his cigarette as I get him change for his Budweiser.

The creaking front door announces two new customers. I greet them as they sit down, one stool between them and Wes. He doesn't appear to know them; nor they him.

In this bartending life, many faces come and go. Some I'd like to see again, while others cannot leave soon enough. Wes is Wes, and that is good.

Several ethnographic, sociological, and cultural studies have attempted to explain the behaviors of those who inhabit bars. The repeated visits of 'regulars' like Wes might suggest a social intimacy with bartenders like me, but I don't always find this to be true. While their face and type of drink are familiar, I usually don't know the people bearing them any more than I do the first time customer.

Yet I cling to these regular faces. They provide a recognized solace on days when it is needed. In a room full of unpredictable behaviors, the regulars can be trusted to be themselves, for better or worse. The regulars balance unknown characters. Their repeated visits allow me to see the individuals within them more clearly, albeit only slightly, and this is comforting. It is part of a continuing process of humans trying to make sense out of an incomprehensible world.

I tinker with these seemingly obvious ideas as I work on my Master's thesis, which attempts to understand people who make bars part of their day-to-day existence, either as patrons or workers. As my research is largely qualitative and subjective, I confront the intersections between my lives as graduate student and barkeep. These worlds may seem disparate at first glance, but I've come to recognize similarities in how people deal with strangers, strangeness, and the unfamiliar. In each world, the familiar often goes unquestioned. The unknown is kept at arm's length, susceptible to limiting assumptions.

These understandings of the service industry have drastically changed since I started tending bars eight years ago as an escape from a corporate path and a means to save travel money.

Being ethnographic in its methodology, my thesis allows me to see my role as bartender being parallel to that of the participant-observer associated in anthropology, if only loosely. I violate many tenets central to ethical scientific research, as I do not give my 'informants' the knowledge that I have been watching and learning. And while I carry neither notepad nor tape recorder, behind the physical buffer of the bar I witness behaviors that seem to disregard my presence a mere foot away: heated arguments, off-color jokes, passionate kisses, and stubborn social wranglings.

I have also noticed many consistent customer archetypes. The 'Panicky Guy' frantically waves down the barkeep to place his order, then takes five minutes asking his friends what they want. The 'Just One More' fellow insists that this beer, right here, is his last. He does this for five beers. The 'Verbal Tipper' insists that he had a splendid time, and hurries out the door before you can see the 10 per cent tip he left. 'Name Guy,' usually trying to impress a date, wants to know my name so he can splendidly recite it each time I pass.

While patterns do emerge, I am reluctant to adhere to them, for they are soon broken. But they allow me to recognize many of the unfamiliar people in the bar, if only in a tongue-in-cheek, superficial way.

I appreciate the way my two lives intersect, yet I also recognize that I am not fully absorbed in either. I made the decision to live away from campus and commute, as it allows me to bartend and pay less rent than I would living closer to school. There are times when I regret the choice, because I see a camaraderie and intellectual bond among my academic peers who live close by. With classes and schoolwork together and time to discuss postmodernity or *The Simpsons* over coffee, my colleagues build upon each other's intellectual musings. Academic life and dialogue hone thought, and these opportunities for intellectual growth outweigh the cheaper rent sometimes.

Customers often ask me, 'Do you do anything besides bartending?' The question seems understandable, but also full of societal expectations that there must or should be something more.

I answer the question, 'Oh, I'm also in grad school.' This often leads to me explaining what American Studies is, usually followed by blank looks.

'So, it's like history?'

'Well, it involves aspects of history, but it also challenges some conventionally held assumptions about history.' They look at me quizzically. Ted Danson doesn't discourse on theories of history on *Cheers*.

I continue, 'It tries to encompass an understanding of how America as a nation and as a notion is represented and understood from national level down to the personal. It works with, and between, traditional disciplines like literature and history, while also using aspects of race and gender studies, material culture studies, and others.'

That explanation would be too fluffy for my professors. But it's too obtuse to fly in bars, where my customers usually pull at their Camel Lights wrappers by the time I'm finished. The gap between these worlds is broad, and my success in bridging this is low.

And to think I taught an introductory course in the subject.

I get similarly blank stares if the discussion turns to my thesis. I explain, 'I'm doing an ethnography of this place, asking both customers and coworkers what meanings they get from the bar experience, and what role this specific bar means to them.' Relating it to the world they know, across wood we both can knock, I usually succeed in distilling these 'strange' concepts into something comprehensible.

Just as many people resist conversing with the stranger next to them, many are reluctant to look at things in new ways. I value American Studies because it emphasizes understandings across boundaries, and lets a variety of materials inform each other. It also looks critically at 'American' institutions, even to the extent of getting people to interrogate how notions of 'nationhood' are constructed. But while it emphasizes the same critical thinking processes and methodologies as traditional disciplines, it is regarded with the same suspicion as the garrulous bar customer on the next stool over.

To ask people what purposes English and History classes serve would likely yield answers such as 'learning about America and the world' or 'learning about writing and literature.' To someone not exposed to poststructuralist thinking, the concepts of 'English' or 'History' are not politicized. Trying to explain in non-academic jargon how novels and histories are the products of power structures and ideologies is not easy.

Often in bars and in academia, confrontations with strangers or new ideas meet resistance. Guards are up, and conversations are not forthcoming. The customer might be a total nut, about to chew your ear off. But maybe the customer has stories to tell that will force a shift in thinking about narrowly held views about the world.

Another familiar customer is not archetypical, but rather one of personal recognition. With combed hair and fancy watch—things I have long since abandoned—he is a peer from high school, or maybe college, walking with a confidence that he played the game right. I recognize a glimmer of who I was, or might have become, and who many of my friends now are. While I am amicable, I also hold this person in chagrin, and perhaps he does the same regarding me. There is a simultaneous warmth and disdain crossing both ways across the bar, passing through money and pints that says, 'When're you going to figure it out?'

Like the challenges American Studies poses, my bartending lifestyle, while not recognized as a success on a résumé, has allowed me to see the world differently and to take a literal step back behind the bar and reconsider not only my own life, but also the worlds of the people I see around me. Before, I would have looked at many customers and written them off as uninteresting. I now look at the people across the bar from me as troves of information. They might look, act, or sound 'weird,' but I see value in the ideas and people that make me re-evaluate my own position in the world. I used to seek out only those who were most like me. Now I talk to them last.

After setting up the bar one recent morning, I went to get a newspaper. On the way, a man approached. His hair was shoulder length, grayish white, and greasy. He looked like any number of panhandlers that frequent the area; his clothes were stained, his shoes laceless. His right eye was swollen and bruised, and I assumed that he had been on the receiving end of a beating for sleeping on the wrong bench, or asking the wrong person for change. I continued to the store for my paper.

Returning to my job, I saw him ahead of me, opening the front door of the bar. This is no way to start the day, I thought. Maybe he just wants to use the bathroom.

As I entered the bar, he grabbed a stool and sat down. While similar folks come in off the street, they usually ingratiate themselves to neither staff nor customers, giving quick reason to be escorted out. There was a time in the recent past when they were the rule rather than the exception at this bar.

As he was the only one in the bar, I reluctantly gave him a chance. I would throw him hurdles, though. The sight of this unkempt, bruised man might deter my lunch crowd, the means to my income. All I needed was one excuse, be it lack of money or unacceptable behavior, and I would ask him to leave.

'How're you today?' I asked. The question was not as congenial as it was a test of his ability to answer. Maybe he was already drunk, and some mumbled words would give me enough reason to ask him to leave.

'Been up since seven,' he said coherently. 'Miller,' he followed, offering up the proper amount of money. I got the beer, and watched him out of the corner of my eye, as others started coming in. They gave him a cautious look, and sat at the tables. Others sat at the bar, though a few stools away.

He finished his beer, and I thought he might leave, but he placed his empty bottle on top of three more dollars. Not a tip, but a mute request for another beer. He placed a sizable wad of cash in his dingy coat pocket. A veritable Howard Hughes.

He acted reasonably and had money to pay for beers. I had no reason to ask him to leave. He continued moderately drinking four beers and eating a cup of crab soup, paying as he went.

He left no tip.

But I was given a more than gratuitous reminder about crossing the boundaries between the two lives I lead in the service industry and in academia. Bartending allows me to make money and pursue my interests outside of a nine-to-five existence. American Studies enamored me with its humanistic outlook and the emphases it places on understanding the multitudes of ways people create and get meaning from their lives. Within each of these worlds, I place a high value on moving beyond a conventional societal outlook. And yet I was still largely unwilling to give this man a chance.

My bar peers might refer to him as a 'bum,' while my academic colleagues might refer to him as 'homeless.' These stereotypical terms are limiting and largely inaccurate, and adherence to these or other labels often causes the ignorance at the core of many phobic thoughts.

And I think back to the man that I so quickly judged. There are times when quick judgments are needed behind the bar: whether or not to serve someone, or to intervene in a heated discussion. These snap judgments run against the deliberate and layered thinking required in academia.

No, I would probably not want him to come in again. Someone similar in appearance might come in at a future date, and might give me good reason to feel justified in my skepticism. But they might not.

The bar, and the world, might seem a safer place if homogeneity ruled. I like to think of myself as someone who craves eclecticism, but I recognize that I only want variance within certain guidelines. I look down at those who live within certain boundaries, while at the same time recognizing the boundaries of my own acceptance level. The two disparate worlds of academia and inebria intersect at odd places to remind me of the need for difference in outlook and opinion.

19
Inside the Idea Factory

Katie Simon

BEGIN WITH AN ANECDOTE THAT WILL HOOK YOUR READER

It is November 21, 1988, three days after my sister committed suicide. I am sitting in my father's office and he is reading her doctors' notes from her medical records. Two weeks before her death she had been diagnosed with Multiple Sclerosis. One day she woke up and was suddenly unable to walk, see, hear, or control her bowels—although she had been river rafting in the Grand Canyon the week before. After her initial diagnosis, she was transferred to a hospital that specializes in physical and occupational therapy. It was from this hospital that my father had requested the notes. A psychiatrist, he thought my sister should have been put on antidepressants and he wanted to sue the hospital for wrongful death.

'Talked with Cici today. Her spirits increasingly low. Reminded her that she was a mountain climber. Offered her antidepressants and she refused.'

My father finished reading and wanted to know my response to this psychologist's note. I was simply filled with grief.

'We have to start crafting this in terms of testimony,' he yelled. 'How do you think your feelings will sound to a judge? We need to start building an argument. This has to stand up in a court of law!'

But what does the law have to do with my feelings? Can a judge bring my sister back from the dead?

Clearly, argument is inappropriate is some instances.

A THESIS IS YOUR ONE RULING IDEA ABOUT YOUR TOPIC
THUS IT IS ALWAYS AN ASSERTION

How did it come to be that the dominant mode of writing in the humanities, at least in the academic study of literature, is the argument? Are we in a court of law? Do we need to garner evidence and convince a jury that our reading of the text is the correct one? It's like a game: develop a thesis, get some textual evidence, and win the 'A.' In the race to 'prove' your thesis you become convinced that this idea actually 'rules' all others you've had about the text.

You rest your case. What impressions and experiences of a text aren't allowed to be expressed or even thought in this context, since they can't be logically and convincingly proven in relation to the main point? Why the need to 'assert' oneself and one's ideas? Why not investigate, explore, enjoy, partake, connect, transmit, exchange?

CONTROL YOUR TONE

I am reacting somewhat angrily to the formal conventions of academic prose that privilege reason over imagination, single-minded linearity over multivoicedness, factual evidence over personal expressiveness. I am a graduate student in English, and I am tired of muzzling my imagination to what I think of as the long arm of the law. Sound a little extreme? Well, academic conventions are modeled on juridical discourse: the language of the courts, the proceedings that enforce the rules we want obeyed.

It might make sense to formulate arguments in court proceedings where there presumably is a guilty/not-guilty question to be solved. In a murder trial where there is opposing council to contend with, it makes sense that your closing argument would, therefore, be contentious and antagonistic in order to undermine the other side's claims. I understand this is how we do things in one of the best legal systems in the world, but if I'm writing and thinking about novels, poetry, and films, I just don't see the need to make and win an airtight case about my point of view.

I have begun experimenting with lyricism in my academic papers. By lyricism I mean the admittedly subjective and sensual use of language to convey exuberance and excess. The use of language to convey realms of experience not neatly fitting into a thesis topic sentence. This has been a scary process, venturing out into dangerous waters. I have begun suspending the need to shape and control the piece as I write it, to censor its tones or impose a structure before it is written.

MAKE CLEAR AND HELPFUL TRANSITIONS

In this experiment with lyricism, I am going back in method and style to my very first year in college. The great scholar Norman O. Brown stood in front of my freshman class and thundered: 'No thesis-topic sentences. The best response to poetry is poetry itself.' We panicked: how will we write? What will we do? 'Make it new,' he countered, after Ezra Pound. It was frightening to be given that kind of freedom and we spent countless hours in the dorms trying to figure out a style, a method. We wrote poetry, aphorisms, manifestos, collages, and collective pieces.

When I transferred the following year to the English Department at UC Berkeley I found that no one was really interested in creative responses to poetry. I learned to make linear, reasonable arguments about Chaucer, Blake, Shakespeare, and Keats. I combed the texts for 'evidence' to support my thesis. I worked in clever allusions to great thinkers. I successfully routed my ideas through the one form allowable and became an 'A' student of literature.

RETURN TO YOUR INITIAL ANECDOTE

When I began writing academic papers at Berkeley, I was able to follow the rules of composition in part because of my particular family background. The world of arguments, evidence, and proof was already extremely familiar to me. I had spent several years in high school in the middle of a raging legal battle between my parents over custody of their kids. I had excellent training in formulating my impressions, thoughts, and feelings about our family situation into credible and convincing testimony. My dad's later impulse to sue the hospital following my sister's death, and his demand that I convert my grief into an argument, made sense to him given our family's history of making high courtroom drama out of otherwise ordinary human failings and pain.

The custody battle years before had been an all-out war: my parents spent hundreds of thousands of dollars on expert witnesses; the case went to trial three separate times. My sister and I were coached by our lawyer before we gave court depositions or spoke to the judges in their chambers: *don't forget the strategy. Do you remember the main points? Mention the supporting points. Leave that out, it's not relevant to the case.* We became masterful at creating effective written and spoken discourse; we framed our words to advance the argument that we should be able to live with the parent we chose. We also presented a unified discursive front to the social workers, psychotherapists, court-appointed mediators, opposing council, police officers, principals, teachers, and curious friends who questioned us about the case.

This unusual early contact with the legal system helped me become Opinion Editor and then Editor-in-Chief of my high school newspaper, and I used my familiarity with juridical discourse to write political editorials and win contests and awards. But it took me a long time to realize that I didn't have to view everything in life through the lens of a legalistic argument justified by an arsenal of evidence and proof.

When I began teaching Composition myself a few years ago I had to deconstruct my own process of writing in order to be able to break it down for beginning writers. I began to question the methods I had so thoroughly appropriated, especially since I noticed that none of the freshman comp textbooks and anthologies practice what they preach. That is, on the one hand the prescriptive instructions for writing a good essay are given, but on the other hand most of the entries are by non-academic writers writing in a non-academic style: Alice Walker, Adrienne Rich, Richard Rodriguez, Virginia Woolf, Joan Didion, George Orwell, Tillie Olsen. The writers generally featured in composition readers write personal essays and narratives that people actually read. They write vividly, with circularity, idiosyncratically, in the form that best suits their particular ends. They may have an argument, but it's often made more through imaginative lyricism and finely noticed details than through the careful assembly of logical, linear thinking and evidence or proof.

We seem to be saying to students, 'You must follow our rules to get along here in college; but if you really want to write, break these rules.' What counts is 'good' writing and it is very difficult to quantify what makes something worth reading. But no one pretends, not even for a minute, that a group of essays written in the academic style would make an interesting read. So why do we promote these conventions?

GIVE CONCRETE EXAMPLES

Let me give a concrete example of the usefulness of these juridically inspired conventions to the research university. As a reader in a large lecture class last summer, I sat down three times to batches of 50 papers. I usually had just a week to read the papers. There is nothing new about my personal experience: it is the standard experience of readers and teaching assistants in large research universities. But I must admit that it was definitely helpful if students routed their ideas through the expository essay form designed purely for the convenience of the academic system, the idea-factory of which we are part.

The myth of the expository essay is that form is an invisible structure acting at the service of the presentation of ideas. And yet form is omnipresent in the academic context because if someone creates their own form they jam the smooth workings of the idea-factory system. A creative expository essay demands to be considered on its own terms; it can't be compared with anything. The standard formal criteria no longer apply; you can't simply mete out the comments: where is your thesis? Use more examples. Watch your transitions.

I learned early on to write what Ruth Behard calls the 'cold-blooded' logical essay, with a formulaic beginning, middle, and end, and I tell myself that my students need to write these cold-blooded essays too if they want to survive in a large research university. I fear that if I encourage them in their imaginative, innovative approaches to intellectual problems, I will only be causing them grief—and perhaps marginalizing them from intellectual legitimacy and future professional or financial success. But I don't feel satisfied with my capitulation to the idea factory, and I don't believe that mass-produced and easily digestible ideas are better than any other kind.

LOOK BEYOND YOUR THESIS IN A CONCLUDING PARAGRAPH

Using juridical discourse in academia is one strategy for a difficult situation: the situation being that I want to get my degree. But there are others. Given that this structure shapes and distorts our research and our ideas and conclusions, we can draw attention to this fact in our prose itself. We can mime that authority back to itself. Venues like *Bad Subjects* open up another possibility, creating a venue where analysis and argument don't 'rule,' but cohabit with autobiographical narrative and experimental prose.

It's worth noting, however, that I haven't broken free here of the constraints of juridical discourse. I have felt compelled to present my ideas as an argument or a case, which leads me to the point that once a structure is so completely internalized it's incredibly difficult to think oneself out of it. I'd like to write an academic prose that stutters in its own language when that language won't allow it to express something. I'd like to undermine rather than reify my own attempt to effect univocality, mastery, authority, and control. That can happen only when I consider the form of academic prose as completely plastic and malleable rather than as a fixed, invisibly powerful set of codes and rules for the expression of thought in language. Language, even academic language, has a texture; it can swing, it can move, it can be felt and heard and sung. We need to admit the presence of language itself, to allow it to occupy a palpable place in our work. To do that we have to get beyond the vilification of the imagination in academia, we have to realize that intellectual activity can take many forms. Only then will we be able to glimpse the possibilities that have never yet come to light.

Part IV

Crossing Borders

INTRODUCTION

When *Bad Subjects* started publication in 1992, its founders aspired to transect borders. The borders they had in mind were both disciplinary and institutional, made literal by the pleasant stroll across Strawberry Creek from the UC Berkeley Department of English's home in the colonnaded neoclassicism of Wheeler Hall to the domain of the social sciences in the defused modernism of security friendly Barrows Hall. Once *Bad Subjects* debuted on the internet the following year, however, it became rapidly apparent that there were bigger, better border crossings to provoke. Correspondence and contributions from around the world demonstrated the demand for thoughtful, concise writing about the politics of everyday life, even if it were published in English.

We have responded to this demand by going out of our way to solicit essays from places that don't exist on most Americans' mental maps. And, although our origin and membership continue to make us an English-language publication, we have pursued efforts both to include foreign-language pieces in *Bad Subjects* and to have our contributors' writing translated into languages such as Korean, Italian, Arabic, and Turkish. In addition, we have made the problem of border-crossing in an era of so-called globalization one of the cornerstones of the publication, encouraging articles that tackle it both literally and metaphorically. This section of the book testifies to that labor, presenting the work of eight authors who address complex boundary spaces that they have encountered or inhabited as they negotiated transnational avenues of experience and communication.

Gretchen Soderlund and Emma Grant open the section by challenging the received idea that international trafficking laws protect women from exploitation. They take a close look at the conflicting channels of rights and protections that affect sex workers, arguing that existing trafficking laws may work to inhibit sex workers from organizing for their own rights. Joel Schalit relates differing relationships of Israeli Jews to their contested Mediterranean landscape in a personal recollection from childhood that is both humorous and melancholy. He describes the cultural misalignments that appear between British Diaspora

Jews and Israeli-identified American-born Jews when his newly formed stepfamily takes a fateful, and nearly explosive, ride through the Judean desert.

The surprising, if tenuous, dimensions of freedom enjoyed by transvestites in Sofia, Bulgaria is explored by Robin S. Brooks in the next essay. The author vividly describes the parameters of self-expression that govern the lives of young and beautiful cross-dressers in this eastern European capital city, where a history of social tolerance counterpoints an atomized society that struggles daily with the legacies of totalitarianism. Frederick Luis Aldama's essay directly challenges the propagandistic notion that a borderless world can be equated with an emancipated world. His critique of the dialectic of globalization encompasses both late capitalists and cultural studies scholars, arguing that scholarly celebrations of hybrid social spaces distract from the relentless economic pressures and prejudices created by capitalist globalization.

Far from any national border, Carrie A. Rentschler looks at the much more personal barriers that Americans are constructing around their private living spaces. In order to write her essay, she posed as a college student concerned about her personal safety, and was given the detailed selling points of the new technical systemization of security available to the fearful who are willing to pay. Rentschler critiques how Americans have relocated the generalized national security threat into their personal spaces. Arturo J. Aldama expands on the theme of fear response at the individual level by looking at the interface between law and the frightened human body. Echoing his brother's arguments, Aldama points out how fantasies of a wildly free postborder world isolate the most fundamental political effects of fear: the silencing of those who are not complicit with neocolonialism, especially those in the United States/Mexico border areas. Finally, Kevin Carollo reflects on the year he spent in Senegal in 1996, finding within his experiences many points on which to critique postcolonial theory. He outlines the layering of economic and racial motivations for transnational identification and migration, in the process illustrating the razor sharp border enforcement so real to most people in the world.

20
Girls (Forced to) Dance Naked! The Politics and Presumptions of Antitrafficking Laws

Gretchen Soderlund and Emma Grant

In the 1910s, during the Progressive Era, sensationalistic stories of white women forced into prostitution at the hands of predatory men circulated widely in the US media. These stories drove home an image of the unwitting, lily white, sexual 'slave' and her deceitful captor. Although 'white slavery' was popularly considered one of the era's most pressing social problems, stories of its prevalence were greatly exaggerated.

In the 1990s stories of trafficked women abound in the news media, but now the women are from so-called Third World and Eastern Bloc countries. Although the geographic locations have changed, these stories conform to the same basic narrative of female victims and male villains. Despite claims that sex industry trafficking has reached record proportions and taken on new characteristics in this era of globalized capital, the rhetoric surrounding trafficking has failed to mature in a similar proportion. In fact, it seems to have ground to a halt sometime in the 1910s during the campaigns against white slavery. Stories about the sex industry are replete with references to sexual slavery, innocent victims, captivity, and deception. Together, these themes form a narrative template for every case of sex industry work involving illegal migrant labor.

For example, a March 24, 1998 article in the *New York Times* entitled '20 Women Forced into Prostitution' details 'the horrors inflicted on unwitting victims' by Mexican traffickers. The 20 women, the article goes on to say, were tricked by the promise of a far different life in the United States: 'It was the American dream of finding legitimate jobs, such as housekeeping and restaurant work, that led to a nightmarish life for women and girls.' Likewise, a *New York Times* story appearing on July 6, 1998, '100,000 Slaves of West's Sex Industry,' makes similar claims about trafficked Ukrainian sex workers: 'Typically, a woman is lured to the West with a promise of work as a dancer, waitress, home help, or often on a promise of marriage.' In a September 11, 1998 *Chicago Tribune* story, 'Victims Forced to Dance Nude at Clubs, US Says,' we learn that while the 'victims' in this prostitution ring knew they would be put to work dancing in the US, they expected to be wearing 'bikinis—not naked or topless,' and to be working in a 'sophisticated nightclub.'

The authors of these stories go out of their way to portray their women subjects as totally ignorant of the work they would be doing in the United States. Of all migrant workers, only undocumented sex workers are portrayed as completely unwitting. Women who migrate illegally to work as domestics or waitresses, on the other hand, are rarely portrayed as being completely ignorant of the work awaiting them upon immigration. The women involved in sex industry rings, however, must be distanced from the sexual acts themselves before tears can be shed for them. In these news stories, women can be viewed sympathetically as victims only if they are first constructed as sexless, as women who would rather scrub a toilet than dance in the nude.

The frozen discourse on trafficking neither advances the rights and agency of workers in the global sex industry nor serves to improve the conditions under which they work. In short, antitrafficking laws are used against the very women they are supposed to protect. Despite media representations of all 'trafficked' women as innocent, unwitting victims, virtual sex slaves at the hands of mafiosos and other unsavory characters, many women are already privy to their job descriptions before arrival at their foreign destination. While the media, antitrafficking organizations, governments, and even human rights groups work in tandem to emphasize the naivety of these women regarding the sexual component of their future jobs, this construction of sex workers ultimately serves ulterior purposes.

The supposedly noble goal of 'protecting the innocent' serves as a smokescreen for the creation of harsh and ultimately moralistic laws preventing the mobility of sex workers. These laws, which often specifically target the sex industry, rob sex workers of their ability to seek out financial opportunity away from their own country, which may be encountering economic depression due to globalization. This image of the virtuous trafficked woman not only undergirds repressive laws, but fails to capture the ways in which sex workers the world over have deliberately and skillfully worked around trafficking laws or used restrictive laws and their own 'victim status' to advantage in dealing with immigration authorities. Since many sex workers are also undocumented migrant workers, they break the law when they work in the United States without permits. By claiming that they are the victims of vast trafficking networks, they may not only avoid arrest, but they may also avoid immediate forced deportation. While we do not want to replace one overly general and stereotyped representation of sex workers with another, that of the 'sly sex worker,' we do wish to stress the ways in which some sex workers actively negotiate their way around less-than-ideal laws. Sex workers are rarely ignorant of their own circumstances and working conditions. On the contrary, they have special knowledge of their own situations.

One author of this essay worked as a health counselor for sex workers on two continents, including the United States. In California she worked with 20 Thai brothel workers. While these workers were undocumented and working in the United States illegally, it became apparent that these women were not 'trafficked' in the sense of being kidnapped and forced into a life of virtual sex slavery. In fact, each of them had a complex story to tell about the circumstances that ultimately led them to sex work in the United States, and all of them expressed the view that their opportunity to perform sex work in the United States was a great improvement over their previous work experiences. Because of the rapport the author developed with these women, and because of the author's own history of having been a sex worker, they were quite candid when discussing these circumstances. The diversity and complexity of sex workers' lives often disappears in the victim narratives of the antitrafficking lobby.

Sadly, there are cases in which women are forced to work in the sex industry under deplorable conditions. These are extreme cases, which should not be tolerated. However, the news media and various antitrafficking groups have a tendency to collapse every story of migrant sex industry labor into one narrative of 'trafficked women.' By wrapping every incident in sensationalist language of 'sexual slavery' and duplicity, these stories fail to address the diverse range of life circumstances that lead women and men to enter the sex industry. To understand the real problems and needs of sex workers, we must avoid such overgeneralizations and instead make a serious effort to understand the different contexts in which sex work occurs.

The tightened regulations for which the antitrafficking agenda lobbies ultimately hurt sex workers in a variety of ways. Domestic trafficking laws such as the Mann Act can be invoked to arrest sex workers as they travel independently across state lines. The Mann Act was instituted in 1910 to prohibit the movement of women or girls across state lines for immoral purposes such as adultery or prostitution. Under this act, it is illegal to purchase train or plane tickets for women sex workers (taxi fares, however, are not covered by the act). More broadly, the act renders a federal crime the 'immoral' arrangements that entail the crossing of state lines for their enactment. Since the act prohibits illegal interstate commerce, arrests are made when the travel actually occurs. In the case of a prostitution offence, alleged 'prostitutes' are arrested at the state level during travel, while 'procurers' are arrested at the federal level. The Mann Act can thus be used to arrest either the prostitute or the third party.

Furthermore, international laws against trafficking make it very hard for sex workers to organize at the international level on their own behalf. Due to strict trafficking laws, known sex workers have been denied visas to travel or attend conferences in foreign countries. Although these problems are not limited to Third World workers, they do appear to affect them disproportionately. In this sense, they mirror many other immigration policies that restrict movement from Third World to First. In that sense, antitrafficking laws are like other immigration laws that deny people with the least capital entry into richer countries. One Latin American sex worker, on her way to the 1997 International Conference on Prostitution in Los Angeles, was detained at the airport because she had a documented history of prostitution. In cases like this one, women who have never been trafficked in their lives were negatively affected by the laws. Some women are indeed 'trafficked' in the sense that they are moved between countries through a brokered deal. However, neither the status quo conceptualization of sex traffic, nor the current laws pertaining to trafficking, make any meaningful distinction between women who knowingly enter these arrangements and women who are trafficked against their will. Moreover, trafficking laws do not distinguish between 'trafficked' women and women who perform sex work without any trafficking, voluntary or involuntary.

Not only are sex workers' movements unjustly curtailed by trafficking laws, but their ability to organize and lobby on their own behalf domestically has, in some cases, been threatened by these laws. For example, in Australia, right-wing attacks against prostitutes' rights organizations have been conducted as part of an antitrafficking campaign. These groups lobby for improved working conditions in the sex industry through the decriminalization of prostitution and the creation of prostitutes' unions.

In Canberra, certain forms of sex work are legal and prostitutes are free to organize. Yet the specter of Asian women working illegally in brothels was recently used there to justify proposed domestic policies that, if passed, would overturn much of the progress made by the prostitutes' rights organization in that area. This progress includes occupational safety laws, health services, sexually transmitted disease prevention training, access to condoms, grievance procedures, and provision of safe places to work. The antitrafficking solution emphasizes deportation and further criminalization, rather than legalization, of both foreign and domestic sex workers. If these policies indeed prevail, years of struggle on the part of Canberra prostitutes will be negated in the name of rescuing 'trafficked' women. As prostitutes' rights organizers in Canberra have suggested, trafficking is not the real issue in these cases: the real issue is that these women were made to work illegally, with no recourse to the services available to legal prostitutes in the city. While the few Asian workers found working in Canberra were indeed doing so illegally, they were not undocumented. Rather, they had tourist visas that allowed them in the country, but did not allow them to work. In this case, the issue of 'trafficking' was used in an attempt to roll back gains made by sex workers.

We contend, then, that to understand the sex industry and illegal immigration we must break out of the straightjacket of the 'trafficked victim' framework. Rarely do 'trafficked women' not have an inkling of the kind of work that they might do in a foreign land. In many cases they are fully prepared to bend or break the law to reach their final goal. When concerned but ill-informed organizations define women as victims of a vast international trafficking conspiracy and call for more laws and legislation to 'save' them, might these laws actually decrease their mobility and opportunity?

The present approach to trafficking is not the solution. It limits sex workers' mobility and creates difficulties for those who engage in sex work of their own volition. Further, it obscures the fact that trafficking is, in part, the product of both illegality in the sex industry and strict immigration laws. Better solutions are available. Decriminalizing the sex industry and creating strong sex worker run organizations to monitor and address concerns about working conditions is a first step toward creating and maintaining safe workplaces for all workers in the sex industry, be they at home or abroad. Decriminalization of prostitution, even when it requires the crossing of borders, should be the ultimate goal. In the meantime, we must work to expand and protect those spaces where borders are still open and where opportunities for travel, albeit technically illegal, still exist.

FURTHER READING

Kampadoo, K., and J. Doezema, *Global Sex Workers*, New York: Routledge, 1998, especially Jo Doezema's chapter, 'Forced to Choose.'

21
Driving Through the Minefields of Love

Joel Schalit

On a frighteningly hot day in the summer of 1977, my father decided to take us on a trip to the place where we had laid my mother to rest two years before, on a desert plateau high above the Dead Sea. This excursion was to be unlike any other because it was the first time my father and I were going to take a trip with my new stepmother, Esther, and her two children, Avi and Elior. It made me uneasy. Why, of all places, were we going to make our first family outing a trip to my mother's grave?

'Are you sure you want to do this?' I nervously asked my father after we finished Shabbat dinner the night before we were to leave for Masada. 'Why don't we just go to the Israel War Museum in Tel Aviv for the day? We could go eat at the Olympia restaurant afterwards.' 'No child,' Elie smiled, patting me reassuringly on my fragile ten-year-old back. 'These people live in London. Even though Esther is an Israeli, her children don't know very much about where they come from. We must teach them. We'll go have a nice Moroccan dinner afterwards in Jerusalem as your reward for being a good boy. Okay?'

Despite my father's appeal to my patriotic sense of educating these *galutim* (Jews from the Diaspora) I couldn't get to sleep that night. I kept thinking about how uncomfortable the car would be, stuffed with young British Jews driving through the Judean desert on a blisteringly hot summer day. I worried that our love of the harsh Biblical landscape would be interpreted as quaint by my new family's cosmopolitan Diaspora sensibilities. I feared that we were going to alienate them by being open about the pain we still felt over the loss of my mother.

Sometime around midnight, I decided to get up and fish through my closet for my collection of Matchbox cars. When I finally found them, I put all of them in an empty green and gold colored Elite chocolate bar box, and took them out to the stairs. From the edge of the staircase I could hear that my father and Esther were still up. They were arguing with each other softly in Hebrew.

I couldn't quite tell what they were talking about because their bedroom door was closed. But judging from the tone of the conversation, it sounded heated enough that I knew it would be a bad idea to turn on the lights in the hallway—

they'd most likely discover that I was awake, and then they would turn their frustration with each other on me.

In the half-light, I slowly unpacked my cars and lined them up at the very top of the typically Mediterranean, cheap marble staircase. Once I had finished making sure that their front bumpers were all carefully aligned with one another, I methodically began pushing each one of them off the edge. As I made my way down the lineup, I began to push them harder and harder, so that by the end I was literally throwing them all the way down the stairs.

By the time I was done, the entire staircase was littered with the upside down shells of all my toy cars. Scared that I'd be heard if I began walking downstairs to pick them up, I left them lying there, thinking that I'd get up earlier than everyone else and clean it all up before my midnight activities had been discovered. It proved to be wishful thinking.

The next morning I was awoken by a very loud shriek. Avi had gotten up before me and had gone to the kitchen to drink hot chocolate. On his way down the stairs, he'd stepped on one of my toy cars, and had been sent flying. I couldn't be quite certain, but judging from the tenor of his wounded-animal like yell, I could tell that I'd upset him. 'Mami, Mami,' I could hear Avi yelling, 'Yoel hurt me with his cars!'

Cowering in fear behind my bedroom door, I could hear Esther running out of her bedroom door, breathless, looking down at her son laying on his side at the bottom of the stairs. 'Yoel,' she yelled, 'Come here right now and clean this mess up.' Scared, I put on my shorts and sandals, collected my Elite chocolate box, and walked sheepishly out my bedroom door. Esther looked down at me disdainfully, trembling. Patches of her dyed orange hair were falling over her face. She pulled a dark brown cigarette out of the pocket of her Mrs. Robinson-look-alike faux-leopard skin nightgown, lit it, and stared at me. Her hands were shaking; 'Mami, Mami,' Avi moaned from below, 'I think my arm is broken.'

'Some way to inaugurate our first family road trip,' I thought to myself. I got on my knees and slowly started to collect my dangerous miniature automobiles. I was in really big trouble.

By the time I'd finished putting my toy cars away, my father had gotten breakfast ready. 'Yoel,' he called up to me, 'we're ready to eat.' I was nervous about putting in an appearance. I knew that everyone except my father would resent my presence at the dining room table. But he knew I was acting out and chose to ignore it. 'There you are kiddo,' he warmly intoned as I sat down, 'I made you your favorite: scrambled eggs and donkey salami.' I was delighted. Elie had decided not to punish me.

We sat there eating in silence. Esther sipped her coffee and stared out at the Arab laborers walking down the street, off to build a new Jewish home in yet another depressing subdivision of Savyon, the rapidly growing wealthy suburb of Tel Aviv that we lived in. My father busied himself with yesterday's newspaper. Elior periodically kicked me under the table, whispering under her breath, 'You stupid ass,' in her English private school accent. Avi appeared to be doing just fine. The arm he claimed my toy cars had broken was miraculously stuffing my father's fried meat and egg combination down his long, whiny throat. I looked at it carefully and thought about how much I wish he'd really broken something.

Finally I decided to break the silence. 'When do we leave for the Dead Sea?' I asked. 'Soon child, soon,' my father replied, staring ever more intently into Friday's *Ha'aretz*. 'Do you think we'll hit another donkey again?' I asked, hoping to get a positive response out of someone at the table. 'Donkey, what donkey, Elie?' Esther replied, sounding rather concerned.

Elie shot a sharp glance at me from across the table. I could tell he was pissed that I had chosen to relate this particular story. 'We hit a donkey at a hundred kilometers an hour last time we drove to Masada,' I said with perverse delight. I could hear my father gripping his newspaper tightly. 'A Bedouin shepherd was moving his flock of animals across the old Roman road near Abu Mousa, but one of his donkeys decided to remain behind.'

Turning slightly red, my father decided to take over the situation, fearful that if he didn't, I might make things even worse than I already had by opening my big, egg and salami filled mouth. 'And we hit the stupid idiot straight in the ass,' he proudly proclaimed. 'If you can believe it, the car was completely unharmed. But the poor creature flew straight up in the air, landed behind us, and headed straight back for Jerusalem.'

Lighting her second cigarette, Esther asked if we could drive a little more carefully this time. My father gripped me under the table by the knee. It was then that I knew I'd manage to piss everyone off that morning. Feeling like my destiny with my new family was completely out of control, I grabbed my new plastic American skateboard out of the hall closet, ran out the front door and repeatedly jumped the curb in front of our house into oncoming traffic.

Peugeots parted to my right. Mercedes taxicabs moved quickly to my left. Seamlessly, I wove my small, agile body in between them, congratulating myself on my dexterity and skill in courting death. The problem was that no one except the oncoming traffic that I was taunting ever bothered to notice. Frustrated, I picked up my skateboard, turned on the front lawn sprinkler, and cried. I was really stressed out.

My father's voice interrupted this brief moment of self-pity. 'Yallah Yoel, its time to go!' I turned off the water, slid my skateboard through the front door, and followed Avi and Elior into our brand new Italian automobile. 'You sit in the middle because you're the smallest,' Esther commanded. 'That's right,' echoed Avi. 'You have the shortest legs of the three of us, you belong in the middle.' I took a deep breath, got in first, and felt the hot leather of a car heated by the early morning summer sun burn the bottom of my tanned thighs. 'Fuck you,' I muttered under my breath as I recoiled in pain from the boiling seats. No one heard me. Elie and Esther soon followed suit, on came the air conditioning, and off we went, speeding toward Jerusalem en route to our final destination, the plateau above the Dead Sea.

'Yoel, Melech [King] Israel,' sang Avi and Elior as we passed the old British military police station in Latrun. I asked them to shut up, so they sang the same chorus over and over again, getting louder with each stupid verse. I was being teased. I reached forward and tapped my father's shoulder, hoping he'd intercede. Without appearing to get involved in the conflict, Elie turned on the radio, and out blasted the British band Deep Purple's 'Smoke on the Water.' 'That's so cool!' yelled an excited Avi, humming the three infamous barré chords that identify this 1970s anthem about the burning of a concert venue in Montreux, Switzerland.

Soon enough Elior joined him, their arms forming air guitars as the song blared out of our car's speakers. Avi and Elior's rock and roll gesticulations grew wilder, their elbows smashing into each side of my face. I was miserable. Finally Esther yelled out, 'Will you kids quiet down? I can't even hear myself talking to Elie.' But her crazed offspring would just not stop. Finally she switched off the radio, and the car returned to silence. I tapped my father's shoulder again. His hand reached around the seat and grabbed my ankle, acknowledging my distress. It was worse than being stuck in the back of a school bus with the neighborhood bullies.

Two hours passed before we reached the outskirts of the Judean desert on the other side of Jerusalem. The old Roman road was crowded with aging, occupied territory-plated Mercedes trucks carrying food and commercial goods from Bethlehem and the West Bank down to Jericho. Much to my stepmother's chagrin, my father put his pedal to the metal to get around them. Like me on my skateboard two hours earlier, Elie wove an intricate, seemingly suicidal pattern on the two-lane highway around these hulking behemoths. Esther shrieked. Her children clapped with delight. My father's racecar driving ritual turned them on. I periodically fell on them as my father dramatically swerved right and then left to avoid oncoming traffic approaching us in the passing lane.

'Elie, Elie, slow down, would you?' intoned Esther. 'Don't worry child, I'm an excellent driver,' my father replied. 'Besides, we're running short on time and there's this place I wanted to take you before it gets too hot.' Suddenly, Elie took an abrupt right turn, and took us up the beginnings of a very steep dirt and stone road, right up the side of a hill covered in flocks of Bedouin sheep looking for non-existent foliage to graze on. Recalling my story of our collision with the donkey, Esther cried out, 'Careful Elie, careful.' 'Listen child,' answered Elie, 'I've been up and down these roads since I was a teenager. We used to hide out from the British army here.'

Everyone gripped their seats in terror. I sat in the middle where there was nothing I could really hold onto, so I abandoned myself to being thrown to and fro between the laps of my larger stepsiblings. Angry at my constant crash landings in their soft, adolescent laps, Avi and Elior tossed me back and forth at one another, while the sounds of large rocks hit the bottom of our new Alfa Romeo. It was built for high-speed driving on the smooth highways of Italian autostradas, not the rugged, stony dirt roads of a barren Biblical geography. 'Why didn't you buy a Jeep?' yelled Esther over the atonal Judean symphony. My father shot her a sharp look and said nothing. Nervous, Esther lit a cigarette, and fumbled through her purse for a cassette to drown out the din of the increasingly crazy voyage we'd all embarked on.

Stumbling upon a copy of British pop singer Tom Jones' *Greatest Hits*, she promptly put it on to shield her ears from the sounds of rocks scraping the bottom of her husband's brand new car. 'What's New Pussycat?' immediately exploded out of the speakers, drowning out the *sturm und drang* of our noisy ascent, as cheap Israeli *Time* cigarette smoke filled the back of our small, fragile automobile. We all began to cough. Esther refused to open her window for fear of all the sand and dust blowing in. Besides, she argued, we had the air conditioning on. It was too hot outside to even think of such a possibility. Rendered silent by the extremity of the proceedings, the lack of air, the constant heaving back and forth, and the combined volume of Tom Jones singing 'Woah, Woah, Woah, Woah,' I felt like I was going to faint.

I was saved from lapsing into unconsciousness when we reached the summit. Elie finally slowed down and we began our sightseeing tour. 'Over there,' he gestured, pointing to a Bedouin camp, 'is where we would hide out as teenagers in the Haganah. From their encampment you can see the road to Jerusalem on your left, Jericho up a bit further, and the Dead Sea and Jordan right in front of you.' Esther was not amused. Avi strained to look out the dusty car window. Elior moaned that from her position she could not see a thing. Sitting in the middle of the back seat, I had the only view that gave me a perspective similar to my father's.

I was excited. My dad and I were alone in our enjoyment of the fruits of our first extended family outing, just as we had been before his remarriage. But it wasn't destined to last very long. As the car continued to roll south across the high desert plateau, an army Jeep sped toward us. When they reached our car, one of them yelled out with a bullhorn for us to stop. An officer clad in a fresh green Israeli army uniform and World War II-era aviator's sunglasses asked my father to roll down his window. 'Slichah,' ['excuse me'] the officer said in Hebrew, 'didn't you read the sign?' My father looked around, pretending not to see the large multilingual billboard in front of us. 'You've started to drive through a minefield. I'd advise you to turn around immediately unless you are planning on taking a quick trip to the cemetery.'

22

Cross-dressing in Bulgaria: Gay Identity, Postcommunist Fear, and Magical Love

Robin S. Brooks

A Chicago journalist once wrote that 'Gay culture is absolutely uniform across the world. A gay bar in Ulan Bator is no different from one in Chicago or Berlin or Buenos Aires. You'll hear the same vapid dance music, smell the same cologne, hear the rustle of the same neatly pressed Polo shirts, and touch the same tanned, well-moisturized skin.'

Buying into this idea, I expected no surprises from Spartakus, the oldest private mix club in Sofia, Bulgaria. Friends billed it as a gay establishment and when I first visited it in the summer of 1997 it was new and fashionable. Entry was restricted to people with exclusive membership cards. The music was indeed vapid, but it was not like any dance music popular in the United States at the time (or ever, for that matter). Scatman John, Era, and other European export bands sang in strangely accented, non-native English over the club's incredibly loud speakers, and the DJ occasionally announced singles by home-grown pop stars in rapid-fire Bulgarian. I did not see a single Polo shirt, but tanned skin did peek out from under every tight muscle shirt and microscopic mini-skirt. The skin covered the lean bodies of a population whose government had plundered their wheat that winter, leaving them poor and without reliable sources of food, in an economy characterized by 1,000 per cent annual inflation and 20 per cent unemployment.

A quick scan of the room revealed that Spartakus was by no means an entirely gay club. Although couples of carefully clad young women on the dance floor moved together to the music, the thick-necked men lining the walls kept a careful eye out to ensure that no one messed with them. Later, threesomes left together in dark BMWs. In the meantime, throngs inside the exclusive establishment blushed and looked away from the stage when the DJ introduced the male erotic dancers. Within a few minutes, however, secret peeks at the stage yielded to enthusiastic applause, and no one in the hall failed to watch the drag queen who came out to lip synch 'I Will Survive' in fishnet stockings and a feather wig.

Who are these people? I asked myself. What does the audience have in common with the transvestite on stage? Is this really a gay club? And aren't people afraid of a police raid?

I had read in the *Rough Guide to Bulgaria* that 'while homosexual acts between men over the age of 21 are not officially illegal, there are heavy restrictions on vague things like scandalous homosexuality or homosexual acts leading to perversions,' which basically means that the authorities have the right to arrest you for any homosexual act. I feared that simulated fellatio and cross-dressing might be considered scandalous, especially in an Orthodox country, and I had heard rumors of a bar raid in Sofia in 1996. I was nervous all night, and I didn't understand why nobody else was as worried as I was. I also didn't understand why the club bothered to hire transvestite dancers if the whole crowd was as straight as it looked.

Two years later, in 1999, I returned to Spartakus. I naively expected time to have transformed the club into something approaching an ideal-typical gay disco with a new Western face. After all, ten years had then elapsed since the fall of the totalitarian communist regime. Bulgaria had experienced two years of relative success with economic and political reforms following the crisis of January 1997. This time in Spartakus there was more standard European music, there were fewer bodyguards, and more youth in the disco. Spartakus had abandoned its members-only policy and was now open to any member of the public who could pass the 'face control' and afford the cover charge of $1.50 (the average Bulgarian monthly salary is $111). There I found an unusual underground culture, and a loosely consolidated community of people simultaneously drawn together and atomized by a set of fears and hopes that is unique to the postcommunist situation. Perhaps even unique to the particular social setting of fin-de-siècle Bulgaria.

Bulgaria historically has been one of Europe's most tolerant countries. In the early 1900s, Bulgaria accepted waves of Armenian refugees from Turkey that no other country would take. During World War II, Bulgaria refused to send its Jews to Nazi concentration camps. In the mid-1980s, Bulgarian citizens demonstrated against anti-Turkish communist policies, and began a process that toppled the totalitarian regime and ushered in a transition to democracy by writing a constitution more liberal than any other in Eastern Europe. Despite what is written in the *Rough Guide*, homosexuality is legal in Bulgaria and has been since 1968. Moreover, the law forbids discrimination based on sex or on HIV-positive status in employment or education. It is expected that the parliament will soon ban discrimination based on sexual orientation.

At the same time, however, Bulgarian society is atomized. The atomization is a legacy of its totalitarian past when a distrust was fostered that destroyed all but the closest individual ties in favor of corporate identities and loyalty to the regime. Consequently, the gay community has also remained unconsolidated. The combined forces of traditional social values and a dire economic situation make public heterosexuality practically compulsory for young people, who often continue to live with their parents until they are married. One informant told me that his greatest fear as a gay man in Bulgaria is that his boyfriend will eventually break up with him in order to get married, even though he knows they will still be in love.

Despite de facto conservatism, however, Bulgaria is de jure one of the most tolerant and inclusive societies in Europe. Gay people there enjoy more liberties and protections than do their counterparts in Britain or France, so there is no pressing reason to unite politically. And widespread poverty means that only a small segment of the gay population has access to the expensive clubs and private bars where people can meet and consolidate their community. The lack of economic resources also prevents the community from producing any printed literature that might bind its members together.

As the Bulgarian government is busy trying to meet the strict criteria for NATO and European Union membership, the country's populace is doing its best to upgrade Bulgaria's image to meet what they think of as European standards. Everyone hoping to get inside Spartakus has to pass the scrutiny of a busty, tattooed transvestite before being allowed entrance. This test unites the successful patrons in the knowledge that they are the best-dressed, most stylish Sofians. At the same time, though, it atomizes the gay community by alienating would-be clients who cannot afford or do not feel like wearing the required fashions.

Bulgaria is the only country I have ever visited where transvestites are at the top of the hierarchy in the gay community. They decide who can get into the exclusive discos, they get reserved tables in private clubs, and everyone else wants to dance with them or be noticed by them. The founders of Spartakus envisioned their creation as a Bulgarian version of Manhattan's Studio 54, a club for the aesthetic elite. This elite includes actors, pop stars, artists, and designers, as well as ultra-hipster youth with avant-garde style. To ensure style quality, the club's management hires transvestites to run the club and to set the visual tone. Aside from the face controller, at least five transvestites mill about Spartakus on any given night. To earn their wages, some of the transvestites tend bar while others put on the stage show. All of the performances are well-rehearsed even though the performers have no paid rehearsal time, and the crowds cheer them enthusiastically but cannot afford to tip them.

Indeed, the audience can barely afford to dress themselves in the style required for entrance to the club. Krâstina, a prominent Bulgarian fashion designer, explains, 'It is interesting to try to make beautiful clothes in a country that doesn't really need fashion or designers, only clothes to wear.' The utilitarian clothing sold from tables on street corners is certainly more affordable to the average Bulgarian than is the haute couture produced by Krâstina, her partner Konstantin, and the eight to ten colleagues who are estimated to be working in their trade in Bulgaria. But inside Spartakus, it is the high fashion transvestites who set an example that everyone else must follow.

Twenty-year-old Persephone, Bulgaria's Miss Transvestite 2000, is lucky that her father runs a successful business and gives her a large allowance without asking her what she spends it on. Persephone competed against 15 other cross-dressers in the Miss Transvestite pageant this March completely on a whim. Konstantin, one of four judges at the pageant, explained that the panel was looking for a combination of 'cosmopolitanism, mysticism, femininity, philosophy, and magical love,' in the winning contestant. Persephone had never cross-dressed before, and didn't expect to do so again. But after she won, the other transvestites pressured her into continuing, at least for the duration of her reign as queen. The 700 Deutschmark honorarium that she won helps, but it will be difficult to build an entire new wardrobe from scratch, especially considering the high standards within the community.

Bulgaria's most famous transvestite, Ursula, has it much easier. Krâstina and Konstantin, her adopted parents, are not only financially better off than the average Bulgarian, but are also supportive of Ursula's cross-dressing and capable of producing fabulously extravagant costumes for her in their own design studio. While Persephone designs her own costumes from inexpensive materials and has her mother sew them in secret, a typical costume for Ursula costs $200 to $300, is designed specifically for her, and is handmade by Krâstina from imported fabrics. It is no wonder that Ursula won the Miss Transvestite pageant two years in a row. Her proud parents want to raise the level of fashion at Spartakus to complement Ursula's beauty, but they cannot do it alone. 'We would like to have more than one transvestite,' explains Konstantin. 'But it is very expensive, and one family simply can't afford it. So we only have one. We put everything into Ursula. She is our only transvestite. The others have to dress themselves.'

With such support, it is not surprising that Ursula is the most famous of the Bulgarian transvestites. What is surprising, however, is the fame that transvestites have even in mainstream Bulgarian society. Krâstina is among Bulgaria's best-received designers, and her transvestite models are accepted as vanguards of fashion for the entire country. At the after-party for the Miss Bulgaria pageant in April 2000 it was transvestite dancers, not the girls who had competed in the pageant, who performed on stage. In a club full of heterosexual businessmen and wealthy, middle-aged Bulgarian glitterati, no one seemed to question the choice of entertainment. And no one complained when Ursula whipped the new Miss Bulgaria away from the edge of the stage with a cat-o-nine-tails.

Aside from the ordinary financial worries that every Bulgarian harbors, Persephone is also nervous that her father might find out she cross-dresses and throw her out of the house. Ursula and her parents worry that Bulgarian privatization will never be completed and their fashion designs will never reach the world market. Still, Ursula dreams of becoming a fashion designer like Krâstina and Konstantin, and of having a career as a model. Persephone would like to go abroad to study. Though Persephone does not see a sex-change operation in her future, Ursula does, and is saving money for breast implants.

The Bulgarian transvestite community is as diverse as any other community in the world, yet its members are tied together at the top of Bulgaria's aesthetic hierarchy. Most of them do not have many straight friends, and they are marginalized within the gay community as well. Still, somehow, it is transvestites, not gays, who can afford to be out in Bulgarian society. They support each other inside the community, and they are famous, well-liked, and respected by people outside of it. Bulgarians follow the trends that they set and conform to their aesthetic taste in order to gain entrance into their unique world of underground clubs and cafes. As a result, Bulgarian gay culture, and indeed Bulgarian culture in general, truly is a bit different from the universal stereotype.

23
Marxing Across the Border

Frederick Luis Aldama

> Finally, there came a time when everything that men had considered
> as inalienable became an object of exchange, of traffic, and could be
> alienated. This is the time when the very things which till then had
> been communicated, but never exchanged; given, but never sold;
> acquired, but never bought—virtue, love, conviction, knowledge,
> conscience, etc.—when everything, in short, passed into commerce.
>
> Karl Marx, *The Poverty of Philosophy* (1847)

There has been much talk on, in so many words, our living in a new, borderless
world order. In Europe, politicians promised an economically more robust
European Union with the collapsing of international trade tariffs and the
movement of bodies within this passportless community. And there are those
who heralded the internet boom as not only a means for corporate CEOs to
increase portfolio dividends, but as a venue for disenfranchised peoples from
around the globe to exchange histories and stories to better understand past
and future acts of genocide (see NetWarriors.com). And, in the name of progress
and capitalism, the US Department of Education instituted the 'Estrella' program
to bring an internet classroom—teaching geography, world history, and algebra,
for example—to the homes of Mexicano farmworkers' children to improve the
drop-out statistics; the internet learning community would provide continuity
while students moved from school to school as the crops and seasons dictated.
And media pundits and academic critics also hail the age of the borderless,
hybrid subject.

In a special issue of *Time* entitled, 'Amexica,' the mixed-race body was held
up as the ultimate erasure of racism and the blendings of musical forms that
make up Nortec as evidence of the arrival of this utopian space of transnational
multiculturalism. And, the media held up the *Exit 2002* music festival in Novi
Sad as the postethnic event that would unite Serbians, Bosnians, and Croats as
well as leading the way to the founding of a democratic political platform. Inside
the academy, there are cultural studies scholars who celebrate a side-effect of
capitalist globalization in the like-identification of racial/cultural/social hybrid
spaces that resist, intervene, and reform oppressive living conditions of the

disenfranchised. In *Magical Urbanism,* for example, Mike Davis writes that 'Tijuaneses are consummate bricoleurs who have built a culturally vibrant metropolis from the bottom up, largely using recycled materials from the other side of the border.'

However, as this so-called borderless world emerges, it is increasingly clear that its reality is limited to the world of profiteering politicians and corporate finance. *Time*'s celebration of Nortec as an example of living in a harmoniously hybrid border reality covers over how it is tied into a US and Mexican government and media rhetoric that applauds the North Atlantic Free Trade Agreement (NAFTA) (the Mexican government sponsored a five day conference titled 'Nortec 2000'), that continues to pass laws denying access to health care, education, and right to representation to the working classes that are forced by economic necessity to traverse the proverbial Tortilla Curtain. Such propagandistic maneuvers are not the only veneer that covers over the way capital fetishizes the disenfranchised. Media advertising—as with those images of Latinos on the border wearing CAT clothing and footwear—creates a Nu Latino Chic image to sell its $150 pair of sneakers and a $300 heavy cotton, proletariat identified fashion ensemble. Few from el otro lado—economically strangled by the International Monetary Fund—can afford such a CAT outfit.

This imagery serves the purpose of hiding the material circumstances in which Nu Latino Chic fashion is produced by capital for a middle-class consumer. For every CAT outfit sold in the United States, there's a maquiladora (US-owned factories pepper the border where working conditions go unregulated) full of workers who are exploited (many are maimed and suffer from malnutrition) and who make $3 a day. And we need to be mindful not only of advertising and the media, but also of the difference between cultural studies theories that talk of borderland 'audiotopias' and transfrontera 'rhythmic cartographies' in their celebration of hybridity and borderless worlds, and the often less emancipatory reality of living within a material, borderland reality.

We also need to be mindful of those politicians who talk of borderless worlds when, as we've seen in the forming of the European Union, this has simply been another way for the bourgeoisie systematically to take away the rights of the working classes. In France, Germany, and Britain, immigration legislation allow politicians (so-called left and right) to control who and what crosses borders (invisible or otherwise): quotas determine how many Moroccans and Algerians can work and live in France, Muslim Gastarbeiters in German, and South Asians and Afro-Caribbeans in Britain.

Indeed, late capitalism has done little to emancipate peoples worldwide. It has led to severe polarizations of class and the massive pauperizing of the proletariat globally. And where there are nation-states that have become borderless—Somalia and the former Yugoslavia, for example—there exists the most denigrated form of capitalism: horrific tyranny over working-class populations. So, while the internet might prove a useful tool for bringing education to those forced to inhabit a homeless state, when a bracero working in California's central valley earns $25 dollars a day, promises of a transnational democratization are more than far fetched.

No musicfest or youth subculture has altered radically the bourgeoisie's exploitation of the working class. Musicians and producers of music want to sell their music; they want people to listen then buy their music. So perhaps we should think twice about identifying Talvin Singh as an 'organic intellectual' who samples Bhangra beats in his Indian-brand of techno/trance to emancipate his hybrid South Asian subject; we should think twice whether Chuck D's 'fight the power' lyric will instill revolution. Perhaps both are simply music. That is, their authors are simply inventing different musical compositions for consumption: one breaks a rhythm by cutting and mixing a Bhangra soundscape to enliven and revitalize its dominant ambient beat and the other repeats a catchy lyric for mnemonic effect.

It's even more dangerous to romanticize disenfranchised groups and their subcultural expressions (music or otherwise) as resistant to dominant paradigms when they feed into globally organized lumpenproletariat underworlds that exercise power to ensure profit margins through violence and exploitation (prostitution, drug peddling, smuggling, and so on). One must be careful not to overstate the power of subcultures—music-based or otherwise—to resist dominant ideologies when much of what takes place here is antithetical to class struggles worldwide.

So our continuing dependence on private capitalist production and distribution trends will restrict to the Haves the capacity to move and to consume across borders. While maquiladora workers can only dream of crossing the border for better paid jobs, US middle-classers can purchase a border 'look' and luxuriate in fantasies of border crossing. Existence within a borderless world seems to be a reality only for the upper and highest segments of the middle class. Waif models from Brazil can catwalk Ché Guevara T-shirts to symbolize a borderless world market, but when Cubans and Mexicans seek political and/or economic refuge in the United States the borders stand strong. Only capital can jump borders; the real people who lie behind capital's fetishes are trapped. In this case, theorists of music might be mindful of the distinction between music, language, and material reality.

Often the counter-hegemonic methodologies theorized by postcolonial and cultural studies critics differ from the methods used to accomplish social change in reality. Certainly, a shared history of colonialism and capital globalization increasingly equates experiences of marginal groups in Los Angeles to those of marginal groups in the San Ysidro/Tijuana borderland. And US ethnic scholars see a similarly North/South American fusion when identifying cultural borderlands. However, this theorizing of a borderless world out there is a problematic abstraction. The destruction of nation-states such as Yugoslavia has given way to the mass-murder of entire populations, and to barbarism. Beyond Europe is a whole continent—Africa—that is being destroyed by the assaults against the nation-states. And when theories such as those of transfrontera 'rhythmic cartographies' and resistant musico-aesthetic epistemologies circulate outside the academy, they risk being used to primitivize and then justify the exploitation and/or genocide of subaltern peoples.

Finally, then, music, music festivals, youth and/or race identified subcultures should not be confused with the real acts that have en masse a 'real' power to destabalize a 'real' colonial/capitalist national power structure. In the case of the music festivals in the Balkans or Baltic states, for example, or Nortec performances on the Tijuana/San Ysidro border, the gathering of young people dancing to techno beats does not exist outside of a parasitic capitalist and Mafia-styled exploitive socioeconomic paradigm that is financed by the European and American governments with European and American tax payer money. Real social progress and reform will only take place when we turn directly toward real politics and make real attempts to organize in the hundreds of thousands to fight for certain basic democratic rights such as equal access to education and the right to representation for all. It will never happen in the often utopian, armchair media and academic formulations rampant today.

24
Securing Profits

Carrie A. Rentschler

A man is not born to run away.
Former US Supreme Court Justice Oliver Wendell Holmes,
in a letter to his friend, political scientist Harold Laski, 1921

In the spring of 1999 I posed as an undergraduate student to visit Melrose Place apartments, a newly developed apartment complex that caters to the University of Illinois student population in Champaign, Illinois. I indicated during my visit that I was concerned about my safety, and that I wanted to learn all about their security protocols. What I learned was very interesting indeed.

I was first treated to a video on Melrose Place apartments, not just the building but also the Florida-based corporation of the same name that built it. The company only builds complexes in mid-size college towns around large universities. The company caters to undergraduates who live away from home and who want to avoid the dormitories. It provides computer rooms, workout facilities and a swimming pool, and large lush lounges with big screen TVs, over-stuffed couches and fireplaces. Residents are essentially offered a luxurious private dorm at a cost of no less than $500 per month. Each resident shares an apartment with either one or three other roommates; the least expensive arrangement costs over $500 per month per tenant.

What makes Melrose Place unique is not only its advertised attention to issues of personal safety for prospective renters, but also the technical systemization of security on its premises. Each apartment comes equipped with a burglar alarm. Each individual bedroom is then wired with panic alarms, which connect the alarm-pusher directly with Melrose's contracted security response company. The resident then receives a call from the contractor to rule out a false alarm before they make a call to the Champaign police department. I was assured the police would arrive within four minutes if I should push the panic alarm. This is a remarkably good response time for the neighborhood in which Melrose Place is located: the 'black' part of town, north of 'the tracks.' The security mentality at Melrose Place apartments no doubt stems from white racist fears about the residents of north Champaign. Each apartment's television hook-up directly connects to the closed circuit television (CCTV) security system located at the gated entrance to the apartment properties, each apartment building entrance, and throughout the main facilities building. At any time, residents can 'tune in' to watch the security cameras that survey the apartment complex properties.

Melrose Place, like many other gated communities around the United States, is literally wired for security. Yet these places are not just new instances of Big Brother peering in on our privacy. Melrose Place is most significant as a site where consumers can learn to experience security as just another household service. Security systems are now available to consumers bundled with direct broadcast cable service (DBS) and telecommunication services. And while studies carried out by security industry analysts say most consumers don't particularly care whether or not their security systems come combined. with their telecommunication and cable service, more and more home-based security becomes available in combination with other telecommunication services.

This service bundling suggests something beyond just getting one's residence wired for internet, long-distance, cable, and home security all at once. It suggests something bigger and much more difficult for us to perceive: the consolidation of security industries with telecommunication industries and the subsequent centralization of the security industry. Consolidation has radically increased the profitmaking potential of security industries and their partners in telecommunications. In 1990, private security (mostly private guard services) was a $4.5 billion industry, with an annual growth rate of 12 per cent (Hallstead Report II, 1991). In 1992, detective agencies and protective service industries (private guards, armored car service, telephone answering services, security system services) had revenues of $12 billion. Security system services alone generated $3.4 billion in revenue; guard services a whopping $7.3 billion. The 1999 *Security Distributing and Marketing*'s 'Industry Forecast' pegged total revenue of dealer and installer security firms at $15.25 billion for 1998, up from $14 billion in 1997. Another security industry trade journal, *Security* magazine, estimated that the total US private security market (including government and corporate spending) amounted to $88 billion in 1998.

Immediately after the terrorist attacks of September 11, 2001, while the stock market lay in shambles, security companies and major defense contractors saw huge increases in their stock values: some doubled, some tripled. Market analysts forecasted annual security sales of $100 billion. In 2002, financial analysts readily doled out advice about which security companies to invest in. Such companies were a 'sure bet' in uncertain times. Yet in just one year after the September 11 attacks, corporations looking for a way to trim their budgets reneged on their security upgrade plans. Expected sales on security systems and technology dropped to $70 billion. Security is all about protecting profits, so when the economy goes sour, so does the supposed need for security.

The profitmaking potential in security, then, depends upon a certain level of financial stability in the corporate world. More generally, it requires corporations and household consumers to perceive that they are at risk for personal and property crimes. Security industry trade journals consistently report stories with themes such as 'Fear of Crime Is Still Up!', which signal good news for the industry. The drastic increase in values of security stock post-September 11 in many ways mirrored news representations of public fear and anxiety. Even Senator Joe Biden, D-DE, recently complained to *Time* magazine that the women he met on the campaign trail during the fall of 2002 only wanted to talk about what he could do to protect their kids from terrorists. 'Soccer moms,' he said, 'are security moms now.'

Consumers' actual perceptions of fear can be described as feeling like they are likely to become a victim of violence or that their home has been targeted for invasion. However, such perceptions are not a necessary condition for the purchase of security systems, and this is especially true when security comes bundled with entertainment and network communication services. The Consumer Survey on Home Security, conducted by Protection One and the trade journal *Security Distributing and Marketing*, shows that the people most likely to fear home invasion are those who already own home security systems: 50 to 59-year-old white males. In the July 1998 issue of *Security Distributing and Marketing*, reported levels of fear among people who already own home security systems were equal to the levels reported by respondents who planned to buy a security system but had yet to purchase one. Buying security appears to be no guarantee against continued fear of crime if that fear already exists.

Individual consumers clearly have some concerns over their personal safety and the safety of their children and home electronics. In contrast, according to security executives, corporations tend to fear employee theft, property crime, and unauthorized access the most, followed by workplace violence, computer security, parking lot security, and burglary (in that order; *Security Distributing and Marketing*, January 1998). On university campuses, security executives rank their top 'risks' in a fashion similar to that of corporations: theft and burglaries top the list, followed by computer security, unauthorized access, alcohol and drug problems, and vandalism. Corporations and educational institutions alike address risks in ways that protect profits and property first, people second. But when the economy overall suffers, as it has been doing since before September 11 in the United States, corporations scale back their security spending. The safety of technology and information can easily be translated into profits, but when profits are already in the toilet, so goes that oh-so-important security spending.

Human safety, on the other hand, is mostly an issue of public image. Just look at the recent decision by the city of Palm Springs, California, to adopt CCTV police surveillance along its commercial corridor. Repeated attempts to adopt such technologies there prior to September 11 failed because residents were not keen to have their shopping privacy invaded and crime rates there are incredibly low. But now Palm Springs police scan the shopping areas because it apparently 'gives tourists a greater sense of security.' According to a managing director of Chubb Protective Services, businesses 'want to look safe. There's a growing need for companies to provide reassurance to their staff and customers and the easiest way to do that is by providing a well-dressed and courteous security officer. This is a highly visible sign that security concerns are being recognized and addressed.' 'Security' is often more image than substance, which makes it particularly profitable. For instance, the going wage rate for security guards is roughly $8.50 per hour, while homeowners spend more than $30 per month, and corporations much more, for alarm and security monitoring services.

Despite the current economic slump, security remains a profitable industry thanks in part to the 1996 US Telecommunications Act. This act greatly increased the industries' profitmaking potential because it enabled the convergence of telecommunication and security corporations. Convergence is the move toward providing telephone, long-distance, cable, security and on-line services from one provider. Ameritech, for instance, owns Security Link, the second largest security corporation in the United States, behind number one ranked ADT and ahead of number three ranked Protection One, each of which has been busy buying up other security firms. AT&T recently won a contract with ADT worth several million dollars to provide telecommunication services to the security company's operations. Most security companies are owned, partially owned, or in joint ventures with telecommunications giants.

While security companies affiliate themselves in more concentrated ways with telecommunication corporations, the security industry has also fractured. Many firms sell off accounts and use third party monitoring, for example Melrose Place apartments and their contract with an alarm monitoring service, because it is more profitable than keeping this service provision in-house. This practice is much like when media conglomerates sell off ownership of some subsidiaries when they are no longer profitable or no longer demonstrate the same growth potential. Conglomerates regularly buy profitable industries while they are profitable, and sell them off when they fail to meet profit expectations.

Where's all this profitability coming from? The majority of security business is in housing, and new housing generally comes wired with security systems. The surging growth in multifamily and upscale housing, such as Melrose Place apartments, provides a ready-made market for the security industry. Thirty-five per cent of the alarm and surveillance security market is in upscale housing markets, and another 25 per cent is in middle-income housing markets. In 1999, a typical home alarm system came at a significant cost: $2,000 to install and another $31 per month to monitor. The most rapid growth in the security market, however, is in the corporate sector. More and more, corporate America farms out its security operations to private security companies, a particularly lucrative market for the security industry.

The security industry also benefits from military downsizing. As military technology becomes declassified and enters the civilian market, security industries can provide services to schools, homes, corporations, and law enforcement that are enhanced with military technology. In the last ten years, several military technologies entered the consumer-based security market. Thanks to groups like the American Defense Preparedness Association, defense contractors can easily make contact with law enforcement and civilian consumer markets to create demand for, and thereby expand the markets for, security technologies. In 1999, for instance, Michigan schools experimented with Department of Defense software that analyzes weak points in security systems. One Las Vegas school has even considered the installation of night vision cameras in its parking lots.

It's pretty clear that fear of crime, and more importantly, the social causes of crime and violence, do not go away because of security systems and monitoring services. Buying security does, however, guarantee the continued fear of crime. Security creates its own demand. Once you have security, the idea that you *need* it is reinforced. It's a bit like upgrading your cable TV service to digital cable with one of those 'it's free for three months' offers; once you have it, it sure is easy to feel like you need it. This is exactly what security industries invest in. They see security as another service they can provide to customers based upon their institutional commitment to increase fear of crime. Today we are hawked all sorts of products in the name of security 'musts,' including duct tape and plastic sheeting thanks to an off-the-cuff remark by Homeland Security Director Tom Ridge. We may not have been born to run away from fear, but we certainly weren't meant to feel fear simply to secure profits for others.

FURTHER READING

Blakely, Edward, and Mary Gail Snyder, *Fortress America: Gated Communities in the United States*, Washington, D.C.: Brookings Institution Press, 1999.

Cunningham, William, John Strauchs, and Clifford Van Meter, *Private Security Trends 1970–2000: The Hallstead Report II*, Boston: Butterworth-Heinemann, 1990.

Klein, Joe, 'How Soccer Moms Became Security Moms,' *Time*, February 17, 2002, 23.

O'Toole, Patrick, 'The Importance of Being Number One,' *Security Distributing and Marketing*, November 1997, 25, 40–2.

Stepanek, Laura, 'Peace of Mind, Piece of Revenue,' *Security Distributing and Marketing*, July 1998, 74–6.

Zalud, Bill, 'Whose Advantage?' *Security Distributing and Marketing*, January 1998, 68–73.

25
Dangerous Bodies: Globalization, the Militarization of Borders, and New (Old) Forms of Slavery

Arturo J. Aldama

> On the eve of the twenty first century, hatreds explode in such places as sarajevo, argentina, chechnya, rwanda, los angeles, and oklahoma city. The hatred embodies a complex set of fears about difference and otherness. It reveals what some people fear in themselves, their own 'differences.' Hatred forms around the unknown, the difference of 'others.' ... Because people grow othered by their racialized, sexualized and engendered bodies, bodies are important to the writing of hatred on history. (21)
>
> Zilah Eisenstein, *Hatreds* (1996)

When bodies feel sudden fear, the adrenaline curve in the nervous system spikes in the first millisecond, provoking a fight or flight response with varying intensities in the physiology of individual subjects. Unlike the spontaneity of an individual lashing out, pushing off and/or running away fast, or the collective adrenaline surges of crowds in protests (for example, the WTO protests in Seattle and the G-8 demonstrations in Italy), the sustained proliferation and normalization of fear in the 'nervous system' of the body politic has different effects. The propagation and internalization of fear in the social body attempts to keep people docile, numb, silent, and afraid to challenge the status quo of racist, sexist, and capitalist order in the United States and Euro-Western nation-states.

Fear of unconformity, fear of race, fear of disease, fear of touch, fear of blood, fear of non-straight sex, fear of workers, fear of desire, fear of women, fear of subaltern rage, fear of color, fear of desire, fear of crime, fear of 'illegals,' and the fear of uprising: 'fear' is both the metanarrative that drives the disciplinary apparatus of the nation-state—the police, the military, immigration authorities, and schools—and the intended effects on the body politic. Fear drives the repression, containment, cooptation, torture, and annihilation of 'unruly' subjects whose class, race, sex, ideology identity differences, and indigenous land claims (for example) are threats to bourgeois, capitalist, patriarchal, and neocolonial orders. Fear drives the militarization of borders, antigay violence, abortion clinic bombers, the CIA, the NSA, xenophobia, the denial of imperial guilt, enslavement, lynchings, police, the Christian right, John McCain and Pat Buchanan's 2000 presidential campaigns, antiaffirmative action policies, California's Prop. 187, racial profiling, and *migra* shootings, to name a few.

DESIRE AND THE EROTICS OF FEAR

In patriarchal family systems that mimic or are bourgeois, young women are taught to fear their desire and feel shame at their bodies while at the same time seeking the 'validating' gaze of 'appropriate' young men. Men are taught to be fearless in their pursuit of desire. The rescue of desire by those seen as objects of desire invokes a desire that does not have to colonize and subjugate bodies to controllable fantasies of seduction, redemption, and disavowal.

In the horrific spectacles of racial lynching, castrated, limp bodies of black/brown men evidence the 'blood erotics' of racial fear—the eugenic purity of the inheritors of America must be protected at all costs. As the antimiscegenation laws of colonial America attest, children produced through rape of women of color, on the other hand, meant an increase in slave stock, a profitable investment. The fear that African, indigenous, and Mexican women were being raped and violated with impunity and without any recourse does not count: it was irrelevant to the operation of white patriarchal power in colonial America. In the case of the colonial genocide of native peoples, Louis Owens (1998) comments on, 'the erotic nature of Euroamerica's desire to simultaneously possess and destroy the Indian,' and argues that, '[it] is nothing less than the indigenous relationship with place, with the invaded and stolen earth, that the colonizer desires.'

FEAR, THE STATE AND RACE

In thinking about 'state' violence toward 'others' on the cusp of twenty-first century—police shootings and beatings of suspected 'illegals,' 'gang-bangers,' an African-American woman shot while asleep in her car, or Mario Paz, a Mexican grandfather asleep and gunned down in his home—'officers of the law' justify their actions with fear. In arrest reports where lethal violence is used, it is common to see the following cited: 'I thought the suspect had a gun' ... 'I saw him reach in his pocket/her purse' ... 'He/she ran away.' In these scenarios, the 'sudden movements' that fear in the 'suspects' produces (an understandable physiological response) are justifications for the exterminating fear of the 'officers.' When officers prove 'fear' of bodily harm on their persons by a suspect, usually by word of mouth and the corroboration by other officers who fear the consequences of challenging the blue wall of silence, then they have a 'clean' shoot, another justified homicide.

In 'The Scriptural Economy' (*The Practice of Everyday Life*, 1974), Michel de Certeau reminds us that, 'There is no law that is not inscribed on bodies. Every law has a hold on the body.' For de Certeau, in 'order for the law to be written on bodies, an apparatus is required' whose tools or instruments of inscription 'range from the policeman's billycub to handcuffs and the box reserved for the accused in the courtroom.' So for those who are criminalized and racialized by dominant bourgeois discourses, their bullet-ridden, handcuffed, kicked, stun-gunned, and baton beat bodies become semiotic generators of fear for subaltern communities in the United States. At the same time, these desecrated bodies serve to appease 'middle-class' panic about the surging of crime of color.

The officers that lead the US-backed death squads of Guatemala and El Salvador are trained in the science of 'torture' (the official term is 'counter-insurgency') at the School of the Americas in Fort Benning, Georgia. These officers are trained to recognize the smell of fear in the subjects that they beat and mutilate as evidence that they are on the verge of being 'broken.' The raped and mutilated bodies of 'suspected' guerrillas are always tossed in shantytowns and busy streets as 'warnings' to spread fear.

The intended effects of these fear-driven desecrations of subaltern bodies echo the flayed and torched bodies of women, Jews, and other 'heretics' of the Holy Inquisition; the decapitated heads of 'criminals' to the queen and the king in Medieval Europe; the severed heads of revolutionary leaders of Mexican independence from Spain in 1810; and the pickling of Joaquin Murieta's head during the California Goldrush of 1850 for daring to confront the growing racial hegemony. These historical spectacles of hegemonic terror put into practice a psychic campaign whose purpose is to spread fear of insurgency to enslaved and oppressed communities: 'How dare you ... Look at the consequences ... This could be you.'

However, at the dawn of the twenty-first century, these spectacles of terror, where 'real criminals get what they deserve,' are now televised in such reality programs as *COPS* and *LAPD: Life on the Beat* and *America's Most Wanted*, further creating a voyeuristic approval between the use of technologically sophisticated disciplinary violence, race, and class. Sloppily panned shots of the run down 'white trash' trailer parks, Spanish speaking families in over-crowded one bedroom apartments, single mother welfare families in the 'projects,' unkempt children, the 'beeping' of profanities, and a general visual tone of squalor are meant to cement the semiological seal between poverty, race, and crime. Close-up shots of tattoos on the hands, arms, legs, necks, and backs of Chicanas/os who are hog tied and face down on the pavement give officers on the *COPS* show the opportunity to narrate directly to camera, 'Just as I suspected ... another gang member.' These 'signs' of criminality on subjects already criminalized as thugs and *cholas/os* provoke further the significatory practices of the law, and its multiphase violating apparatus. On the cusp of the twenty-first century the paranoia of the racialized panoptic regime in the United States is directed inwards on the 'domestic' terrorists of inner cities (gang-bangers) and at the edges of the US/Mexico border—to survey and contain what Pat Buchanan calls, 'the invading Mexican hordes,' and now to all those suspected as being 'terrorists.'

As we enter this new millennium, Western nation-states attempt to seduce subject citizens into believing that we live in a borderless cyber-utopia, a cosmopolitan free market of e-commerce, and anonymity. The cyber-consumers and fantasists in the 'fearless' cyber-world continue the 'false' magic of global capitalism, marking further the distance between elite consumers and hyper-exploited producers of goods. The simulacrum of e-commerce masks the multidirectional movements of 'free market' manifest destiny and depends on the learned fetishes for material commodities. You add to your 'shopping cart' the latest and best commodity fetish—DVDs, digital zoom-cams, and $49.99 Gap khakis. However, we must ask: who makes them and under what conditions? What happens to the eco-systems strip-mined, clear-cut, and irradiated by toxic waste? What happens to workers' children who drink water contaminated by unregulated industrial waste produced by the maquiladoras on the US/Mexico border? What happens to the young women in El Salvador, Honduras, and the Philippines who are fired, beaten, raped, and disappeared for protesting the horrific work conditions of 'free trade' zone factories such as the Gap, Old Navy, and Nike? What happens to the 'software' producing ghettoes of south India? What happens to social responsibility, to the hyper-exploitation of subaltern workers, mainly women and children? Do they disappear with a click of a mouse? The 'fearlessness' of cyber-wealth is the fruition of the phantasmagoria of the 'free market' whose violence of predatory capitalism is deadly.

The global proliferation of neocolonial predatory capitalism and its accompanying panoptic regime requires one to be politically creative and self-reflexive in our privileges, margins, and differences (race, nationalities, class, gender, and sexuality), to our cultural assumptions, and our epistemologies. To resist the violence of predatory capitalism, we must learn to forge transnational and transethnic opposition coalitions that are fluid, multilevel, and sustained without becoming autocratic. Confronting 'our' fears that alienation and neocolonialism produce will allow us to enter into new collective adrenaline surges of local and global political resistance.

Do you fear, 'Fear?' I do!

26
The Race to Be Mobile

Kevin Carollo

In summer and fall of 1996, French television broadcast the expulsion of the 'sans-papiers' (the 'without papers') from Paris. It was widely understood that this media affair was solely and specifically targeted at black Africans. The white immigrant workers in France are apparently a separate issue. I was in Senegal when French telejournalists interviewed the dispossessed, displayed protests and hunger strikes, and spoke to administrators who called for a more organized, lawful approach to immigration. Senegalese TV is basically French TV: in 1996, when I was in Senegal, there was only one regularly transmitting local channel. Because of this, I found myself trying to assess how Senegalese people were watching this assertion of colonial power against African migrant workers.

They didn't like it. People did not need to be personally acquainted with any deportees in order to identify with the plight of the sans-papiers in Paris. The representation of race on European television was an act of peculiar proportions. In Senegal, I rarely had the feeling that people spoke in collective terms that extended beyond local boundaries of culture, geography, and perhaps nation. In general, international identities seemed to form around religion before race.

The 1996 transmissions from France, however, allowed the French to assert their Frenchness, and also unified Africans as (once again) the oppressed. But it's a classy affair. Race in Africa these days, I surmised, often seems more driven by economic mobility than by naturalized notions of ethnic coherence. Racial unity arises when a particular group cannot freely go where others have gone before. The display of expulsion on TV uneasily equated having no papers as having no humanity. In other words, Africans with access to television experienced a collective othering, though it happened far away on another continent.

Pan-African unity and postcolonial subversion are both present in this appraisal of the French clampdown. Africans unite to decry the injustices perpetrated on their brothers and sisters abroad. In so doing, they fracture the colonial powers of representation that seek to defuse racial issues by couching them in legal, bureaucratic terms. However, this media representation should also remind us of the current economic impetus to maintain mobility in the world of globalized labor. We must consider some of the reasons why so many

Africans wish to remain on European and American soil, and why expulsion becomes an issue precisely when the immigration department looks at the urban poor.

In general, postcolonial theory and Pan-Africanism have endeavored to explain the effect of migration on diasporic peoples via different hermeneutic routes. Contemporary postcolonial theory concerns itself with ruptures, hybridity, and sites of ambivalence. Generally, this type of critique tries to assert that something (choose your something) which does not quite fit into a category can rupture or subvert that category. Pan-Africanism, on the other hand, strives to link up dispersed groups of people across ruptures of space, time, nation, and language.

A central problem of postcolonial theory is its tendency to find subversion everywhere. After all, as all categories are crude approximations of the diversity within, something within will inevitably rub the category the wrong way. A central problem of Pan-Africanism is its tendency to find African commonality everywhere. Although essentialist notions of identity have been thoroughly critiqued, classicists and others have begun to acknowledge Africa's debt to their disciplines and Westerners now benevolently understand that 'our' American standard of living is higher than 'theirs.' Yet in spite of these three evolving truisms, Africa remains a place usually referred to in terms of race. Class inequalities within Africa are often assumed to be either unilateral ('that other level of subsistence'), or unimportant when discussing what really keeps blacks together. When we in America discuss Africa, race is perceived as something people may either believe to be self-evident, or rely on as a substantial indicator of commonality.

The appeal of race as a determining factor of identity cannot be hastily dismissed. Rather than wondering how we might move beyond this tendency (a postcolonial problematic), we are better equipped to complicate the notion of race as an inherited given, as something to claim without effort. What does this mean for those Pan-Africanist visions of a home within racial identity? It may frustrate the assumption of commonality between the lived situation of black Americans and that of the people on the other side of the Atlantic. To be sure, some African Americans might assume that the ways in which they differ from Africans do not really make a difference. Because most Americans do not usually encounter many Africans in their daily lives, it remains relatively easy to deny that 'there is no going home.' A good history lesson on contemporary Africa helps to complicate these assumptions of commonality without denying the need to belong. People from diverse global locations can easily gain a deeper understanding of sociopolitical situations within Africa, and that is the critical point in which the assumption of race as a grounds of comparison must be checked.

On the other side of the Atlantic, many people desire to adventure to first worlds unknown. This wanderlust is directed by economic angst, not by currents of race. Because 'everyone is rich' in America, some youths in Africa find it difficult to critique the image of the United States as the pinnacle of cool. In this sense, the linguistic subversion contained in literary texts written by Africans in colonizer languages, or the critical acceptance of Africa's hybridity, has little to say to customs officials and the dearth of job opportunities in parts of postcolonial Africa. America looks particularly appealing to those coming of age across the Atlantic. We in America may well wonder if our conceptions of Pan-Africanism presume too much racial commonality to address global class inequalities.

A month in Dakar convinced me of the need to complicate assertions of postcolonial subversion. I had many conversations with male Senegalese youths, all of whom constantly dreamed of leaving their families and homeland to get rich in America (young women in Dakar, for the most part, appeared less interested in leaving). A father with a decent job told me that if 'they' would only bring development to Senegal, hardly anyone would desire to leave. This seemed true enough, although for the moment the desire for work remained inseparable from the emotional investment in America as cool. It was hard for me to hear people proclaim that full-scale acceptance of Western industrial practices was the solution to familial separation and cultural fragmentation.

But who could blame the youth of Dakar? If people have to go where the money is to feel like an active part of humanity, then the Senegalese will maintain a more coherent sense of community if money comes to where the community already resides. Understand the conflicting senses of exile in this 'should I stay or should I go' predicament: either a) you are exiled from family and friends in search of prosperity in the first world, or b) you stay at home feeling exiled from the imagined benefits a place in the hip world economy would grant you.

In general, the young Senegalese guys I talked to about their American dreams were not all that interested in the savage inequalities America perpetrates at home between peoples. Most of them quietly disagreed with me when I tried to acknowledge my native country's hypocrisy, because many of them had brothers who had 'made it' in Europe or the United States. In addition, my rather low annual income (by American standards) would have left them unconvinced, as the fact of my visit to Africa in some vital way proved my affluence. The power to visit a foreign country and continent is proof of being well off. Even if I had not been white, there would have been no denying my relative wealth and privilege. Of course, you do not have to leave the United States to find people who literally and figuratively do not have the power to go anywhere. But literally and figuratively 'going somewhere' in Senegal is an altogether different experience than in America.

It was striking to me how the reciprocal desires for mobility and wealth fuel one another in Senegal. I often felt that while I gave people hope that they might visit me in the United States (in order to find work), I also confirmed their lack of mobility. The reasons for the Senegalese youths' interest in me were unsettling; they were contingent on my arbitrary birthplace and all that it signifies.

Despite the large-scale dispersal of American corporations into multinational sites of cheap labor, we still find America at the center of production. The use of Africa, via Pan-Africanism, or postcoloniality in theoretical discussions of capitalist exploitation is often inaccurate. Racial politics and their subversion both exist in Africa, but like mobility, they manifest themselves differently from country to country, and from group to group. In addition, the ability to classify and specify seems frustratingly unimportant at times. It is certainly unimportant to an acquaintance of mine in Senegal, who woke me up early one morning in February of 1997 to accept his collect call. He was wondering if I had succeeded in taking the necessary steps for him to come to America. I hadn't, but I had been trying. The rare human voice at Immigration and Naturalization Services always tells me to order the forms by calling a certain number. The recorded voice at that number says they are too busy, and that I should call back.

At the time of writing it has been six years since I traveled outside the United States. I find myself astonished that media attention was given to the plight of immigrant workers in 1996. Maybe France's old world approach to global politics means they actually feel compelled to give attention to the newsworthy issues of race and mobility? Of course, on either side of the Atlantic, the issue is rather black and white. Immigration is primarily important for presidential elections across Europe and America; witness media coverage of France's support for Jean-Marie Le Pen and other National Front candidates. But it is always a surprise to see any national coverage of immigrant workers in America after the platforms have been folded up and stored for four more years.

Behind the back-page fanfare of clandestine detentions and the Patriot Act, the Immigration and Naturalization Service (now assimilated into the Department of Homeland Security) still has a Green Card Lottery each year in which they raffle off 55,000 permanent resident visas. They currently have around 20,000 people detained on any given day of the year, three times as many since 1996. The US Border Patrol has swelled to 8,000, double the 1993 total. The mobility-privileged are afraid to go abroad in a post-9/11 world of 'us' and 'terrorists,' while the migrant poor of the world strive to make a living outside their native countries.

Estimates suggest that there may be as many as 5 million Africans living in France. As bureaucracy struggles to tighten legal reins, immigrants may become more harried, but they will not be deterred. The deportations continue, as do the sans-papiers protests. Air France, the same airline that flew me to and from

Senegal, has recently taken over the European deportation business from KLM. Immigrants periodically die while being forcefully deported. For example, Ricardo Barrientos of Argentina, age 52, died on December 30, 2002. On January 16, 2003, Mariame Getu Hagos of Somalia, age 25, was deported despite claiming that he was too sick to travel. He died in the hospital two days later. The list of deceased since 1998 includes people from Nigeria, Palestine, Sudan, and Cameroon. After a broken arm and a beating, a woman from Togo who resisted her deportation was told by an Air France pilot that 'we will bring you back to your jungle.' Such are the stories of the borderlands. Makes me want to take the first ticket out of here. But the question remains for us all: to where?

Part V

The Personal Is the Political

INTRODUCTION

From its earliest days, *Bad Subjects* has made room for writing that is unapologetically personal, even as it strives for political relevance. To be sure, this has caused us to fall into disfavor with people who still adhere to the tenets of the old left, for whom the privilege of using the first person singular always comes at the expense of the first person plural. But this is a price we are willing to pay. We are informed by the more useful insights of poststructuralism and influenced, probably more than we realize, by the positive aspects of American individualism—exemplified in our low-budget, do-it-yourself approach to the publishing. Our political task is not to transcend the individual, but to make the individual both recognize and feel a connection to the pluralities of which she or he is inevitably a part.

The essays in this section are connected by their authors' narration of family histories and their reflections on how those histories have affected their political awareness. Tomás F. Sandoval's essay opens the section by describing his development of a politicized sense of ethnic identity in college, and why he has since chosen to identify himself as a Chicano. He then tells how, as a graduate instructor, he learned to teach his own process of self-discovery to his students. In a politicized, autobiographical article about her sexual experiences, Kim Nicolini explores how communities devoted to alternative gender and sexual identities are not always welcoming and can contain internal hierarchies that can be just as exclusive as the dominant societal paradigms. Nicolini's experience of negotiating her sexual identity with social acceptance has powerfully marked her emergence from an abusive family.

Viet Thanh Nguyen's family was torn apart by the Vietnam war. His essay describes his family's experiences and their resulting antagonisms toward Marxism, and contrasts that story with his own developing appreciation of the power of Marxism as social critique. The result powerfully reincarnates the immigrant's tale of generational conflict within the framework of ideological point and counterpoint. Nguyen's piece makes us realize, with an intensity few scholars' work can match, just how difficult it is for someone who has suffered the effects of 'actually existing socialism' to develop and sustain a leftist politics.

The tale of rape and response told by Cynthia Hoffman in the next essay challenges many conventional assumptions about the therapeutic role of the law in assisting sexual assault victims. Hoffman argues for a distinction between rape laws and reporting laws, particularly when the reporting law makes it impossible to get state funded medical or therapeutic care unless the victim complies with legal strictures with which she may not agree. Inevitably, Hoffman discovers she has been raped not only by an individual but also by the state.

Zach Furness relays the spectacular experience of having had a father who was a sports star who appeared regularly on television. As defensive end for the Pittsburgh Steelers American football team, Zach's father was regularly recreated as a television persona. Furness shows how the conflict between real-life parents and their idealized counterparts on television became painfully literal for him, as he had to triangulate between 'TV dad' and the dad of his lived experience to find his 'real' father.

27

On the Merits of Racial Identity

Tomás F. Sandoval, Jr.

Teaching at a university, I work with students at a crucial point in their intellectual lives. At a time when their identity is beginning to take concrete and passionate shape, they may encounter me in a lecture dealing with the intersections of race, gender, and class. I hope they learn to think critically of the world around them and to strive for an intellectual position that questions the simplistic notions that dominate this world. Especially concerning race, I teach them that it is all too easy for us to fall into the essentialist constructs of past generations and further impede their well-intentioned goal: progress for all people of color.

What I learn is something even more profound. My students often remind me that you can't overlook the obvious in your quest for intellectual growth, even if it is a little limiting. Sometimes we can acquire a strength to be used for a greater good if we learn to understand race in ways that go beyond or even contradict the skills we develop as scholars. Ultimately, there is still a difference between the 'real' world and the intellectual one. What makes sense in one doesn't always make sense in the other. No matter what intellectual constructs we devise, however persuasive and sensible they may seem when applied to observations about the world outside the university, people living in that world continue to hold fast to their own belief systems.

In a race-conscious world, this is still true today. Scholars increasingly agree in their criticisms of essentialist identity politics. The notion that people must conform to certain political ideals and maintain some cultural ideal while being 'true to their race' is simplistic when considered within a complex understanding of how 'race' itself is a social construct. But the experiences of many of my students suggest that sometimes it is good to be too simplistic. Often, their experiences suggest a need for simplicity for the purpose it serves. My own story may serve to illustrate.

I am a Chicano. The second of three children born to two second-generation Americans, I grew up in a typical Los Angeles suburb of tract housing and strip malls. Perhaps not so typically, people of my ethnicity all but dominated the landscape; we always seemed to be surrounded by people of Mexican descent. In the greater La Puente area of the 1980s I lived in a diverse area marked by a Mexican majority.

Then, in 1990, I began my undergraduate career at a small, liberal arts college in Claremont, California. While only about 15 miles east of my hometown, Claremont seemed an entirely different planet. Despite the difference, it took me no time to acculturate myself to the well-planned cleanliness of quaint Claremont. The population of my microcosm within the town was quite another adjustment. For you see, at Claremont McKenna College I became part of a small Mexican minority in a primarily wealthy, Anglo student population.

That's when I became a 'Chicano'; when my ethnicity assumed a more developed, precise, political, and personal meaning. The name 'Chicano' became the term that I, like the politicized generation of Mexican Americans before me, chose to reflect that change. Before that, I was most often 'Mexican.' At times we were 'Mexican Americans,' some were even 'Hispanics,' but the terms rarely served to describe more than our historical nationality and, at times, level of acculturation. Of course, those qualities have a very real political aspect. The difference was that when we used one of them to describe ourselves, we didn't necessarily mean to argue racial politics.

Beyond the label, we related to our ancestries in different ways. My Mexican-ness differed from that of my second-generation friends as it did from our racially mixed or immigrant colleagues. We were not cultural relativists. We lived in a world of cultural standards. In that world some were more Mexican than others. Sometimes being too Mexican or too American caused social anxiety. Still, we all shared some ambiguous connection to each other, perhaps best expressed through our cultural practices.

In Claremont, there were very few of 'us.' I found that my views in the classroom, or in the dining hall, produced a different effect than they had before I came to college. I, like my 20 or so other college mates, represented the 'Mexican view.' White students—many surprisingly never having had much contact with Mexicans—listened to our views not merely as another opinion but as the 'Mexican opinion.' In ways this inspired confidence in my own beliefs. Those beliefs were more than the product of books or family, they were also products of culture and other life experiences. By observing how others considered my views, I was able to grow in my understanding of what made me different from the students around me and what did not.

Even more striking, 'our' views were rarely desired. Whereas high school teachers made race a frequent issue in discussions, I now found that professors rarely included it except as some footnote or special case. How can we learn about the welfare system and not discuss the interplay of race with class? How can you understand civil rights and not portray the struggles of Mexican Americans in the 1960s and 1970s?

My professors didn't teach these things because they were not part of their experiences. While at Claremont I first appreciated the way societies can mask acknowledgment of the racial 'other' and, at the same time, portray a knowledge that is as singularly complete as any. I understood that most people approach the learning of the unknown through the gaze of what they do know. For people who never experienced strong emotions because of race or ethnicity, ignoring those in other aspects of their life was natural. That didn't mean their learning was flawed compared to mine, just different. So, what rang 'true' to the majority of students in a class seemed problematic to me because of my racial/ethnic past.

Feeling that many of my classes minimized a student of color perspective, I not only became more vocal, I also increasingly felt an obligation to represent 'my side' as accurately as possible. Unexpectedly, I felt a weight upon me realizing that I spoke for those whom I had never met, yet were tied to me by history. A once loose association with other Mexicans became a firmer and more political bond in an environment labeling our views as those of 'our people.' This circumstance naturally contributed to my developing cultural nationalism. By understanding how my views and experiences differed from others' I also learned more about who I was and where I came from. My ethnicity clashed with the world I encountered in Claremont. That world reduced it to a reflection of my 'race.' I quickly realized that politically, and personally, it was more advantageous to go with the flow.

I began to study Chicano history. If professors wouldn't include the information in class, I made a point to include it on my own. Every term paper became an opportunity to research the Chicano experience. A major preoccupation of mine became inserting the Chicano experience into every place I could, to both satisfy my quest for 'truth' and to complicate everyone else's.

Moving onward in my studies, I felt advantaged not only from the body of knowledge I accumulated on the Chicano experience but because I lived in a society that made me learn it in order to feel normal and content. I believed the world that ignored my 'race' was hardly race-blind. Instead, it was a white, upper-class standard; a highly racialized environment. By ignoring race altogether, the majority was failing to grasp the ways they themselves were racial beings.

These intellectual changes forged close bonds with other students of color at Claremont. We shared feelings of marginalization and the burden of being representative of our larger communities. We all also shared an experience of cultural withdrawal, missing what we had previously been used to on a daily basis. As these feelings met with the frustrations of higher education, some of our identities became more public as their expressions became more significant to our peace of mind and feelings of solidarity. In the process, ethnicity became political and, for some, essentialized.

That's how I became a Chicano. The label I now ascribe to my ethnicity suggested much more than culture to me and, I hoped, to others. It conveyed a historical consciousness, a strong sense of pride, and a commitment to assuring those qualities of my life would never be devalued. Furthermore, it said I shared the cause of political activists who first began using the title widely during the Chicano Movement of the 1960s and 1970s. By calling myself Chicano, I was telling the world who I was culturally and what that meant to me politically and professionally.

The meanings of my identity continued to evolve throughout my graduate career studying history at UC Berkeley. As before, the classroom helped to transform me but now it was doing so from my position as instructor. What I learned rested in the conflict between an intellectual understanding and an emotional one. My program taught critical analysis to challenge simplistic notions of the past. In the area of cultural history, this produced a revolution in my thinking. The more I learned in this new environment, the more intellectually sophisticated I felt. As I became more conscious of my political and cultural identity, I also became more aware of the ways my varied environments helped to construct it. I knew that there wasn't anything essential about being Mexican. The more I learned about Chicana/o history the more I saw the variety of experiences and cultures within my own community.

Once these beliefs took concrete shape in study, I wanted others to appreciate the complexity of some common assumptions we make about race in our society. When I stood before my students, I sought to lead them through my own intellectual journey by: complicating the meaning of 'Chicano'; suggesting we shouldn't have to conform to society's ideas about who we are, or the ones imposed upon us by our own communities; and emphasizing the formation of a multiracial, inclusive movement rather than a narrow, nationalistic one. In time, I sensed that my fervent desire to educate them came at the expense of respect for their own learning pathways. In my fourth semester as a Graduate Student Instructor I was hit with the realization that my students were going through what I did at Claremont. Instead of providing them a free space to develop, I robbed them of a crucial process so we could all start from the same place. I wanted to spare them my experiences, but I couldn't. Every person of color in this society will have to confront these emotions at sometime in their life. Society sees and acts through race. Eventually, we must all make sense of that in our lives.

For many, making sense of it means becoming culturally nationalistic. I'm not sure that in the long run cultural nationalism is the best solution for increasing social justice, but I can see how it might be necessary on two levels: as part of the process of becoming culturally (and politically) aware, and as a means of survival. Because our world works from simplistic beliefs about race and culture we need to make sense of our place from within those beliefs before we deconstruct them into oblivion.

Members of my family, living out in the world beyond academics, call themselves everything from Mexican to Hispanics. Happily, more and more of them are adopting the term Chicano or Chicana and with it, a dedication to social change. But no matter what we call ourselves, we, like all Mexicans in the United States, must come to some realization of how race continues to affect our American experiences. The conclusions we draw and the strategies we choose for survival may differ, but they will not be void of political significance.

And they should not be. To separate the two is to place oneself at a disadvantage. In my classes, I encourage strategic simplicity along with a critical appraisal of race. I do it for my students, so they can gain confidence in discovering themselves. I do it for class dialogue, so none of our discussions will ever serve the intellectual at the expense of the experiential. I do it for all of my students. When all of our pasts are told and appreciated, we can each learn more about ourselves.

When all is said and done, I do it for myself. I've learned that I can't separate my politics from my identity or my profession. The personal is political, and so is my profession as a scholar and teacher. The most important thing I've learned is that the process of development is an intimate part of my students' critical understandings of race. To analyze race we must understand it in all of its manifestations and, on some level, learn to accept why people situate themselves where they do.

28
Outside In:
the Failings of Alternative Communities

Kim Nicolini

SEX I AM

I've always been 'different,' been one of those people who never quite fits in and is therefore labeled as 'weird.' It started when I was a little kid and has persisted until today, when I am a middle-aged professional. My weirdness has been difficult to pinpoint and categorize and has led me through many attempts at trying to join a community and fit in, attempts that have consistently failed. What I've learned through my travels through alternative communities, especially those based on sex and gender, is that prejudices, ridiculous codes of behavior and fashion, and rigid re-enforcement of the status quo can be just as insidious and persistent as in mainstream society. My experiences with sex and gender-based alternative communities point to a huge problem in organized groups that need to classify people and put them in their place on the basis of who they are instead of what they want to do. They 'essentialize.' By talking about myself here, I hope to show the need for postessentialized communities that are more flexible in their classifications and more open to the many 'others' that populate our world.

I grew up in an abusive household. This is not the place for gut-wrenching melodramatic memoir. Nevertheless, being ritually abused in a middle-class suburb, where the neighbors could hear the fights, the crying, the beating, on a daily basis, automatically marked me as an 'outsider' in our tight-knit community. My friends' parents did not want their children in our house. Our house was a dangerous place; it was the evil 'other.' No Brady Bunch or Beaver Cleaver there. Just a huge tyrant of a man, a hell of a lot of alcohol, and three very scared kids.

That's what my home life was like. To spice up my life outside the home and to take control where I thought I could grab it, I became 'funny.' I was not the traditional girl. I wore my brothers' hand-me-downs, played in the mud and dirt, got in fist fights, talked a lot in class, pulled faces, and cracked jokes. I was the clown, the feisty fighter, the girl with a dirty mouth. For this reason, I fitted in nowhere. I wasn't a nerd. I wasn't the popular girlish girl. I was the one who was hard to pin down. The kids in my school didn't know what to do with me.

Still, I didn't seem to care. But when I became an adolescent all that changed. My gender started becoming more of an issue. My girlfriends tried to dress me up and put make-up on me, and the boys started identifying me as sexual. Suddenly I was referred to as 'the slut,' even though I was a stone cold virgin and had never even kissed a boy. In the tight-knit circles of suburban adolescents, definitions of what is 'normal' are quite narrow, and I didn't fit into any of them. I was a girl, but I was also loud, strong, and funny, and I didn't seem to care what people thought of the way I acted.

Communities cannot stand it unless everyone is labeled and in their proper place, so the only way my peers could define me was through sex. If I wasn't the traditional well-groomed and well-behaved girl, then I had to be a slut. Fine, I figured. If they want slut, I can show them slut. I didn't understand that my sexualization as a 'slut' was the effect of a larger problem, not the cause of the problem itself. I became obsessed with Bad Girl books: *Carrie*, *Go Ask Alice*, *The Exorcist*, and *The Happy Hooker*. All these books somehow equate girl sex with bad behavior, and they all had a strange allure to me. I started writing in my diary about how I was going to be a prostitute 'when I grew up.' This was all fantasy of course. But somehow, in these books I finally found a community of girls (all be it fictional) where I felt I belonged.

When I was 13, my family uprooted and moved away from the town where I had spent most of my life. Suddenly I had no control over my environment. At least in my hometown Pacifica, regardless of my outsiderness, I had my friends and I lived in a hippie-ish environment that was more willing to accept 'different' people. I had places outside my home where I felt safe and where I felt like I sort of belonged. But when we moved, suddenly I was completely alien both inside and outside of my home. There is nothing worse for an adolescent girl who has a completely fucked-up home life than to have to be the 'new girl' in class. So what did I do? I took the books I loved so much and turned them into my reality. I became the 'slut' that people had categorized me as for years, following the typical teen runaway narrative: teenage girl starts taking drugs, hangs out with the wrong crowd, has sex with lots of older boys, runs away, becomes stripper, becomes junkie, becomes prostitute, etc. That's what my teenage years were like, but that's not what I'm writing about here. Suffice it to say that once you've had that kind of experience, spending your entire high school years in the sex industry instead of geometry and history, you're marked for life. So I tried to find communities of people with whom I could identify.

Looking for a place to belong, I turned to alternative communities based on sex and gender, since my experiences and my sense of otherness were determined by them. But instead of offering solutions to my problem of outsiderness and alienation, providing me with a network of support and bonding, those communities reproduced the very problems that had screwed me up in the first place. Because sex played such a key role in my otherness and because my history in sex work made it fairly impossible for me to ever identify myself as a 'normal heterosexual,' my natural inclinations were to head toward the gay and lesbian community. Here I was sure I would find comrades. After all, wasn't the gay community somehow also alienated from mainstream society by sexuality? Wouldn't its members be able to identify with my alienation and experience? What I found instead was disappointment after disappointment. I found enforced stereotypes, classism, and a structure that nurtures a society of the elite. I also found that, for the most part, people in the gay and lesbian community did not want to deal with my sexuality—it was too loud, too much on the surface, and too much based in the heterosexual world. The gay community seemed more interested in maintaining its own version of the status quo than in actually promoting an alternative to mainstream society.

Too frequently, gay and lesbian communities create a mirror image of the very mainstream society from which they have attempted to escape. These communities become a highly essentialized gay and lesbian mainstream, where you have to do all the right things to belong. Take San Francisco, for example. In the Castro, the hippest gay and lesbian neighborhood around, queer culture and consumer culture seem to be interchangeable. To really belong in this community, you have to go to the right gym, wear the right clothes, have the right haircut, eat at the right restaurants, go to the right clubs. But the problem goes deeper than this kind of queer consumerism. I used to live in the working-class town of Vallejo, California, which happens to have a pretty big gay and lesbian population. Time and time again, I headed down to the local gay clubs looking for fellowship and camaraderie. Time and time again, I found the same stereotypes and rigid codes of dress and behavior that perpetuate themselves in the heterosexual world. I couldn't hang with the girls because I'm not butch enough, don't play on the softball team, don't have a truck, and simply am not part of 'the group.' I couldn't hang with the boys because, well, I'm a girl. I could talk with them a little bit, but ultimately a wall would come up between us.

Individuals aren't the problem here. It's the communities in which they participate. I guess that's where people really get fucked up: in groups. Suddenly, they want to classify everyone, put them in their caste, and fight for the 'in' spot. Figuring out who's in and who's out, who's got power and who doesn't, becomes more important than building relationships and developing a community of support. Well, I've always been 'out,' and what I've learned, especially by writing this essay, is that I have built and preserved my strong sense of self and integrity by embracing my 'outness.' I have no use for the status quo except to analyze myself and others in relation to it.

FEMINIST OR FOE?

Living in the San Francisco Bay Area and hanging out with 'Berkeley types' for most of my adult life, I found myself on more than one occasion in the midst of feminist communities. Now here, I would think, is a place where I can get support: women supporting women, understanding the atrocities of patriarchy, the abuses we suffer at the hands of the men in power. But I was always wrong. A few years ago, I was invited to a party hosted by a radical Berkeley feminist political group. I jumped at the opportunity to meet other women and participate in a community where I could share a sense of commitment to bettering women's lives. Over and over, throughout the evening I tried to meet and converse with the women at the party. But as soon as I mentioned prostitution, empowering the sexuality of all women regardless of orientation, or anything that was not within the narrow parameters and guidelines of their 'group,' I was met with ridicule, repulsion, or utter disregard. I was shocked. It was like a huge slap in my face. If these women couldn't relate to and accept me, then who would?

What I found in these types of feminist communities is that the women also could not deal with my sexuality. I would talk to them openly about my experiences, thinking I would open the door for a discourse about sex, identity, oppression, power, etc. Instead, the door slammed in my face. For the hard-line, antimale feminists who policed these communities, I was way too deep in the heteronormative world and way too tainted by sex and men. For the punk, hip, neofeminists, I was a threat to their 'alternative' world, which carefully maintained a miniature elite structure with the ruling divas on top. My 'alternative' lifestyle was a little too real and dirty, and of course a little too 'authentic' in a hipster culture that strives to prove who is and who is not authentic.

BAD IS GOOD

A few years ago I connected with *Bad Subjects* and found a community that actually was somewhat utopian in its views. With *Bad Subjects* not only do I feel accepted, comfortable, and respected for who I am, but by being involved with people who think about the complicated workings of social structures, I've been able to learn more about the forces that have affected my life and to understand better my identity. It took me years to understand that my sexual identity was not the cause of my problems and situations but was an effect of forces in my life that go far beyond my sexuality. I'm still trying to understand that as I write this piece. What I see now is that although I thought my hyper-sexualized history defined me, it doesn't. The social situations that led to my sexualization played an even larger role. That's why I have a hard time fitting into gay and feminist communities.

There is a great need to address the problem of categorization that proliferates in all groups, particularly those that are organized around sex and gender. We need communities that embrace a wider sense of 'otherness' and queerness and that actually practice the tolerance which they preach. We've reached the place where we identify social problems of a singular nature (for example, homophobia, patriarchy, racism). Now let's go to the next step by combining forces to create an alternative community that really is an 'alternative' to mainstream society and not its microcosmic mirror image.

29
Marxism After Ho Chi Minh

Viet Thanh Nguyen

Reading Marx and Marxist theory produces in me a mixture of excitement and discomfort. I think this is a healthy reaction, given that my conflicted but respectful thoughts about Marxism are rooted in my family's history. In 1954, as Vietnam was about to be partitioned along the 17th parallel, my parents were devout Vietnamese Catholic peasants who had never finished secondary school. They fled from the north during the partition, fearing religious persecution as much as economic deprivation. In the south, with no education and little capital, they started their own business. Through hard work and good luck they became, in succession, tailors, merchants, auto dealers, and jewelers. If they had lived in the United States, we would call their adventure the successful pursuit of the American dream. The ongoing war would provide my parents with the opportunity, under duress, to discover the truly American version of that dream.

In 1975, as the south collapsed under northern invasion, they had to flee once again, leaving almost everything behind. Their hard work and good fortune were once again compounded with more luck, this time disguised as near tragedy. On the eve of the invasion my father had gone to Saigon with enough gold to buy a house. My mother, brother, and I had stayed behind in our hometown of Ban Me Thuot, a town famous for its coffee. It was also the first town captured in the 1975 invasion of the south. When the town was captured while my father was away, my mother made the difficult decision to flee town with my brother and I, leaving our adopted sister behind to take care of the family business. My mother somehow managed to take us to Saigon and onto a barge, while my father decided on his own that he, too, would jump on a ship. Many families were separated for decades as a consequence of decisions made in those fateful days. But my family was reunited by accident days later on a ship in the South China Sea. We were all reunited except for my adopted sister, who to this day I have not seen since. My family's story of dislocation and hardship is all too common and forms the bedrock of anger against communism in Vietnamese communities overseas.

I grew up in San Jose, California, in a concentration of Vietnamese refugees that was strongly, even violently, anticommunist. I lived within this anticommunist environment that was compounded by a deep familial obligation, filial piety, and Catholic guilt. Spoken and unspoken gestures of the sacrifice of the parents for the children, along with my Catholic elementary and Jesuit prep school education, constantly reminded us of our divinely sanctioned good fortune. The combination of traditional small business, immigrant family capitalism with devout Catholicism did not bode well for an individual drawn to Marxism. Yet Marxism has always been an ideology that attracts rebels from the middle class.

My disaffection from middle-class values had something to do with the familiar constrictions of an immigrant's life—the fact that my parents, who worked constantly to secure our family's future, ironically had little time left for me. My estrangement stemmed partially from my atheism, which arose despite (or perhaps because of) all my Catholic education. And if anyone has spent time in San Jose, they will also understand that it is the embodiment of a suburban America bent on work and leisure, with little inclination to foster countercultures, artists, radicals, or world travelers. Or so it seemed to me as a teenager struggling to define my angst.

When my parents warned me about the communist proselytizers at Berkeley, they had more to be concerned about than they realized. It wasn't the Socialist Workers' Party they needed to worry about, however. I received my first doses of Marxism in Asian-American Studies, through a Gramscian analysis of race, class, and American history. This initiation was soon to be supplemented by Marxist-influenced studies of ethnic and postcolonial literature in the English Department. The department was not exactly a hotbed of Marxism, but there were a couple of avowed Marxists and a few more who dabbled.

The materialist analysis of ethnic studies filtered to the undergraduate political types, who without any self-consciousness resurrected the rhetoric of the United Front in order to work toward minority faculty tenure and multicultural curricula. We had ourselves arrested in the name of diversity, and we called ourselves people of color and organized 'new social movements' based on race and progressive interests that challenged the university. We were, however, unaware of the contradictions between a fast-growing multiculturalist agenda and the Marxist-based Ethnic Studies classes that helped politicize us.

For a brief moment in my undergraduate life, it seemed as if my dreams of youthful rebellion were coming true through an intellectual awakening whose ramifications I scarcely understood, and through a political practice whose contradictions escaped me. The road that led to this moment was highly personal, as it is for everyone who comes to grapple with Marxism. Indeed, Marxism is an ideology that can be both highly personal and impersonal in its implications.

Most people who come to Marxism earnestly seek an answer to pressing questions concerning economic inequality and social injustice. The seduction of Marxism lies in its ability to provide total answers; even Marxist theories that refuse the teleological destination of an end to history nevertheless form a consensual platform against capitalism. Marxism is thus highly personal in its ability to harness the emotional energies we bring to it. It provides answers to the passionate questions that allow us to build bridges between theory and practice even within the rarefied world of the academy. Marxism is also highly impersonal, as is any ideology: human beings count only in the abstract, only in their status as members of classes and ideological positions. How does anyone reconcile their theory with the possible reality that one day their family and friends may be taken out and shot, or taken away and imprisoned because they belong to the wrong class?

While Marxists after Lenin, Stalin, Mao, and Pol Pot have struggled to answer this question, their results have not been satisfactory to me. My discomfort stems not only from an inherent distrust of any ideology that claims to provide all the answers, but also from my family and communal history. The fraught history of attempts to institutionalize Marxism should make the experience of reading Marxist theory and using it difficult for anyone. In the historical example of Vietnam, the devastation wreaked upon the economy, culture, and society after 1975 was partially due to an American embargo, but also due to Vietnamese economic policy. The human weaknesses that led to corruption, discrimination, and persecution in Vietnam are pervasive and latent in all societies, and certainly manifest themselves in capitalist, democratic nations. Nevertheless, corruption, discrimination, and persecution have served capitalist methods and designs much more ably than they have communist goals.

In capitalism, corruption, discrimination, and persecution produce profits, at least some of which benefit the middle class and, arguably, the poor. In communism, only the party benefits. Marxist apologists may argue that Vietnam never had a chance to develop properly its economy due to the 20-year US embargo, but this is essentially an idealist defense. If certain conditions could be realized, then communism may prosper. It's better to consider that the military-industrial complex of capitalism is far better suited than communism to wage the wars and run the profitable economies that were mutually interdependent in the Cold War.

From the perspective of historical hindsight, it can be said that capitalism has not yet run its course (which was the precondition, according to Marx, for a successful, international communist revolution). The legacy of communist efforts in the Soviet Union, China, Cambodia, and Vietnam to fuel the international revolution leaves me in severe doubt about the ability of Marxism to provide a blueprint for the postcapitalist future and the operation of state, culture, and economy. Marxism has proven to be an effective tool for addressing the ability of capitalism to exploit and reify; in short, Marxism remains more useful and convincing as a negative critique than as a positive program. The power of Marxism's critique, along with its consequences, make working and living with it a practice of discomfort.

Yet it should not be a discomfort that compels disbelief, once we consider that Marxism is not the only doctrine that believes in the gun as a final solution. Living in a society bombarded with capitalist values, assumptions, and history, it becomes easy to forget the ways in which capitalism also counts human beings only in the abstract, only in their status as members of classes and ideological positions. The examples are many: slavery, colonialism, imperialism, patriarchy, industrialism, and current US migrant labor practices. The body count of capitalism is high; capitalism is just as willing as communism to take people out and shoot them when it comes to the bottom line. Keeping this in mind puts Marxism's errors in perspective. In the end, Marxism is a tool we use to shape an unknowable future—a potentially sharp tool—and one of the only tools that has the necessary imagination to confront the global sweep of capitalism.

30
Reporting Rape v. a Woman's Right to Speak: I Won't Get Fooled Again

Cynthia Hoffman

Feminist anti-rape initiatives directed at the social contract afforded a rich opportunity for law enforcement to rehabilitate itself, to display its gentler role as protector of the besieged citizen's body. [...] In helping to redeem the police and the law, rape sensitivity and legal reform demanded of the rape victim herself that she take an active interest in 'confessing' and reporting the rape to the state authorities. 'The victim support program will be designed to guide and direct women through the public or private agencies available to provide any counseling,' the Conference of Mayors concluded. 'The purpose will be to reduce trauma ... and to increase the likelihood of the victim's following through with prosecution ... Encouraging women to report assaults to the police should be a priority item for criminal justice agencies and citizen's groups.'

> National League, 1974, quoted in Pamela Haag, *differences* 8:2

> When they had sworn to this advised doom,
> They did conclude to bear dead Lucrece thence,
> To show her bleeding body through Rome,
> And so to publish Tarquin's foul offence;
> Which being done with speedy diligence,
> The Romans plausibly did give consent
> To Tarquin's everlasting banishment.
>
> Shakespeare, *The Rape of Lucrece*, lines 1849–55

> We won't get fooled again.
> Pete Townsend, 1971

On October 24, 1991 I made a decision to defend my life by not fighting back because the man who was assaulting me had a knife at my throat and if I had fought back I'd be dead. I know this to be true like I know my own name. By the time the police got to my house, there was blood everywhere, I had a dislocated shoulder and a dislocated hip and that's only part of what he did just because he felt like it. I cooperated with him because he was crazy, a foot taller than me and there is no question in my mind that when he left me on the floor of my house, tied up in telephone wire and stereo cords, he thought I was dead and that's exactly what he wanted me to be. I have scars on my neck, shoulders, back, and face from that man, and I have scars inside that will never fully heal. But because I chose not to fight back then, I am alive today and can fight back now in the only way I know how: by using words and my truth to educate people about what rape really means and how it affects lives more than five years after the fact.

This particular experience of being raped was profoundly life changing, not because I was assaulted—I'd been assaulted before—but because in the course of that evening I came to understand that I was not, in fact, the kind of pacifist I had always believed myself to be and that if I had been given a secure opening (believe me, I was looking for one), I would have taken that bastard's life without a second thought. That was a hell of a discovery to make about myself, that I was capable of killing a person. I didn't know that until that night.

In the aftermath of being raped, it didn't occur to me not to call 911. I was bleeding and I was scared and I needed help. It certainly never occurred to me that silence was an option because I no longer know how to stay silent and because I knew I hadn't done anything wrong. In fact, I could articulate that truth more clearly in the first days following the rape than I could even a month following it. 'Tell everyone,' I said to a professor who wanted to know who she could share the news with, 'I've got nothing to be ashamed of.' Who or what taught me that I was wrong? That I was responsible? That somehow what I knew instinctively in the moment was something I had to go through hell to relearn months later? That's what confronted me as a result of both the rape and my decision to call 911, which was unexpected to me because that night I simply assumed that justice as well as help were available to me. I made that assumption because I'd been told for years through women's centers and rape crisis handouts and through everything that I had learned over years of feminist activity that the justice system had changed and that it now served me in ways that it might not have 20 years earlier. I had forgotten that the work of the justice system was revenge and it never occurred to me that no one had ever inquired of me what I thought justice looked like.

In the movie *Billy Jack*, there's a sequence where Jean Roberts, the heroine and founder of the Freedom School, is sexually assaulted by the town bully's son Bernard. Bernard ties her down and rapes her while his buddy watches, all the while commenting that in spite of his bragging, he has never made it with a woman because he has trouble getting an erection. This time, however, he assures himself, will be different; and it is. When Jean is rescued by one of her students, she insists that the rape is a test of her commitment to pacifism and that her student can't tell either Billy Jack or anyone else what Bernard has done to her: she must 'turn the other cheek' and learn to live with and accept what has been done to her. Her determination is to no avail and as anyone who has ever seen the movie can assure you, Bernard is finally killed by Billy Jack, while in the midst of having sex with a child. But there is no question that it's Billy Jack's revenge; the movie makes it quite clear in scenes leading up to Billy Jack's killing of Bernard that Jean's priority would have been taking care of the 13-year old girl.

Billy Jack was released in the early 1970s and contains what I believe is the first on-screen depiction of a rape from a woman's point of view. What interests me in this particular sequence of events is two-fold. First, it's a statement about the distance women have come since 1971 that a so-called progressive film would insist that a woman's best recourse is silence and pacifist acceptance; but second, and perhaps more importantly, it's a statement about revenge and its value in our society that I would rewatch this movie from a distance of 25 years and be angered by a scene that moved me to no end as a teenager. And yet still, this scene that moved me as a teenager now challenges all of my deeply held beliefs about what it means to be a victim of sexual assault as well as pointing up what society thinks being a victim means. For Jean, revenge is apparently of secondary importance and upon rewatching the movie last fall, I found myself asking questions I hadn't let myself ask myself in a very long time: why did I report the rape and agree to press charges when I don't believe in revenge? And when did my right to speak out turn into the expectation and finally the demand that I report and press charges?

I need to make it abundantly clear here that I make a distinction between telling and reporting. I'm not challenging telling; in fact, I advocate screaming from rooftops. What I am challenging are reporting laws, laws that make it impossible to get medical care or therapeutic care if one isn't interested in pressing charges, laws that benefit the justice system at the expense of those that same system purports to represent.

Six months after I was raped, the State of California executed Robert Alton Harris. He was the first person executed by the state in decades, and while today executions seem to generate little or no notice in the news, his execution was a big deal and everyone was talking about it, had a theory about it, was demonstrating against it, or otherwise had an opinion that they were sharing vociferously. I'm not proud; I had an opinion too and I didn't hesitate to share it. Capital punishment offends me. When asked how I felt, my standard line was, 'How dare the state execute someone in my name. I do not give them permission to do that.' The state, however, didn't ask my opinion, and Harris was executed as planned.

What I was asked, which stunned and confused me, was whether the experience of having been raped had somehow had an effect on my opinion of capital punishment. At the time, I didn't understand why people made this connection and I absolutely didn't understand their certainty that being raped had to have affected my thoughts on state sanctioned murder. Rape, after all, is not a capital offence. I think now that the people asking me those questions on the eve of the execution were asking if somehow the experience of being a victim of a violent crime had helped me to get comfortable with the idea of capital punishment as just revenge. The answer is most adamantly no. But it's still not so simple as all that. For me, it has become a question of whether revenge works at all.

And make no mistake about it, the work of the justice system is revenge. It is punitive, mosaic law, eye for an eye activity that to me works only in the moment, but afterward is worthless. Once the act is done, nothing can undo it. We don't ever, for example, question someone's choice not to report a robbery; why is choosing not to report a rape such a no-no? In 1994 my car was broken into somewhere in the realm of ten times; I only ever reported it once, and then only because the video store needed a report number to generate an insurance payment. No one ever asked me why I didn't report these break-ins. That question simply never came up. When I say I've been raped, 'Did they catch him?' is almost invariably the first question I'm asked. What's the difference? Why is it that I'm allowed choice about my car and not allowed the same when it's my body that has been violated? Why is my car accorded more respect than I am?

Again, I'm not talking about silence here; I'm talking about contacting the justice system and reporting. In my mind these are two very different things. I may never report again, but I will never be silent. Where did rape crisis go wrong in getting in bed with the criminal justice system? Did a choice to go with the money divorce us from fulfilling our needs?

The night I was assaulted, I was put in a private room in the hospital, the one reserved by law for assault victims ostensibly so they will feel safe. As near as I can tell the major gift of my private room is that I can smoke here without going outside in my shift; my clothing has been confiscated as evidence. In fact, there is no 'I' in this room: what I have become is evidence, of no intrinsic value at the moment beyond my body's ability to tell an evidentiary story that will lead to the arrest of the person who did this to me. The court case, should there be one, will be called *The People of the State of California* v. *John Doe*. I am only evidence. It is not my case. It is theirs.

Case in point: I have a series of bruises on my thighs and as those bruises age and become colorful the police want photographs of them as physical evidence and the investigator wants to know what gave me bruises in such an odd place. The police photographer gets his pictures; the investigator gets to discover that Perry was wearing 501s. I, however, still have ugly and painful bruises and can't sit down.

This is only problematic to me. I am not by myself an advocate of victims' rights. I've been criminalized before and being victimized does not impugn new status to me. The system doesn't care who I am or how I feel. That's my job. But my victim status makes it more difficult to do that job and that makes it my business; the system that is ostensibly responsible for taking care of me has requirements and one of those requirements is that I have to agree to press charges. Jean's option of staying quiet is not available to me if I also need the financial assistance that the state offers through victims' assistance.

For instance, at the time I was assaulted, I had only minimal health insurance. I needed major medical assistance. My choice was simple, and was presented to me materially in the hospital in the form of a hospital bill coupled with a police report with an agreement attached to it stating that if this man were caught I would press charges, and this admonition: if I agreed to press charges, the state would pay my medical bills, no matter how large they got. Faced with this material, how can I say no to them? I can't afford the hospital bills. So from minute one they had me: you want your face sewn back together? Sign here. It isn't enough for me to report the rape; I must agree to press charges.

In 18 more months, I won't have to worry about Perry any longer. Of course, in 18 more months, he doesn't have to worry about me either since the statute of limitations will have run. In the interim, however, my life is circumscribed by police reports, victim assistance disability counseling, district attorney questioning sessions, HIV testing, Social Security Insurance and testing. I lose my job so we can add to this list State Disability Insurance. My life is mine but my body and my experience are held hostage to the legal system. I am evidence.

I still resent that I had no choice in whether to press charges. I wonder at the people who on finding out that I was raped ask, 'Was he caught?' before they ask any other questions, questions like, 'Are you okay?' The assumptions have certainly changed in the last 25 years; pacifism is no longer the only option. Now it's not even an option at all.

There's an attempt to make us all complicit in this shift. As a victim, I'm supposed to assume that things like victims' rights are different and better than my regular rights get and I'm supposed to ignore that to have 'victims' rights' my regular rights disappeared. Even the local rape crisis center wants me to revel in my victim status, and its support system is based on that assumption.

Only by embracing my status as a victim am I able to be empowered. It's an insidious system that's designed to keep me in line and in control under uncontrollable circumstances. The final and largest way they make me complicit is by insisting that it is somehow my responsibility if he should choose to do it again. 'Press charges' we are told, 'so he won't hurt another woman.' As if by pressing charges we have somehow actually done something to change the fact of rape in the first place.

When I started writing this piece, I thought I wanted to write about revenge and how I didn't get it. What I've ended up with instead is the quite frightening conclusion that if this happens to me again, I'm not going to report it. How did I get here? And what does it mean that I, a self-identified radical feminist, have diverged so far from the expected feminist norm that I would advocate not reporting as a viable and even empowering option in the case of rape?

Revenge is what the state wants because arresting, trying, and imprisoning the man who raped me would allow everyone the illusion that things have returned to pre-rape normal. I can never have that; no matter what happens to him. I have been raped and putting him in jail doesn't change that. Andrea Dworkin would say that the problem is that we have to stop rape altogether (and I'm certainly not going to argue against her) but what about the rape crisis system that has allowed itself to be subsumed into the justice system—a system that supports itself at my expense?

Last fall I met someone in the flesh with whom I had only ever corresponded virtually. She's an artist of some burgeoning reputation and my partner and I met her for sushi dinner in the Mission and in the course of the evening discussed life, NYC, punk, and art as well as things like impending marriage (hers), and dealing with worker's compensation (mine). On the walk back to her studio I mentioned in passing that I had once been sexually assaulted. Without missing a beat, she said, 'Me too' and proceeded to tell me about it.

Sexual assault is becoming a universal language for women, not in the 'we're victims, take care of us' sense but in the sense that no matter how little we know of each other, we have a common experience. The judicial system continues to support revenge-based law that ignores what those of us who have been raped know: it's the structure of society that's the problem and imprisoning an individual rapist only gets the rapist raped, it doesn't change the fact that the next woman I meet might also have been raped and have a better idea of what I need than the justice system that's set up to meet my needs ever dreamed of.

First I was raped by a man; then I was raped by the system; some people get raped by the press; but I continue to be raped by a social structure that insists that my rape is its property. My rape is my property and I'm taking it back. I'm taking it back by stating that putting someone in jail won't help me; it will only hurt him. Hurting him does nothing for me. The idea that it should is an illusion I now flatly refuse to accept. What will help me is if we put the kind of energy into changing the world that we put into criminal justice. Changing the world and a system that makes assaulting me seem like a good option in Perry's mind is the kind of work that justice should be attempting, not incarceration and eye for an eye illusionary punishment that solves nothing.

After more than five years, all I have left is a scar on my chin. It's a small scar; the physician's assistant who stitched my face back together was quite good and unless I've been in the sun it's rather difficult to find. My partner barely notices it. I see it every day in the bathroom mirror. I like my scar. When the state offered to pay for surgery to remove it, I declined. I want this small talisman; it reminds me that my past is real.

31
My Dad Kicked Ass for a Living

Zach Furness

When I was a little kid I used to have a ritual designed specifically for days when I was home sick with the flu. After consuming a modest amount of buttered toast and tea, I would plant myself in front of the television screen and watch a consistent pattern of recorded movies including *Mary Poppins, Star Wars*, and several films that documented the adventures of *Herbie the Love Bug*. On one such occasion when I was enjoying the benefits of a newly settled stomach, I watched static fill the screen after one of Herbie's wild escapades and I lazily drooped off of the couch with a finger extended toward the stop button on the VCR.

Suddenly the static disappeared and the screen was overtaken by a swarm of football players, green Astroturf and the audible banter of Brent Musberger, a quasi-legendary sports broadcaster. Among the scattered bodies of Houston Oilers and Pittsburgh Steelers I immediately picked out the black and gold embroidered number 64, and realized for the first time that I was watching my dad on television. And holy shit, there he was in the flesh and blood! He was chasing the Oilers around the field using his body like some medieval ramming device, clubbing his opponents with taped fists and padded armor, grabbing at jerseys with his crooked football fingers. After several minutes of action he received a 15-yard penalty for slamming the quarterback to the ground after he had already thrown the ball.

During a replay of the penalty the announcers were offering up their formulaic doses of commentary, saying things like, 'Furness should have known not to take that penalty,' and, 'You don't expect those type of mistakes from a veteran player,' and other statements that were intended to decry my dad's bone-crushing hit on the quarterback. The camera then switched from the reply to a close up shot of my dad, a man who only hours earlier had read me a story before bed, and here he was the subject of the almighty close up shot of the NBC cameras—a shot that either meant you had done something exceptional or you had fucked up. In this case, the camera angle was attempting to create a sort of multifaceted mug shot of the temporary villain ... the man who could have given that poor quarterback a concussion ... the man who should have known better ... the man who kicks ass for a living ... the man I call dad.

Through his facemask and enormous beard I could tell from his stoic expression that he was proud to play this modern role of half-villain, half-hero, and he certainly wasn't showing any visible signs of remorse. And although I knew the intricacies of this man's life, had eaten his breakfasts, had watched him lift weights, had hung from his extended arm like a small monkey, here he was being *created* by the television set. His actions were framed, admired, dictated, and conformed to the spectacle of the screen his character was developed through instant replays, audience noises, and violent clashes with the Houston natives. While my house was plastered with black and white stills of him making a tackle or standing on the sidelines, it was not until I saw him on the screen that it all added up to greatness in my mind. On that day, my dad became immortalized alongside the likes of Darth Vader, The Great Grape Ape, and other such characters that lingered in my four-year-old television world of mystery, action, and enchantment. But on that day, he ceased to belong only to me and became part of a much larger world that I could have imagined only in terms of crowds I had seen at the mall or the local amusement park.

Over the course of my pre-teen years I witnessed the development of my TV dad on a number of different occasions—usually during dinnertime. When he appeared on television, I would watch intensely as he offered brief statements concerning the Michigan State football team, or more specifically the defensive players that he coached. On the screen, his mustache would bounce up and down with the rhythm of his lips as he talked, and his green athletic gear would give off an aura of prestige and respectability that seemed naturally to evoke the term 'coach.' What was even more uncanny is that I often watched this TV personality together with the real life version of my dad, becoming ever more enamored by his presence as I passed him the peas. During our years in East Lansing my friends would tell me when they saw him on television. Some of them even remarked that he looked like Magnum P.I., which was a pretty badass compliment in the mid-1980s. Given my age at the time, I sometimes wondered whether Magnum P.I.'s family ever saw my dad on television and thought about how their dad looked just like Steve Furness.

Throughout the next ten years I became more familiar with the life of my TV dad by watching his eloquent statements about leaving Michigan State, his eventual return to the Steelers as a coach, and his thoughts on being fired from the Pittsburgh job a few years later. I watched this character with a keen interest because I had never heard these exact thoughts articulated to anyone within my immediate family, and I always found it remarkable how the living room background of these miniature press events looked so much like my own. Still, there was a gap between these two lives, these two characters that I had become so familiar with over the years. They gave different reasons for major life decisions, they spoke to different audiences, they wore different types of hair products, and they expressed different emotions.

My Dad Kicked Ass for a Living

Perhaps the most difficult aspect of this situation was the attempt to extrapolate some type of authenticity from these various televised segments. Which decision was the *real* one? Which comment was truthful and which one intended for an audience? I began to realize that one of the distinguishing features of my TV dad was his ability to deliver a particularly TV-style series of comments concerning his situation. His speech was informative but to the point, confident but also humble, and willfully constructed with a series of specific nods and eyebrow movements. An awkwardness would sometimes emerge after such TV moments when my real dad would say something to one of us and I could swear that it had been rehearsed before a TV audience at some previous time. Because of the apparent disjunction between my real life and TV dads, I became acutely aware of the screen's ability to conform reality to its own selfish standards. Each of us has witnessed these effects firsthand when we gauge our tragedies, heroic acts, or amazing feats through experience of the screen, leading to eyewitness accounts of people who describe a given event as 'surreal'—'like I am watching TV.' Most of us realize that the screen possesses no motivation of its own, however we undoubtedly grapple with the effects of the screen like cavemen might have initially grappled with their shadows.

While we attempt to dissociate ourselves from such comparisons, it is all too evident that our ability to distinguish between the real and the reproduction has not, and will not, come to fruition within our lifetimes. Yet, we operate under the assumption that such decisions will inevitably have to be made if our species will continue to thrive. Our lives thrive within, evolve from and are inextricably bound to what Philip K. Dick calls 'irreal' relationships and mediated life-forms. For Dick, life is an irreal presence that thrives within the seamlessly jagged juxtapositions of the natural and the mechanical—forces that simultaneously imitate one another with no beginning or end in sight. Perhaps I learned the lessons of irreality so early on that I couldn't keep track of where my life ended and the screen began. Like many of Dick's characters, I could never identify the exact separation of the real from the irreal and I eventually gave up trying.

Sometime after I first had to confront these bizarre circumstances, my TV dad became movable, controllable, and pixelated within the video game world of John Madden Football—a virtual conglomeration of various TV dads from different eras whose speaking parts were swept away in favor of repetitive motions and 16-bit touchdown dances. I played his character on several occasions, watching his movements, examining his build, comparing his athletic prowess to my memories of the real version. They just had it all wrong in the game though. He could rush the passer much better in real life and he was quite a bit faster. However, his extra point blocking ability on the screen was Herculean in nature, providing thousands of people with a false sense of what his strengths and weaknesses were like during the heyday of the Steelers. But on the other hand, he won my friend Brian $25 when his last-second-kick-blocking skills prevented an overtime victory against the 1985 Bears—a team that was assembled long after his retirement. Several months later I taught my dad how to play the video game and remembered to tell him that Brian said 'thank you' for the money. During the 15-minute game I clobbered my dad with the video version of himself, leaving us in near silence, partially amused, partially confused, but definitely entertained.

Unlike the experience of watching my TV dad on a newscast or sports show, the video game version of him was not all that unsettling. One might imagine that the game's distortion of his figure, skills, size, or complexion would have provoked some uneasiness on my part, but the synthetic quality of the game actually created a more succinct split between my real dad and the creation displayed on the screen. Because older games lacked the ability to create a realistic image, they were also stripped of the pretenses associated with regular TV—a format in which the editorial procedures, make-up applications, lighting coordinators and out-takes are hidden in the attempt to reproduce/produce reality for mass consumption. In the most basic sense, we weren't meant to believe that the little, square-headed people of SEGA's world were real. They didn't drink water, they didn't sweat and they didn't get tired ... these were the conditions that were not only acceptable, but desirable.

For a two day span in February 2000, the discrepancy between the real and TV versions of my dad became fully realized as the former departed quickly from this earth, while the latter was exalted through video clips, photo stills, and polished commentary from several different Pittsburgh newscasters. I watched the television when I returned home from the hospital, disappointed to find my TV dad so cramped within the MTV-style editing of various games played throughout the 1970s. The quick shots attempted to summarize particular eras of his life within seconds of video footage, but it couldn't reproduce the blissful sensation of seeing him pulverize that quarterback some 20 years earlier. Still, I relished the experience of seeing my dad receive a television eulogy— apparently the highest honor that media can provide. All of his television pasts were spliced together in order to create an immortal TV superhero who wore his jersey with pride and made his family proud.

Every year when it comes time for the Super Bowl to be played, I inevitably receive a late night call from one of my friends who has spotted my TV dad within the hours of old Super Bowl footage that ESPN runs in order to keep all pot smokers and insomniac football fans entertained for the three days preceding the game. I always take a few moments to share in the nostalgia with my excited friend and take solace in the idea that somewhere in a far off video game, highlight reel, or rerun, my dad still kicks ass for a living.

Part VI

Media and Response

INTRODUCTION

This book's final section covers the territory that *Bad Subjects* first staked out over a decade ago: the critique of mainstream popular culture. Back then, scholarly works on Madonna, *Star Trek*, and action movies were all the rage. Perversely, though, few of these treatises were written accessibly. Indeed, they were often so burdened with the jargon and syntax of poststructuralist criticism that they were often harder to read than pieces on 'difficult' works such as James Joyce's *Ulysses*. *Bad Subjects* set out to intervene in the academy's infatuation with popular culture by demonstrating that it was possible to write short, insightful analyses of television, movies, and pop music without abandoning the hard-won insights of theory. Over time, the academy proved less receptive to the study of popular culture than it once seemed. And *Bad Subjects* turned more of its attention to other phenomena, from religion to the politics of identity. But we have always retained a soft spot for well-executed readings of popular culture, particularly because we know from both our correspondence and from our experience in the classroom that text-based cultural criticism is good pedagogy.

To the extent that our approach to popular culture has changed over the years, it is in recognizing that this kind of close reading works best when it is coupled with a rich sense of context. Our best pieces in this vein are able to take the individual text seriously—be it a popular song or a theoretical tract—without losing sight of the politics of the medium. All the pieces in this final section draw attention to the way in which response to the media shapes critical consciousness. They pull readers into the authors' personal explorations of the songs, commercials, and movies that swirl around Western culture, and the theory that accompanies them.

Charlie Bertsch opens the section with his close look at the Eagles' song 'Hotel California,' which was omnipresent on FM airwaves in North America during the post-Watergate era. He wryly relates the significance of this song to the historical consciousness unique to his generation: the regret at having been born too late for the excesses of the 1960s. His piece then concludes on a more sober note, making a plea to redeem the broken promises of previous generations by telling their story differently than the mainstream media have done. The Sex Pistols were also very famous in the 1970s—they were, among other things, a reaction to the rock establishment exemplified by the Eagles—and have suffered as signposts in narratives of decline ever since. Mike Mosher's essay pulls their lyrics out of the din of history-as-unquestioned-fact and re-energizes them in relation to the contemporary battle over abortion rights. He correlates the outrage he feels about the horrific danger of illegal abortion with John Lydon's lyrical expression of similar thoughts in the song 'Bodies.' Jonathan Sterne takes a more abstract approach to media and response, analyzing Marxian contributions to media theory and pointing out their continued relevance. He makes a straightforward assessment of their potential: that new media, while intensive capitalist projects, are still human institutions and are therefore able to be reshaped. Although this point is a foundation of Marxism, it is one we must work hard to recall in this age of reality television.

Analyzing a TV commercial and its unsettling historical textual implications, Robert Shaw and Megan Shaw Prelinger (father and daughter) frame their discussion in terms of the use and abuse of historical traumas. They dissect the corporate marketing strategies that would attempt to profit from the collective tragedy of the Vietnam war and they expose the ways that the current fetishism of communications technology leads to distortions of past realities. Finally, in the concluding essay of the book, *Bad Subjects* cofounder Annalee Newitz goes to the movies and dissects several 1990s Hollywood films about heterosexuals who fall in love with homosexuals and form families with them. In these supposedly liberal films, she sees a dangerously reactionary trend in which homosexual characters are redeemed by flirtation with heterosexuality and their insertion into chaste but otherwise traditional family structures. Her piece is a perfect example of how *Bad Subjects* has used the analysis of popular culture to make political points that are both simple and sophisticated, a testament to the power of writing accessibly.

32

'Hotel California': Learning How to Read

Charlie Bertsch

> The concept of progress must be grounded in the idea of catastrophe.
> That things are 'status quo' is the catastrophe.
>
> Walter Benjamin

It's hard to get the overeducated, underpaid intellectuals in my circle of friends to agree on anything. But I've learned how to produce solidarity in their ranks. When the discussion turns to music, I make a startling confession: I like the Eagles. And I love the album *Hotel California*, particularly the title song. The response to this declaration is as predictable as the hourly reprise of Eagles' hits on classic rock stations: 'You're kidding, right?'

No, I'm not. Even on a bad day, I brighten when I hear the words 'Standing on a corner in Winslow, Arizona.' I always turn up the volume at the sound of Joe Walsh's squiggly guitar at the beginning of 'Life in the Fast Lane.' I suppose that if I were a middle-aged Boomer in an SUV, this affection for classic rock would make more sense to people. Unfortunately, I don't even have this sort of nostalgia as an excuse. When the Eagles were flying highest, I was in second grade, playing make-believe in the back yard. The only music I listened to regularly was my father's, on Saturday broadcasts from the Metropolitan Opera. Hell, in 1976 I knew more about Georges Bizet's *Carmen* than I did about anything on the pop charts.

So what explains my soft spot for the Eagles? It's true I've become fond of music that mixes country and rock in recent years. But my attachment to the Eagles goes beyond this affection for the genre. I liked them long before I could stand country. The reason? 'Hotel California' taught me how to read. Not literally, mind you. I owe that favor to the brightly colored SRA workbooks in Mr. Johnson's open classroom. But it was through listening to the Eagles' monster hit that I learned to 'read' for something more than plot. Growing up in my middle America, I couldn't avoid the song. 'Hotel California' was everywhere during the Carter administration. And so, since I had to listen to the song anyway, I turned my mind loose on it. The song became my mental gymnasium, where I would work out my interpretive powers with the diligence of someone pumping iron.

'Hotel California' combines a story familiar from Alfred Hitchcock's *Psycho*—person gets tired, stops at hotel, never leaves—with the impression that there is more to the story than the storyline alone. The song is the product of a time when the horror genre was enjoying unprecedented mainstream success, from *The Exorcist* to Stephen King's *Carrie*. But unlike most horror hits of the 1970s, 'Hotel California' doesn't indulge in graphic excess. The only explicit violence comes at the banquet, where 'they stab it with their steely knives, but they just can't kill the beast.' Compared to gory scenes of the era, however, even these lines seem muted. The horror in 'Hotel California' must be activated by the listener's imagination. Perhaps that explains the song's long instrumental coda. It encourages you to think about the song for a minute or two before moving on to the next song on the album or radio station. If I identified with the narrator of 'Hotel California,' it was in his capacity to spin a tale that solicits reading between the lines. I didn't fear for his safety; I feared the situation he is trying to make us see. This explains why the most important part of the song for me was not the invocation of the beast itself, but the scene that precedes the banquet: 'I called for the captain, "Please bring me my wine." He said, "We haven't had that spirit here since nineteen sixty-nine."'

Already as a child I was afflicted with a sense of my belatedness. Born in May of 1968, I didn't become conscious of world events until that tumultuous decade had passed. My earliest historical memories are of the hangover from the 1960s: the terrorist attack on Israeli athletes at the 1972 Munich Olympics, the OPEC oil embargo, the Patty Hearst kidnapping, and Watergate. Long before I had a clear understanding of what had actually happened in the 1960s, I sensed that the 1970s represented a turn for the worse. As I started to learn more about the major events of the 1960s—the revolt against conservative social mores, the resistance to the Vietnam war, and, above all else, the Civil Rights Movement—my nostalgia for the decade grew stronger and stronger. The paradox was that, like many people of my generation, I longed to relive a time that I hadn't lived through in the first place. For me, the upheavals of the 1960s seemed like the first steps toward a better world, one we had betrayed, first with the inward turn of the 1970s and then the reactionary politics of Ronald Reagan and company.

All through my teenage years, I kept returning to 'Hotel California' as confirmation of my sense that the United States had passed its peak. In order to interpret the song in this way, it was necessary for me to read between the lines. The captain wasn't really talking about wine when he said, 'We haven't had that spirit here since nineteen sixty-nine.' *Spirit* had to have a double meaning. I was sure it referred to the spirit of change that inspired the social movements of the 1960s, the belief that anything was possible, that we wouldn't get fooled again, the belief, finally, that we were really a 'we' distinct from 'them.'

Once I had interpreted *spirit* in this way, the whole meaning of the song changed. The Hotel California wasn't a real hotel, but a metaphor for the state where the revolution had progressed and, consequently, retreated the furthest. More than that, it was a metaphor for the state of mind produced in California, one that no longer had any vision of the future. It's no accident that, right after the lines about the missing 'wine,' the song continues with a ghostly siren song: 'And still those voices are calling from far away.' To be sure, they could be coming from the future. Yet, following on the heels of nostalgia for the spirit that died in the 1960s, it is far more likely that they are coming from the past.

What I found most disturbing in my interpretation of 'Hotel California' was what it implied about the song's last line. If you find yourself in a spiritually deprived state, the natural impulse—conservatives have this right—is to 'find the passage back' to the place you were before, to turn around. But if it is true that 'you can check out any time you like, but you can never leave,' then this possibility is foreclosed. Despite what the Margaret Thatchers of this world will tell you, there's no going back.

As I sit here today, informed by years of reading philosophy, this point seems laughably obvious. Even when we sift through our memories, we are still going forward within the space of linear time. To a twelve-year-old, though, the idea that there is never a 'passage back' seemed horribly bleak. I wanted so badly to live in a future projected from the most extreme point of the 1960s (for which my birth month, May 1968, was as likely a candidate as any), yet found myself in a far less hopeful historical situation. This was the horror of 'Hotel California' for me. And, though I admit to being scared by the horror films of the 1970s, I was less disturbed by the slamming of that steel door in *The Texas Chainsaw Massacre* than by the realization that the door to the past had been shut for good.

In the end, though, the fear that 'Hotel California' inspired was less important than the confidence it gave me in my interpretive powers. By inviting me to look for the deeper meaning in its tale of a desert vacation gone wrong, the song alerted me to the possibility that every story might be the vehicle for another, different story underneath it. In short, the song introduced me to the concept of allegory. Now, some 20 years later, I have made reflection on allegory a cornerstone of my scholarly work. I spend countless hours pondering the different, contradictory definitions of the term. I read novels, not only for their concealed politics, but also for the insight they provide us into the act of reading for something concealed. And 'Hotel California' has to shoulder much of the blame.

My favorite theorist of allegory is Walter Benjamin. He was interested in the perception of decline, the way artists have confronted the feeling of belatedness that seems to be an integral part of the modern experience. For centuries, people have been afflicted with the sense of having been born too late. The strange thing, as Benjamin noted, is that this feeling goes hand in hand with the relentless 'progress' promoted by a capitalist economy. Not surprisingly, the perception of decline often has been most acute during periods of political regression.

Denied the opportunity to transform the social order, people turn their attention to transforming their personal lives. They give themselves the 'makeover' they can't give to society. But these attempts at personal transformation are shadowed by the prospect of what could have been. No matter how many fads they run through, no matter how many items they purchase in order to refashion their identity, they can never completely escape the political tragedy of the recent past. This was true of the German Baroque that Benjamin pondered in *The Origins of German Tragic Drama*. It was true of Paris during the Second Empire, to which he devoted his vast, unfinished 'passage-work,' the *Arcades Project*. And it was true of the post-World War I era in which he conducted his analyses. The 1970s have much in common with those periods.

Benjamin was no pessimist. At one point in the *Arcades Project*, he declares his goal to be showing that, in reality, 'there are no periods of decline.' He believed that, even though you can't literally go back in time, you can still make good on the promise of the past. But in order to do so, you have to keep it alive in the present. Benjamin called the process *Eingedenken*, which translates literally as 'remembering into.' *Eingedenken* makes it possible to actualize the potential in what could have been. Where a more conventional approach to history sees refuse, *Eingedenken* sees raw material. It redeems. For Benjamin, it would still be possible for us to connect with the 'spirit of 1969.' The trick is to distinguish between what we can't change—our forward motion in linear time—from what we can—our attitude toward a million dreams deferred.

This is the lesson I take from 'Hotel California.' The song is surely in need of some redemption. The materialism of the 1970s that 'Hotel California' both exemplifies and condemns—the Eagles were no less 'Tiffany-twisted' than their fans—is still with us, only without as much hope for personal transformation. And politicians around the world are still trying to take us back to the place we were before the 1960s happened. Yet there's still hope. As long as we are able to 'read' for politics, we still have the chance to find a different, better narrative within the one that holds us prisoner. We can be free. But it will have to be a freedom of our own device.

33

'Bodies': Sex Pistols and Abortion Art

Mike Mosher

Coffee helps, but I need punk. On sleepy Mondays I pop in the Sex Pistols' 1977 album *Never Mind the Bollocks* while driving seven miles to the university where I teach. Kicking off the work week with the opening song 'Holidays in the Sun' is bracing, but it's the high-energy second track 'Bodies' that is always the most fun and thought-provoking.

> She was a girl from Birmingham
> She just had an abortion
> She was a case of insanity.

I assumed the next line 'Her name was Pauline, she lived in a tree' was just a throwaway, and nowadays can't help but think of eco-radical pinup Julia 'Butterfly' Hill perched high atop the Headwaters forest. Yet in his 1994 autobiography, *Rotten*, John Lydon, known as Johnny Rotten when he was the Sex Pistols' singer, remembered that Pauline, 'actually had a treehouse on the estate of this nuthouse. The nurses couldn't get her down, she'd be up there for days.'

He continued, 'She turned up at my door once wearing a see-through plastic bag. She did the rounds in London and ended up at everybody's door ... Like most insane people, she was very promiscuous.' I suspect the band enjoyed Pauline's sexual favors, and later were a bit remorseful when they realized that a troubled mental condition lay beyond her punk outrageousness. In my first teaching job, in the loosely managed art program of an inner-city drop-in center with many clients in and out of the mental health system, another male teacher had the habit of bringing home deeply troubled women. He would later bemoan their clinging and emotional dependency. 'I want to bear Buddha's babies' wrote one on a drawing he showed me. I can imagine Pauline.

> She wasn't the only one who killed her baby
> She sent letters from the country
> She was an animal
> She was a bloody disgrace
> Mommy! I'm not an animal!
> Bodies! An abortion!

In the early 1970s, abortions may have been prevalent among university-town women in Michigan but required inconvenient travel out of state. I was in high school then. In my ninth grade class, one faculty-brat friend disappeared twice from school for that purpose, then finally bore a daughter sophomore year. That same year, an older girl in the neighborhood asked me to take care of her dog, while she dealt with a pregnancy resulting from bored trysts with fellow employees in her job as a hotel maid.

Then came the January 1973 *Roe* v. *Wade* decision that effectively legalized abortion across the United States.

There was fear at this new order of women's reproductive rights among traditionalist young men, for whom removal of the threat of unwanted pregnancies and shotgun marriages should have brought nothing but relief. That fall, I went to college, at a school that had only matriculated its second co-ed class. A pre-med sophomore bemoaned unverifiable 'facts' that the year before 10 per cent of the newly admitted women had college-provided abortions. This year, he said, the number was so high the college wouldn't release its statistics. He seemed disappointed at my shrug and lack of outrage.

> Dragged on a table in a factory
> Illegitimate place to be
> In a packet in a lavatory
> Die little baby screaming
> Screaming fucking bloody mess
> It's not an animal, it's an abortion.

'The fetus thing is what got me,' said Lydon. 'She'd tell me about getting pregnant by the male nurses at the asylum or whatever.'

Like Lydon's, my outrage comes from stories such as those contained in Marge Piercy's novel *Braided Lives*, a tale of women attending the University of Michigan about 1960. Unwanted pregnancies and abortions figure heavily in their lives. The disastrous consequences of its illegality at the time are described in wrenching detail: the agonizing pain of self-induced methods or those performed by sympathetic doctors without anesthesia. Piercy's autobiographical narrator explains

> Buhbe [grandmother] had twelve children and at least five abortions; Mother three children, at least two abortions and a miscarriage that almost killed her—doctors can't help you when you're miscarrying until the fetus is out, for fear of being an accomplice to abortion. Buhbe, my mother and their sisters always chose illegally and dangerously which of the endless possibilities for fecundity they would bring to birth, which of the multitude of possible

children they might feed, clothe and love. So women have always done in societies everywhere, with or without male knowledge or aid, with or without the help of official medicine and law. Such was the province of midwives and witches.

On the rolling drive toward work, even the mid-Michigan environment conspires to make 'Bodies' resonate. Halfway to my university, along the M-84 near I-75 and across from a Lutheran church, there stood for several months last year a notable outdoor installation. Dominated by the billboard 'Bay City Population—38,000. Michigan Abortions 1999—26,600.' was a roadside field of numerous white popsicle-stick crosses. Twenty-six thousand? Sorry, didn't count. As a piece of political art, it was quite impressive—reductive, conceptually clear, spiritual, and somber like the military cemeteries that sprang up in France for World War I dead. Like the entertainer Madonna, who grew up in and fled this region, it's high concept, showy, and in your face. And the work is straight-out wrongheaded, if it intends to promote any reduction in women's right to choice.

This wasn't the only antiabortion public art in Michigan last fall. A group called the Genocide Awareness Project set up for two days a display of what the conservative student paper *Michigan Independent* called 'disgustingly huge' photographs. The thirty 6' x 13 display boards were set up on the University of Michigan's central campus by Chi Alpha Christian Fellowship. Developed by the Center for Bio-Ethical Reform in California, its grisly medical photographs attempted to morally link abortion to mural-sized images of the slaughter of whales, the lynching of African-Americans, and the Holocaust. Even students sympathetic to the antiabortion cause said they were grossed out by the overkill.

> Bodies I'm not an animal
> Mummy I'm not an abortion
> Throbbing squirm gurgling bloody mess
> I'm not a discharge
> I'm not a loss in protein
> I'm not a throbbing squirm.

Here Johnny turns Pauline's dilemma into a Halloween pantomime, the Demon Barber of Fleet Street waving his sharp instruments above his blood-soaked apron, or Elephant Man John Merrick stumbling away from the tormenting crowd sobbing that he's a human being. As guitars and drums thrash, the band maintains a characteristically male distance from the fluids of life.

In Britain, John Lydon was born into an immigrant Irish Catholic family, a people for whom unwanted children have caused much misery. With a not-easy life to lead in a not-welcoming place, Lydon's autobiography *Rotten* is even subtitled 'No Irish/No Blacks/No Dogs' after a sign he once saw. Though many US Catholics are stalwarts in the antichoice movement, British and European Catholics are not so rigid on the abortion issue, aware that there were never even Papal pronouncements on the issue until about a century ago. In Ireland, abortion was finally declared a crime in 1861 and remains illegal, despite an active Dublin Abortion Rights Group. Ireland made sure no provision of the 1992 Maastricht Treaty would bind the nation to European Union rulings on women's rights, and an abortion doctor was shot in Ireland in 1998. For the procedure an inconvenient trip from Ireland to England is necessary. Fortunately, even the most severe foes of choice have done nothing to prevent this travel or the publication of information on abortion services in the press and on the internet.

At the end of the second verse and chorus of 'Bodies' there is a false stop to the song. Then with a slap to the snare drum like a starter's pistol, Cook slams down the gauntlet and Rotten lets loose, goes ballistic.

> Fuck this and fuck that
> Fuck it all a fucking fucking brat
> She don't want a baby that looks like that
> I don't want a baby that looks like that.

In the 1980s I occasionally worked as a bartender for a publican from Dublin who was equally effusive in liberal use of the f-word. More recently, on Inishbofin island off Ireland's Galway coast I heard an angry teenager in a boat dockside cuss as emphatically and carnally—'Fuck! Bloody shit! Fuck it all fucking fuck!'—when he found someone had messed with his fishing tackle. In 'Bodies' there is none of the good-hearted family humor about the turmoil an unplanned pregnancy causes, as in the Irish movie *The Snapper*. Instead, Pistol Johnny takes an ugly turn, cursing the world and its cruelties and expediencies.

The flipside to such magnanimous spirituality is Johnny's exasperated scapegoating confusion. He speaks first as the woman's confidant to a story he wishes he hadn't heard; then as the abortionist; now as a spectator to Pauline's fast operation on a steel table (as efficient as whatever quickies the band enjoyed with her); then back to his growling status as the woman's lover and impregnator, or perhaps even her angry father (think Danny Aiello in Madonna's 'Papa Don't Preach' video); and most emphatically, the yowling embryo itself.

Perhaps out of fear, Pauline's voice is the one that Johnny and group never speak. By going so over the top, Johnny effectively lampoons all opposition as coming from a male mouth to Pauline's abortion decision. In *England's Dreaming* (St. Martin's, 1993) Jon Savage notes how 'Bodies' has no fixed narrator, its story told in both third and first person, from 'an almost schizoid viewpoint' that may even mirror that of troubled Pauline.

'Bodies' was the last song the Sex Pistols recorded in the studio, the only all-new song on *Never Mind the Bollocks*, written and assembled by the band in the studio, and inspired by their fan's letter and later in-person appearance in their lives. Propelled by his band's beat, Johnny Rotten rages at this young woman's abuse, rages at sex and death and birth, and even at those fans seeking solace in sexual congress with and confession to a rock band. In those three minutes two seconds he rages at everything else too. What are you rebelling against? Whaddya got?

Many hoped George W. Bush would be moderate on the issue of abortion, but one of his first acts as president was to deny federal aid to any group that provides abortion counseling in 'developing' countries. His actions, like his campaign rhetoric, placate his party's radical fundamentalist Christian wing, though his party is far from united against choice. A recent feature article in the *Ann Arbor Observer* discussed that city's Dobson brothers, pointing out that though the octogenarian millionaires are staunchly Republican, they dislike their party's antichoice position. In the 1940s and 1950s Republican women like Dobson wives were strong supporters of Planned Parenthood, whereas the Democratic party included more Irish- or Polish-American Catholics who steered clear of it.

Despite *Roe* v. *Wade*, abortion remains unavailable in 86 per cent of the counties of the United States. RU-686 (mifepristone) is a drug that induces miscarriage and is now available in the United States through physicians, though small-town doctors have expressed skepticism and fear of reproach if they were to prescribe it in conservative communities. Antichoice activists claim they will fight the drug as they do surgical abortion.

> Body I'm not an animal
> Body I'm not an abortion
> I'm not an animal mummy.

'Bodies' would make a great wicked animated cartoon, in perverse early Disney or *Ren and Stimpy* style depicting all the animals that Johnny is not. The Sex Pistols came along too early, and despite their manager Malcolm McLaren's cinematic efforts after the fact, they were spared the budget to make effects-laden rock videos. That gloss is unnecessary, for a perfect three-minute rock song is art enough. And it is women, not those young male Pistols, who, when universally given their right to choice, can finally assert they're no longer animals domestically penned for breeding.

I believe 'Bodies' remains the most important song to deal with abortion. Three decades after *Roe* v. *Wade*, abortion rights remain contested, though I don't believe John Lydon was out to curtail them. Beyond simplistic (albeit powerful) propaganda like the churchyard or campus installations, deceptively simple art like the choppy, frenetic multivoiced 'Bodies' is one way to deal with the contradictions and difficulties of serious political issues. The Sex Pistols, in their macho bravado, vent their panoply of feelings from the outside of Pauline's decision, which must never again be given force of law (nor be allowed to harass abortion doctors, clinics or clients).

The Sex Pistols' compact rock 'n' roll explosion is more nuanced and contradictory than the expansive propaganda put forth in the churchyard to seize the attention of passing cars, or the campus square to alarm blasé students. 'Bodies' is thus deeper and more lasting, more fun and more true. May its subject Pauline be safe and content today, warm in the knowledge that she inspired one of the great songs of '77 punk.

Fuck this and fuck that, indeed.

34
Marx's Media Corps

Jonathan Sterne

From both left and right, we hear daily of the novelty of today's media environment. We are told that new and purportedly global communication technologies, most notably the personal computer (which is not new) and the internet (which is not global) demand that we rethink our fundamental conceptions of what the media are and how they work. While the specifics differ, these writers more often than not agree on the basic terms: capitalism has won, or at least is almost invincible in our age. Nicholas Negroponte, corporate consultant, and Manuel Castells, critical information theorist, have no significant difference of opinion on this matter. As the globe is traversed by microwave relays, satellite link-ups, and fiber-optic cable, finance capital and the power of capital itself will become more and more mobile, more and more powerful. The media enhance capitalism, capitalism feeds the media. This is what we are told.

What can a writer from the middle of the nineteenth century tell us about the end of the twentieth century? Though he wrote for newspapers and the popularity of his ideas was helped greatly by their publication and print dissemination, Marx had relatively little to say about the media and communication in general. This has led to casual dismissals by many media analysts: because he doesn't give the media a lot of attention, they argue, why should someone concerned with the media give him attention? Since his analysis neither anticipates nor takes into account the massive transformations in communication that happened during and just after his lifetime—so the argument goes—he's useless for understanding media.

For all its classic red-baiting style, this argument has a rigidly literalist approach to reading Marx's texts. By this standard, only living thinkers who are able to account for the very latest in social transformations are worth reading.

Marxists are in fact blessed with a rich tradition of media criticism, ranging from the Frankfurt School to the Birmingham School, from the political economists to the postmodernists (though they love to hate each other), and well beyond. Media criticism retains an essential pedagogical importance: people live as if their media environment is a natural environment. By showing that meaning is itself constructed and implicated in power relations, media criticism—

if nothing else—provides a basic consciousness-raising function. If we show that the world is made, we show that it can be changed. Both the left press and the business press know all too well that the symbolic, institutional, and economic organization and function of the media affect the fundamental possibilities for everything from personal experience to large-scale political action. That is why both *The Nation* and the *Wall Street Journal* provide extensive coverage of media industries and technologies.

Even if the new media are massive, they are still human institutions, and if people made them, people can and should change them. Call it a simple, dramatic, and ethical insight—and one that is often left by the roadside even by the most 'orthodox' of Marxist media theorists. 'The point is to change it': Marx's oeuvre remains the most effective statement of the meaning and promise of total social transformation; a society based on need and ability rather than the ability to make money and exploit others.

This simple insight—that people make history but not in conditions of their own making—is especially relevant for thinking about the transformations in our contemporary media environment. While we find almost unanimous assent that the media are changing, few critics are willing to look at this as a purely social phenomenon. Hip cyber-propheteers declare that the technology is changing us and that machines will make our world quicker, cleaner, easier. Yet they remain silent about how that technology came to exist in the first place and the social forces behind it—or for that matter, inside of it.

It is not simply enough to say that the media are capitalist projects and leave it at that. As Robert McChesney and others continue to argue, it is impossible to have a truly democratic society when access to all the major modes of information and communication is controlled by a tiny elite. Even in the age of the free [sic] computer, the internet remains a denizen of relative elites. The vast majority of people live in a world where the only media they even barely control are their own telephones (notwithstanding the phone company owning all the lines and the relentless press of telemarketers) and their outgoing mail (though this too should be qualified by the fact that a lot of outgoing domestic mail consists of bill payments and other non-voluntary communications).

As cultural Marxists have long argued, ownership and access alone do not guarantee the meaning and power of media. Their dynamic shapes, as 'cultural technologies' to borrow a term from Jody Berland, have tremendous effects on how we experience them and with them our relationships to other parts of our social world. The workings of the mass media at a purely functional level make a difference in their social significance. To take an obvious example, the context of an experience of synchronized light and sound makes enough difference that the English language has clear semantic distinctions between television, film, and video—though of course those categories are often crossed. This too is an area where leftists need to think carefully in terms of social transformation. It was not enough for the communists in the then-new USSR to take over the assembly lines in order to effect a truly egalitarian working environment—they were still assembly lines, and the people who worked them were still exploited.

The same holds true for media today: for a truly just and egalitarian media system, we need to transform the character of media as cultural technologies— as *ways* of communicating. Again, Marx offers the kernel of this insight: 'the forming of the five senses is the labor of the entire history of the world down to the present.' Media are not simply institutions and conduits for messages, but rather they are a product of immense collective labor by people to shape their own sensory relationship with the world.

Marx's writings offer an essentially hopeful model of history, and this is perhaps the point at which even the most poststructuralist reading of Marx has to concede to humanism: people can and should change the world to make it all the more humane (rather than, shall we say, 'all too human'), and in thinking about the media, it is this basic ethical principle that should guide all Marxist analysis of the media. We may understand media as massive institutions that are out of the control of the average man or woman, but we must keep alive the hope that motivated and active groups of people can still transform them. We should make our analyses count toward this end. We should work together to transform our five senses.

35
Fetishizing the Communication Gap: the AT&T 'Vietnam' Commercial

Robert Shaw and Megan Shaw Prelinger

An open-canopied passenger boat glides up a wide river bound by jungle-covered banks. Crosby, Stills, and Nash's tune 'Long Time Gone' starts playing. Inside the boat a young black man looks out on the water intently, surrounded by traditionally dressed Vietnamese people of all ages. In the next shot he lies on his back on the boat looking across the river at the palm-clad shore. His shirt is open and dog-tags loll on his chest, marking him as a military man. 'It's been a long time coming ... ' sings David Crosby. The soldier disembarks onto a dusty shore dotted with bamboo structures and filled with playing children. The soldier's voice narrates over peaceful scenes of rural Vietnamese life: 'My dad was here ... he never talked about it much—he said you had to be there.—Well, here I am.' While the melody peaks in the background, the scene cuts to the soldier, indoors, leaning against a public telephone. 'Hey old man!' he says. He is holding an AT&T calling card. A graying man answers the phone back in America and says, 'Tye! You still in Singapore?' Tye replies, 'No, I'm on leave. I'm in Vietnam.' The older man replies, 'Vietnam' and purses his lips and rolls his eyes upward. Lowering his eyes again he continues, 'Let's talk, son.' Close-up of Tye as he replies, head bowed, 'Yeah.' David Crosby sings: 'And it appears to be a long ... ' Fade to a black screen pierced by the silver AT&T logo with the underlying slogan: 'It's all within your reach.'

THE AT&T 'VIETNAM' COMMERCIAL: A VIETNAM VETERAN RESPONDS

At first this looks like just another expensive American commercial filmed in an exotic location in order to grab the viewer's attention. Music of the 1960s is frequently used in advertising to make those of us who came of age at that time feel bonded to the contemporary culture. The lyrics of David Crosby's song 'Long Time Gone,' which he rerecorded for this commercial, reinforce this bond, as does the underlying back beat, which reminds me of Marvin Gaye's 'I Heard it Through the Grapevine.'

After a few seconds, the landscape becomes recognizably Vietnamese. The *National Geographic*-style photography in the commercial makes the landscape look quite serene. It did always seem to look serene, though it never was. For me it held terror. I find it ironic that the scenery in which the commercial is set includes landscapes that hosted some of the most intense fighting of the war. Navy patrol boats were regularly ambushed from those beautiful riverbanks as they poled up the rivers as the boat in the commercial does so blithely. And I climbed several hills in Vietnam like the one the man walks up in the commercial. When walking up a hill like that during the war one didn't just pray to live through the day, or the next hour, but through the next few minutes. There were a hundred ways to become maimed or to die hiking. We called it 'humping those hills.'

It is interesting that the man in the commercial is black. The white Americans who fought in the war had in general no respect for the Asians, typically referring to them in derogatory terms. 'Pappa-san,' 'slopes,' 'ginks,' 'gooks,' or just 'v.c.,' and of course treating them like shit. Statements like 'We'll bomb them back into the Stone Age (and it won't take long)' and 'We had to destroy the village to save it' were often heard among GIs. We did massive population relocations and tried to destroy the forests with defoliants. So who did the white US government send to fight the war? Blacks. The ratio of blacks to whites in Vietnam, if I remember, was about one in four or five, while the ratio in the US population as a whole was about one in nine or ten. The blacks, after the Vietnamese, where the most exploited race in the war. When the war was lost, instead of taking responsibility for the greatest US fuck-up of the twentieth century, those in power violated the social contract that had been in place at least since the Peloponnesian war. The social contract states that those who go and risk life at the behest of the state will be accorded honors in proportion to their risk. But in the United States, since the war ended, the soldiers who fought the war have been either forgotten or denigrated in public.

I notice that the commercial shows the traditional conception of the 'look' of the country. It doesn't show any neon lights, humming factories, or the colonial cities of Saigon or Hue. Instead it shows the dirt roads, river roads, and small villages of the rural agrarian people. This vision of the Vietnamese countryside echoes the policy maintained by the US government for 20 years after the war of hindering Vietnam's every effort to modernize and become a productive member of the developed world. I feel horribly embarrassed for the vindictive attitude that the United States took during those two decades. After 20 years, finally, the United States lifted its trade embargo.

Since the embargo has been lifted, Nike has set up shop there exploiting the people. And AT&T is now exploiting our cultural amnesia about the war. 'Son, let's talk.' Damn right! The US government needs to recover its memory of the past 30 years and talk to its citizens about what an onerous error it made by getting involved in the war, and do some healing on the issue. Maybe it would be possible to bring some of those hawks to accountability. Let the Pentagon and the old senators learn a few lessons. But if that's going to happen it needs to happen soon, because like for the father and son in this commercial, it is almost too late. The talking should have been done long ago.

THE AT&T 'VIETNAM' COMMERCIAL: A VIETNAM VETERAN'S DAUGHTER RESPONDS

The AT&T 'Vietnam' commercial was filmed on the Mekong river delta by a director of television advertisements who had fought there and won decoration during the war. The commercial is an example of 'emotional advertising,' which seeks to reach markets by using dramatic narratives to appeal to audiences' heartstrings. The commercial turns the communication gap between Vietnam veterans and their children into an object of fetishization that is condescended to, beautified, and sold for profit. It gives grave offense to those of us who were raised by parents who carry a burden of memory that is too painful to recall, much less retell. This communication gap, which exists even for those of us who are close to our veteran parents, is presented as a tragic half-told tale: ripe to be redeemed by the Midas touch of the commercial sphere like a Disney movie of a grisly tale from Brothers Grimm.

This dramatization of the very private, difficult work my father and I have done to make sense of each other's painful histories is deeply offensive. The nature of this offense is twofold. First, the story invokes the history of the Vietnam war generation at the expense of my own generational experience. Second, the story was told for profit. In addition to the ways in which this commercial offended me in particular, it is also offensive in ways that are not specific to my experience. These ways include the use of African-American actors to portray the father and son; the use of a narrative that parallels that of the film *Apocalypse Now*; and exploitation of the invisibility of Vietnam veterans as a group.

The main character of the commercial's story is not the Vietnam veteran, it is the veteran's son. The ad-makers may have assumed that they were aiming at a veteran audience, but that would be naive. No doubt veterans will notice the ad, triggered to identify with it by the sound of David Crosby's voice. But it would have been more appropriate to use 'Smells Like Teen Spirit.' That would repair the contradiction of using a child of a veteran to grab the attention, and the market share, of the vets and their cohort. The ad-makers have invaded the privacy of the family relationships that have been affected by the war, and veterans' children are equal partners in those relationships.

That this privacy should be invaded at all is offensive, but the use of African-American actors to do so is troublesome in a different direction. As my father correctly points out, the Vietnam war troops were disproportionately African-American. This was true for a number of reasons, including lower levels of employment in African-American communities that made military service an inviting option, and high rates of re-enlistment. The result of this high population density of African-American soldiers in elite units was that their casualty rates increased proportionately, as they were chronically on the front lines, performing the dirtiest, most difficult fighting to advance the United States' campaign.

The ratio of non-whites to whites in elite combat units peaked at around one in four in 1966 and 1967 (Bates, p. 55). This accounts for my father's recollection of the large population of African-American soldiers, as my father fought in a construction brigades unit that was attached to the Green Berets in 1968. The commercial's use of African-American actors to portray the characters echoes the war's tendency to exploit them by offering them opportunities for 'front line' positions. Such positions offered prestige, but at the cost of life and limb. It is critically important to feature non-whites in the mainstream culture to increase the visibility and participation of non-whites in the culture. But after watching the commercial I felt an uneasy suggestion that a history of exploitation was being invoked.

It is likewise inappropriate for the ad to invoke cultural icons that reinforce the negative public image of Vietnam veterans. By paralleling the narrative of *Apocalypse Now*, the AT&T commercial does exactly that. Like *Apocalypse Now*, the commercial tells the story of a young American military man who arrives in Vietnam and journeys inland by river-boat on a quest for a distant, older, military man who had made the same journey years before. As in the film, the action of the commercial takes place in a rural Vietnamese landscape that is dominated by the Mekong river. Also as in the film, the action only moves indoors when the younger man makes contact with the object of his quest. When Tye gets on the phone to call his father, the action moves out of the jungle, into a building, and zooms in to a head-shot close-up first of Tye, then of Tye's father on the phone in America. The father is filmed in shadow, his disembodied head appearing in extreme close-up, just like Marlon Brando was filmed in *Apocalypse Now*.

The narrative parallels between the commercial and the famous film are unmistakable, and they are disturbing because they imply a correlation between Vietnam veterans in America and the character of Kurtz played in the film by Marlon Brando. This correlation plays hard on the marginalized status of Vietnam veterans. That such an alignment could be made in a prime-time commercial is an indication that veterans' status as the exiled 'Other' in American society has not dissipated in the least over the past 25 years. Quite the opposite. This commercial is evidence that the marginalization of Vietnam veterans has been dressed up and shown on prime-time. Their exile has been mainstreamed.

This commercial was screened for members of the executive committee of the Vietnam Veterans of America who reportedly found it 'memorable.' David Crosby's active support for the commercial perhaps gives us a clue why they might have approved of it. It is understandable that veterans and former antiwar activists like Crosby might be charmed by the respect that is superficially implied by the use of veterans as a marketing tool, and the inclusion that cannot be denied. But the inclusion of the veterans' experience into the commercial culture comes at the expense of their children. This 'respect' cannot be accepted at face value. A closer look tells us that respect motivated by profit is rarely respect.

REFERENCE

Bates, Milton J., *The Wars We Took to Vietnam*, Berkeley: University of California Press, 1996.

36
Heterosexual Love

Annalee Newitz

Gazing out across some early twentieth-century British estate, the esteemed cultural critic Lytton Strachey sees a group of boys playing soccer. They run to and fro, their young bodies muddy and colliding in homoerotic splendor. One in particular strikes his fancy, the loud one with blonde curls. 'Ah,' he intones with great satisfaction, 'What a beautiful young man.' But the young man, it turns out, is no man at all. He's Dora Carrington, the wild, androgynous female painter whose lifelong relationship with the utterly queer Strachey is the subject of the 1995 movie *Carrington*, one of many 1990s films about heterosexual romance between people whom one would hardly wish to call 'straight.'

The queer tragedy of pining after oblivious heterosexuals was immortalized in movies such as *The Children's Hour* (1961), *Kiss of the Spider Woman* (1985), and *Maurice* (1987); now Hollywood is exploring how this specific sort of unrequited love cuts both ways. Parodied and mourned in recent fare such as *Chasing Amy* (1997), *My Best Friend's Wedding* (1997), and *The Object of My Affection* (1998), the homo-infatuated heterosexual has emerged as one of the latest heroes in the romantic genre's ongoing quest to recreate the medieval thrill of courtly love. Idealized during the Middle Ages as a passionate yet entirely chaste form of desire (usually between a knight and his king's wife), courtly love has underwritten a great deal of what counts as 'romance' in centuries since. After all, it is still generally the case that we value a prolonged period of yearning and waiting in 'true love,' even if chastity is out of the question. This holds for both homo- and heterosexual love—think, for instance, of the charming despair and angels-are-singing fulfillment in the ultra-queer *The Incredibly True Adventures of Two Girls in Love* (1995) and the ultra-straight *Swingers* (1996). Both indie flicks work so well as romantic tales because their protagonists must languish almost interminably before meeting The Right One and dancing off into the proverbial sunset.

But what does it mean when fuddy-duddy courtly love is coupled with super-contemporary issues like sexual identity? And why is middle-of-the-road Hollywood placing heterosexuals in the ideologically weird position of falling for sexual minorities? One might easily claim—particularly in the movies I've just mentioned—that these are actually stories about converting homosexuals into 'normal' people. *Chasing Amy*, after all, has lesbian Alyssa (Joey Lauren Adams) fall happily into bed with the alterna-macho dork Holden (Ben Affleck). *Carrington* features an ambiguous sex scene between Carrington and Strachey, just as *My Best Friend's Wedding* concludes with the seriously romantic dance between Julianne (Julia Roberts) and her gay friend George (Rupert Everett). And *The Object of My Affection* depicts hero Nina (*Friends* pinup girl Jennifer Aniston) in a hot almost-sex scene with her gay room-mate (another George, played by Paul Rudd), whose sexual orientation is literally saved by the bell: right before consummation, his ex-lover calls and derails what appears to be a blow job in the making.

So perhaps these films are reactionary heterosexual fantasies about teaching homosexuals the 'true' way to love; or, more generously, liberal fantasies about having your sexual diversity cake and eating it too, letting the queers be queer unless some nice straight person actually wants to bed one. I'd wager that most of them are doing both things, with a film like *Chasing Amy* taking the most reactionary perspective (nice boy converts lesbian), and *The Object of My Affection* (which, after all, ends with George firmly choosing his male lover over the weepy Nina) providing a liberal counterpoint.

But I think there is also a third possibility for these movies, one that helps explain their relationship to a contemporary trend in heterosexual thought. They offer audiences a new form of sexual conservatism in which your orientation matters less than whether you choose to form a family, become monogamous, and procreate.

Looking at movies like *The Object of My Affection* and *My Best Friend's Wedding* with this in mind, it becomes clear that what's at stake is less the conversion of homo into hetero, and more the conversion of queer families into traditional ones. As critic Kath Weston has explained, the queer family is a 'family we choose,' a group of close-knit friends who support and nurture each other in ways that biological families often spectacularly fail to do. Driven from their own families by prejudice, homosexuals historically have formed queer families to regain a sense of home and community that they miss. But in the post-Reagan era of job mobility and 'rootlessness,' the queer family has become a kind of norm for straights and gays alike. Celebrated on TV shows such as *Cheers*, *Seinfeld*, and *Friends*, the friends-as-family idea is both comforting and pragmatic. When so few people have the luxury of living near their families, we are forced to form other kinship ties. In addition, it seems that pop psychology has finally taught us that biological families are mostly dysfunctional anyway, so why would anyone want to depend on them to 'be there for you,' as the *Friends* theme song says? And yet the queer family, often highly unconventional and rife with sexual ambiguity, is hardly traditional enough to qualify as having what Republicans call 'family values.'

Hence the need to find socially acceptable ways of bringing homosexuals into traditional families. According to *My Best Friend's Wedding* and *The Object of My Affection*, the easiest way to do this is to reinstate chastity as the norm in adult relationships. Both films are concerned principally with intimate but non-sexual relationships between straight women and gay men who are at the center of extended, mostly non-biological families. Abstinence in both films is romanticized, and all the most passionate, 'marriage' style relationships are between platonic friends. *The Object of My Affection* is quite explicit about how this desexualized state of affairs is the best situation possible in which to have children. When Nina gets pregnant, she knows instinctively that her obnoxiously sexist boyfriend is the wrong father for her child, and she asks the sensitive George to help her coparent the baby instead. George, a first grade teacher, has been longing to raise babies all his life, and falls in love with the idea of family that Nina offers him.

As Nina and George's relationship develops, they accumulate a 'family' that includes Nina's relatives, their spouses, and George's gay lover and friends. None of the domestic partners we meet ever have sex: George's lover lives with an older man who adores him but is just 'too old'; George lives with Nina; and Nina's mother lives in a postsexual marriage. Implicitly, the best family homes are run by celibates. In the film's epilogue, which takes place six years after Nina's child is born, we see that Nina and George's family has blossomed. Everyone has a long-term monogamous lover, everyone thinks of themselves as 'family,' and they've all come to watch Nina's daughter dance in the school play. 'I had the most people come to see me!' the little girl exults to 'Uncle George' on the way home. Of course it's great to see homosexuals treated like ordinary 'family,' but what kind of family is this? Elder members of the clan offer condescending, snarky comments to the younger ones; no one is allowed to have sex; gender roles are strictly enforced (women are emotionally fragile and men have jobs); and making babies becomes the source of all fulfillment. What we have is a slightly more colorful version of the Brady Bunch.

Similar sets of 'happy' circumstances adorn the endings of *My Best Friend's Wedding*, and *The Object of My Affection*'s indie precursor *The Wedding Banquet* (1993). In *My Best Friend's Wedding*, Julianne's family becomes her now-married best friend Michael, and her unbelievably devoted gay pal George. After she unsuccessfully attempts to woo Michael, Julianne realizes that the real pleasures in life come from platonic family bonds, and she and George dance at Michael's very traditional wedding through a sea of sparkly, bourgeois relatives. George even notes that, 'There may be no sex, but there is dancing.' Ang Lee's *The Wedding Banquet* also carves out a niche for gay men in the traditional family by providing them with a pseudo-wedding and children. To please his highly respected family, the gay Wai-Tung throws a wedding for himself and Wei-Wei, a friend who wants to get residence in the United States. But the fake wedding ends in a drunken night of sex between Wai-Tung and the besotted Wei-Wei, who immediately gets pregnant. Wai-Tung and his lover Simon, whose charade pleases Wai-Tung's family no end (although they know what's 'really going on'), ultimately do their duty as men and patriarchs in a traditional Chinese family.

Oddly enough, the addition of homosexuals and their queer families to the traditional family makes taboos against sexuality even more rigid. If anyone— not just biological relatives—can become your potential family member, then taboos against sex are virtually forced to skyrocket. You never know when the prick of love might become the sting of incest. Traditional families are, in essence, the locus of sexual taboo in our society: they are the first place we learn about prohibitions against homosexuality (babies are made by mom and dad), and prohibitions against incest. Blending queers into the traditional family relaxes taboos against homosexuality only to expand incest taboos to the point where one can't imagine sex except with a long-term monogamous partner. Everyone else is 'family' and therefore off-limits. Queer families, while not always any less dysfunctional than traditional ones, at least have the advantage of allowing for the open expression of sexual desire between adults who are not biologically related. What we get from a film such as *The Object of My Affection* or *The Wedding Banquet* is the idea that open sexual expression is always a bad idea, particularly if you want families and children. So 'family values' remain, in essence, unchanged.

Chasing Amy is perhaps the most ideologically heinous film in this respect, in that sexual taboo-breaking becomes the source of all social disruption. Alyssa's lesbianism is connected to her 'sluttiness,' which turns out to include a past episode in which she had group sex with men. Repulsed and confused by Alyssa's polymorphous perversity, Holden breaks up with her, and then rudely attempts to involve her in a mini-orgy with himself and his best friend/business partner Banky. Alyssa and Holden's family of comic book artist friends—which includes straights and gays—is torn apart by Alyssa's refusal to be sexually conservative. Had she just been a nice lesbian girl who happened to be hetero for Holden, we assume, things might have worked out. But she threatens their family with open sexual expression, which finally destroys her relationship with Holden, as well as Holden and Banky's long-term friendship. Here we find that homosexuality is acceptable only so long as everyone engages in highly selective serial monogamy.

Not surprisingly, films in which we find gays and straights sharing an overtly sexual—and often non-monogamous—queer family usually end with the family's dissolution or its recombination into traditional families. *Three of Hearts* (1993), about the non-sexual room-mate romance between lesbian Connie

(Kelly Lynch) and straight guy Joe (William Baldwin), is emphatic about keeping its characters out of family situations. Although there is the requisite wedding sequence, in which Joe pretends to be Connie's boyfriend, it's less a celebration of family than a statement about Connie's distance from it. Joe is a gigolo whom she's paid to accompany her, and Connie is still madly in love with her bisexual ex-girlfriend Ellen (Sherilyn Fenn). After Joe and Connie bond over a mutual infatuation (and fornication) with Ellen, the film ends with the two living together but utterly without extended family. Ellen has left both of them, and while Connie and Joe seem happy together, they are not comfortably nestled within the kinds of kinship networks formed in *The Object of My Affection*, *My Best Friend's Wedding*, or *The Wedding Banquet*. *Carrington* ends even more tragically, with Carrington and Strachey leading bitter, unfulfilled lives at the center of a highly sexualized queer family that provides them with intellectual sustenance but little in the way of *The Object of My Affection*'s, warm fuzzies. *Threesome* (1994), a college dorm romance between a gay man and his straight male and female room-mates, allows its nubile young protagonists to have group sex, but only because we understand this is a 'phase' that they all grow out of as soon as they graduate into job and family.

So heterosexuals are falling in love with homosexuals because sexless relationships are the cornerstones of any family with 'values.' And queers are welcome into traditional families precisely because their presence actually de-escalates the possibility that people will be engaging in what was once called free love.

Certainly there's also a more utopian possibility—that these are films about heterosexuals learning to love homosexuals without trying to make them straight. Save for *Chasing Amy*, every film I've described allows its homosexuals to remain happily queer (if somewhat inexplicably overattached to their straight friends). Straights are forced to accept the reality of homosexual love, even if they do it ungracefully and sometimes only after trying to make the homosexuals have heterosexual sex. This even seems to be the message in the übernormal Kevin Kline vehicle *In & Out* (1997). But if these recent Hollywood heterosexuals are sacrificing a wish to make everyone straight, they are only doing it because they have a chance to absorb everyone into conservative family-driven communities where all the bad old values of sexual and social repression run rampant.

Although these movies think of themselves as 'straight but not narrow' liberalizing forces, they are draining away the transformative possibilities created by radically queer families in which sexuality is treated as a part of everyday life. *The Object of My Affection*, which I believe typifies romantic comedies devoted to redefining heterosexuality, never attempts to question the way its family constrains erotic desire, reinforces gender norms, and directs us all toward child-rearing as a domestic goal. Although heterosexuals may be learning to redefine love, this is hardly a radical breakthrough if we never question the problems posed by families formed under conditions not of our own choosing. Going back to traditional families—even if they include homosexuals—is a cultural step in the wrong direction.

Notes on Contributors

Arturo J. Aldama is a member of the *Bad Subjects* collective and is currently Associate Professor of Ethnic Studies at the University of Colorado, Boulder. His publications include *Disrupting Savagism: Intersecting Chicana/o, Mexican Immigrant and Native American Struggles for Representation* (Duke University Press, 2002). He is editor of *Decolonial Voices: Chicana and Chicano Cultural Studies in the 21st Century* (Indiana University Press, 2003). His third book is *Violence and the Body: Race, Gender and the State* (Indiana University Press, 2003).

Frederick Luis Aldama teaches modern US and British literature and film at University of Colorado, Boulder. He is a freelance writer and author of a number of books, including, *Postethnic Narrative Criticism* (University of Texas, 2003), *Dancing With Ghosts: A Critical Biography of Arturo Islas* (University of California Press, 2004), *Arturo Islas: The Uncollected Works* (Arte Publico Press, 2003), and *Critical Mappings of Arturo Islas's Narrative Fiction* (Biligual Review Press, 2004).

Lisa Archer is the alter ego of a Brooklyn based writer, whose pseudonymous musings have appeared on Eros-Guide.com and in *San Francisco Bay Guardian* and a variety of anthologies, including *Best Bisexual Women's Erotica* (Cleis Press, 2001), *Best Woman's Erotica* 2002 and 2004 (Cleis Press), *Five-Minute Erotica* (Running Press, 2003), *Awakening the Virgin 2* (Alyson Publications, 2002), and *Pills, Thrills, Chills, and Heartache: Adventures in the First Person* (Alyson Publications, 2004).

Charlie Bertsch (cbertsch@u.arizona.edu) is Assistant Professor of English at the University of Arizona, Tucson, where he specializes in twentieth-century American prose, cultural studies, and the history of aesthetics. He also teaches film. In his free time he contributes interviews, features, and reviews to *Punk Planet* magazine and a number of free weeklies. His abiding obsessions are trippy noise-pop, college basketball, cookbooks, and whatever movies his daughter Skylar is watching at the time.

John Brady is a political scientist and writer living in California. A long-time member and former codirector of *Bad Subjects*, he works on theories of public space, immigration, and the politics of multiculturalism. Besides *Bad Subjects*, his work has appeared in *Punk Planet* and *Mother Jones*.

Robin S. Brooks is a Ph.D candidate in political science at UC Berkeley, and is finishing a dissertation on ethnic politics in Bulgaria. Her academic career has been colorful and delightful, and her publications include articles in the *East

European Constitutional Review, Peace Review, and the *International Journal of the Sociology of Language.* Her contribution to *Bad Subjects,* however, has been the most fun. Robin next plans to become a diplomat.

Kevin Carollo has a Ph.D in comparative literature from the University of Illinois. He teaches world literature at Minnesota State University, Moorhead.

Jason M. Ferreira received his Ph.D from Berkeley's Ethnic Studies Department in 2003. He is a University of California President's Postdoctoral Fellow in residence at the University of California, Santa Cruz, and is completing a manuscript preliminarily titled *All Power to the People: A Social History of Third World Radicalism in the San Francisco Bay Area, 1960–1980.*

Zach Furness is a Ph.D candidate in communication at the University of Pittsburgh, and a member of the *Bad Subjects* collective. In addition to *Bad Subjects,* Zach has been published in *Punk Planet* and *New Voices.* He is currently working on a dissertation project about culture jamming groups and techno- logical discourses. Zach has performed and recorded with several punk bands and is an avid bicycle rider.

Emma Grant is a prostitutes' rights activist whose visa status is tenuous.

Wayde Grinstead wrote the essay that appears in this book while pursuing a Master's degree in American Studies at the University of Maryland. Since finishing that program, he has worked as a substitute teacher and as a writer and editor for a trade magazine, in addition to continuing his life in the service industry. He has been working with the New York City Teaching Fellows since the fall of 2003.

David Hawkes is Associate Professor of English at Lehigh University. He is the author of *Ideology* (Routledge, 1996) and *Idols of the Marketplace* (Palgrave, 2001) and his work has appeared in such journals as *The Nation,* the *Times Literary Supplement,* the *Journal of the History of Ideas* and *In These Times.*

Doug Henwood edits the *Left Business Observer* (www.leftbusinessobserver.com) and hosts a weekly radio show on WBAI, New York. He is the author of *The State of the USA Atlas* (Simon & Schuster, 1994), *Wall Street* (Verso, 1997) and *After the New Economy* (New Press, 2003). In January 2003, he attended the POR's 50th anniversary banquet; read all about this alarming event on *The Nation's* website (www.thenation.com).

Cynthia Hoffman (choff@lmi.net) recently relocated to Los Angeles in order to become a Rabbi, and pursue her brand of social justice from within the system that means the most to her. Not surprisingly, she hasn't noticed an appreciable difference in relative air quality. She has been a member of *Bad Subjects* for ten years, which coincidentally is as long as she has been without cigarettes.

Elisabeth Hurst (lizyjn@earthlink.net) doesn't live in Canada any longer, but left for reasons unrelated to APEC '97. Current events only convince her that the attitudes which created the events of APEC '97 are still prevalent. She sometimes spends far too much time trying to figure out whether it's possible to change that.

Joe Lockard is Assistant Professor of English at Arizona State University. He teaches early American literature and directs the Antislavery Literature Project. Joe has been a member of the *Bad Subjects* collective for ten years and has coedited issues on internet culture, aesthetics of violence, Marx, labor, race, and writing.

Karl MacRae lives, works, and organizes in Oakland, California. He maintains regular visiting schedules with two prisoners, including one on death row, and has communicated by mail with prisoners all over the country. Karl urges folks to build bridges with prisoners either through the mail or by visiting them. He is hopeful that change will come once people have connected their own humanity to the humanity of those inside our prisons.

Mike Mosher (mosher@svsu.edu) is Assistant Professor of Art/Communication Multimedia at Saginaw Valley State University. His publications include the textbook *Creating Web Graphics, Audio and Video* with Roger L. Shepard (Prentice-Hall, 2002), illustrations for *Orwell for Beginners* (Writers & Readers, 1999), and visuals and texts for *Bad Subjects* since 1994.

J.C. Myers is Assistant Professor of Political Science at California State University, Stanislaus, and has also lectured at the University of Cape Town. He is the author of several articles on ideology.

Annalee Newitz is the culture editor at the *San Francisco Bay Guardian*. She writes about technology, pop culture, and sex for *Salon, Nerve, Wired, Alternet. org* and various other magazines and newspapers. Annalee is a founding editor of *Bad Subjects*, and the editor of *The Bad Subjects Anthology* (NYU Press, 1998). Get the gory details at www.techsploitation.com.

Viet Thanh Nguyen is Associate Professor of English and American Studies and Ethnicity at the University of Southern California. He is the author of *Race and Resistance: Literature and Politics in Asian America* (Oxford University Press, 2002). Currently, he is working on a comparative history about the postwar cultural production of Vietnam and the United States.

Kim Nicolini is a third generation San Francisco native who now lives in Tucson, Arizona, with her partner Charlie, daughter Skylar, two cats, two turtles, and a fish. In between working full-time and being a mom, Kim explores the abstract interior of the body in a variety of art media, obsessively goes to films, serves on the International Arts Society committee on film at the University of Arizona, and speaks out loudly against the current Bush regime's foreign, domestic, and environmental policies. She can be reached at knicolini@comcast.net.

Ewa Pagacz was a college teacher in Bielsko-Biala, an industrial town in southwest Poland. She recently completed a law degree in the United States. She can be reached at ewadob@hotmail.com.

Megan Shaw Prelinger focuses her scholarship and artwork on land use history and American social history. She is partner in the Prelinger Archives, a collection of ephemeral films and a library of natural and social history. She has been a member of the *Bad Subjects* collective since 1997 and served as codirector from 1999 to 2001. She is also a wildlife rehabilitator.

Rick Prelinger founded Prelinger Archives (www.prelinger.com), a collection of over 48,000 'ephemeral' (advertising, industrial, educational, documentary, and amateur) films depicting life, culture, and industry in twentieth-century America. He has partnered with the Internet Archive to make rich media materials available online for free. He has worked in television and film production as producer, writer, and conceptualist, and produced CD-ROMs and laser discs with the Voyager Company. He is now working on an all-archival feature-length film.

Carrie A. Rentschler is visiting Assistant Professor of Women's Studies at the University of Pittsburgh. Her work examines media coverage of public safety, crime, and security. She wrote her dissertation on the US crime victims' movement and the emergence of 'victim's rights' approaches to crime. She studies media portrayals and autobiographies of wounded journalists as narratives of masculinity in the present political context. She also kickboxes, gardens, and participates in the antiwar movement in Pittsburgh.

Tomás F. Sandoval, Jr. is Assistant Professor of Chicana/o and Latina/o Studies at California State University, Monterey Bay. He holds a Ph.D in US history from the University of California and is currently at work on a book about the formation of the Latina/o community of San Francisco. He is an avid consumer of popular culture and various soy products, and awaits the airing of an authentic Chicana/o sitcom on a major network.

Scott Schaffer is Assistant Professor of sociology at Millersville University of Pennsylvania, where he teaches courses in social theory, cultural sociology, and social change and everyday life. He is also a member of the *Bad Subjects* production team and the managing editor of the online *Journal of Mundane Behavior* (www.mundanebehavior.org). His first book, *Resisting Ethics*, which uses the practice of resistance to develop a new social ethics, is forthcoming from Palgrave in 2004.

Joel Schalit is codirector of *Bad Subjects* (1997–99 and 2001–03), and associate editor of *Punk Planet*. He is the author of *Jerusalem Calling: A Homeless Conscience in a Post Everything World*, and editor of *The Anti-Capitalism Reader: Imagining a Geography of Opposition*, both published by Akashic Books in 2002. Still an editor of *Bad Subjects* Joel contributes to many publications and is currently working on his third book, *Israel Versus Utopia*. In his free time, he processes digital audio in the San Francisco–Seattle group, Elders of Zion.

Robert Shaw is a Vietnam war veteran who served with the US Army Combat Engineers in the central highlands of Vietnam. He is now an architect in private practice focusing on energy-efficient and green architecture. He shares a home with two cats in Eugene, Oregon.

Katie Simon is a graduate student in English at UC Berkeley. Her work has appeared in *The East Bay Express*, *The Berkeley Poetry Review*, and *Terpsichorean*. She can be reached at mskatiesimon@hotmail.com.

Gretchen Soderlund is a Mellon Postdoctoral Fellow in Communication and Society at the University of Chicago. Her primary research is on early twentieth-century print culture. She also studies panics over commercial sex in past and present contexts. In her spare time, Gretchen enjoys hanging out in hotel bars with her friend and coauthor, Emma Grant.

Jonathan Sterne has been online since 1982 and a member of the *Bad Subjects* collective since 1994. He currently teaches in the Department of Communication and the Program for Cultural Studies at the University of Pittsburgh and he is author of *The Audible Past: Cultural Origins of Sound Reproduction* (Duke, 2003). Learn more at www.pitt.edu/~jsterne and hear his two-bass postrock band at www.lo-boy.net.

Mark Van Proyen is an artist and art critic who since 1996 has been Associate Professor of Art History, Painting and Digital Media at the San Francisco Art Institute. Prior to that appointment, he held the position of migrant academic laborer in the art departments of no fewer than four large California universities.

Richard D. Wolff is Professor of Economics at the University of Massachusetts. Author of many books and articles in the fields of critical social theory and Marxism, his latest, with frequent coauthor Stephen A. Resnick, is *Class Theory and History: Capitalism and Communism in the USSR* (Routledge, 2002). He can be reached at RDWolff@worldnet.att.net.

Matt Wray, a former member of the *Bad Subjects* collective, writes on issues of class, race, and ethnicity, particularly poor whites. He has coedited *White Trash: Race and Class in America* (Routledge, 1997) and *The Making and Unmaking of Whiteness* (Duke, 2001). His next book, forthcoming in 2005, focuses on the sociohistorical emergence and development of the 'white trash' stereotype. He is Assistant Professor of Sociology at the University of Nevada, Las Vegas.

Edmund Zimmerman, performer, poet, and cofounder of TongueMagazine. com (which makes an oft-disputed claim to compassionate conservatism), lived in Italy from 1986 through 1996.

Index

Compiled by Sue Carlton

Bush, G.W. 22, 66, 87, 193
Butler, Judith 92, 94–5

Calhoun, John Caldwell 30
California, Vietnamese community 167–8
California Department of Corrections
    (CDC) 12
Canada, and APEC summit 77
capital punishment 173–4
capitalism 29, 49–54, 59, 79–80, 170
    and exploitation 51–2, 53, 89–90, 91,
    153
    future of 78, 79, 80–2
    global 38, 81, 82, 102, 120, 137–40, 149
    and media 195
    and rationalization 80, 81
    state 52–3
Carrington 203, 204, 207
Carrington, Dora 203, 204, 207
Castells, Manuel 195
Castronovo, Russ 21
Catholic Church
    and homosexuality 48
    and materialism 47–8
    power of 10, 44–8
    and social control 45, 48
Center for Bio-Ethical Reform, California
    191
Certeau, Michel de 148
Chasing Amy 203, 204, 206
Chi Alpha Christian Fellowship 191
Chicago Tribune 121–2
Children's Hour, The 203
China, repression 56, 75–6
Chowchilla Prison 16
Chrétien, Jean 73, 77
Christian Democrats, Italy 40
Chubb Protective Services 144
Civil Disturbance Collection Plan 66, 67
civil rights, and APEC summit 73–5, 76,
    77
Civil Rights Movement 186
class 49–54
    and property and power 50, 51, 52–3
    surplus labor theory 49, 51–4
Clinton, Bill 73
closed circuit television (CCTV) 141–2,
    143–4
    see also surveillance

Cold War, end of 78–9, 98–9
commodity fetishism 36, 59
communism 50–1, 52–3, 167–8
    collapse of 78–9
    and organization of surplus labor 53–4
COND. (Condemned) 12–13
Connery, Chris 92, 93
conservatism 10, 29–31
    and traditionalism 29–30
Consumer Survey on Home Security 143
copyright law 10, 23–8
    and access to works 25–8
    extension of 24
    and freedom of expression 25
    reform 24–5
Cossiga, Francesco 42
Craxi, Bettino 40
Creative Commons 27
Crosby, Dave 198, 202
CS gas 64

Davis, Mike 13, 138
Death Row 13
Debord, Guy 36
decline, perception of 187–8
Deleuze, Gilles 13–14
Delta Force 63, 66
Department of Homeland Security (DHS)
    63, 66–7, 153
deportation 150, 153–4
Deukmeijian, George 15
Dick, Philip K. 180
Didion, Joan 116
Digital Millennium Copyright Act 2000
    (DMCA) 24
Döblin, Alfred 58
Domestic Security Enhancement Act 2003
    20
Dortch, Vaughn 12–13
Dublin Abortion Rights Group 192
Durrant 16
Duvalier, François ('Papa Doc') 32, 33, 34
Dworkin, Andrea 176

East Berlin, communist legacy 59–60
Economist, The 39
Eichmann, Adolph 41
Eisenstein, Zilah 146
El Salvador 148

internet 137, 139, 195
Iraq War (2003) 10, 18–22
    and international law 22
    and US social expenditure cutbacks 18
    see also war culture
Ireland, and abortion 192
Italian Communist Party (PCI) 40, 42
Italy
    corruption 40
    fascism 10, 37, 38–43
    media ownership 40, 41
    see also Berlusconi, Silvio

James, Lawrence 19
Japanese-Americans, incarceration of 66
Jews, and Israeli landscape 119–20, 126–31
JFK Airport 14
Jiang Zemin 73, 75–6, 77
Jonestown, Guyana, mass suicide 64
Judea, trip through desert 120, 126–31
justice system, and revenge 172–4, 176–7

Kerr, Clark 69
Kiss of the Spider Woman 203
Kissinger, Henry 42
KMD 16
Kolakowski, Lescek 47
Koresh, David 64
Kruger, Daniel 19
Kuroda, Barbara 12
Kurtz, Stanley 19

Le Pen, Jean-Marie 153
Left Conservatism 92–7
    effect of debate on students 96–7
    as reaction to theory 92, 93, 95–6
Lega Nord (Northern League) 40
Lenin, V.I. 52
Lennon, John 24
lesbians see gay and lesbian communities;
    homosexuals
Lockhead, Carolyn 87
Lydon, John (Johnny Rotten) 184, 189,
    190, 192–3, 194

McChesney, Robert 196
McLaren, Malcolm 193
McLaughlin, Herbert 16

Mancuso, Liberato 42
market, and political direction 34, 36
market capitalism 29, 81–2
market multiculturalism 9
Markus, Thomas A. 13
Marx, Karl 9, 56, 106, 137
    class analysis 49–51, 52–3, 54
    criticism of 78, 79
    and future of capitalism 80–2
    and internationalism 82–3
    market ideology 36
    predictions of social revolution 78, 83
    and source of social order 79–80
Marxism 11, 89, 94, 167–70
    class analysis 49–54
    and media theory 184, 195–7
    as social critique 155, 169–70
    structural 97
Maurice 203
media
    and capitalism 195
    control of 196, 197
    Marxist analysis of 184, 195–7
    transformation of 184, 196–7
Melrose Place 141–2, 144
Mengele, Joseph 41
Mexico 138
MI-4 66
Michigan Independent 191
migration 150–4
millennium, celebrations in Berlin 57–62
Milton, John 35
Mondadori 40
Movimento Sociale (MSI) 40–1
multiculturalism 9, 137, 168
music festivals 137, 139, 140
Mussolini, Benito 38–9, 41
My Best Friend's Wedding 203, 204, 205,
    207

Nation, The 92, 93, 196
nation-states, destruction of 140
National League 171
national security
    and repression 19–20
    see also security
nationalism 82–3, 160
Nazism 30
Negroponte, Nicholas 195